"There have been few books that rightly assess and analyze . . . ican church leaders are managing in our current cultural moment. In *Inalienable*, the authors not only provide a proper assessment and analysis of these issues, but more importantly, they also offer a way forward. If you care about what the next generation of American Christianity looks like and how marginalized voices are shaping the future of American churches, I highly recommend this book."

Ed Stetzer, executive director of the Wheaton College Billy Graham Center and dean of the School of Mission, Ministry, and Leadership

"This is a book for our times, some strong-but-needed medicine. The authors write, 'Many in the American church have replaced worship of God with idolatrous pursuits of wealth and power, at the cost of our integrity.' In many ways, much of the American church has lost her way in consumerism, political idolatry, and shallowness. As a result, the church in America is feeble. This book is a clarion call for American Christians to listen to and learn from our brothers and sisters in the global church. The future of the American church depends on it."

Derwin L. Gray, cofounder and lead pastor of Transformation Church, author of *How to Heal Our Racial Divide: What the Bible Says, and the First Christians Knew, about Racial Reconciliation*

"This book, by some of the most thoughtful leaders in the church today, points us away from fear and panic and toward promise and hope and joy. Jesus is building his church, and doing so, as he always has, using those who are at the margins. This book will help ready you for the exciting next generation of the Spirit's work through the church."

Russell Moore, Christianity Today

"As 'the most substantial threats to American Christianity are not those from outside but from within,' Costanzo, Yang, and Soerens in *Inalienable* employ the voices of world Christianity to call the American church to account. From the outset, the authors employ a global hermeneutic to revisit biblical concepts of the kingdom, image, word, and mission of God from the perspective of marginalized people to address the blind spots in American Christianity. Every pastor and Christian leader in the United States should read this book."

Gina A. Zurlo, codirector of the Center for the Study of Global Christianity at Gordon-Conwell Theological Seminary

"The US church is in sharp decline. As in the days of Jesus of Nazareth, however, hope sometimes springs from unexpected and forsaken places such as 'Galilee of the Gentiles.' Costanzo, Yang, and Soerens point us to those voices of hope from the global and rapidly growing immigrant church."

Robert Chao Romero, associate professor in the departments of Chicana/o studies and Asian American studies at the University of California at Los Angeles, author of *Brown Church*

"This is a must-read resource for church leaders and church members, for missionaries, and for any of us living in what feels like a world turned upside down. The answer to whether God is still at work in the American church lies in its capacity to grow and learn from those outside our borders. *Inalienable* is a guided tour by seasoned and dedicated travelers into what it means to be a church that is both locally rooted and globally minded. It's the journey of a lifetime."

Mindy Belz, author of *They Say We Are Infidels*

"The church is flourishing in many parts of the world today, but it's easy for those of us in the West to feel a sense of hopelessness as we see the churches we attend, love, and perhaps lead mired in scandals, materialism, consumerism, and nationalism. Our brothers and sisters around the world, however, are tackling the challenges of poverty, forced migration, trafficking, and natural disasters, pointing a broken world to a better way, and we in the Western church have so much to learn and receive about the good news being proclaimed in both word and deed from the broader church. This book helps us do just that, sharing the incredible work that God is doing around the world, pointing us to a better way to listen and learn from our brothers and sisters who are living out the ways and truths of Jesus to transform their communities and ultimately point people to Christ. The Bible is the story of God centering those on the margins, and this book teaches us as the church to do the same."

Jenny Yang, senior vice president for advocacy and policy for World Relief and coauthor of *Welcoming the Stranger*

"This is the book I've been waiting for. Each author is writing from different disciplines and ministry backgrounds, each grateful for their tribes yet seeing something far more important—kingdom citizens made of every tribe, tongue, and nation. Until we see ourselves as one people with one King and one mission, we will forever undermine Jesus, the One we claim to worship. It's time we stop talking so much and start listening a lot more—to God and one another. The church is broken and lost—this book points to the path back home. May we get on our faces before God and repent of our deepest sin, a failure to love with abandonment."

Bob Roberts Jr., founder of Glocal.Net and Northwood Community Church in Keller, Texas, and cofounder of the Multi-Faith Neighbors Network

"Costanzo, Yang, and Soerens have given the American church a tremendous resource with this profound and needed book. Their impassioned call to us is to listen to our brothers and sisters in the Majority World and minority churches in the United States. These authors recognize that White American Christians can no longer act as the dominant partner in missions and theology, but rather we need to adopt a vulnerable and listening posture. This is a must-read for all Christians who long to see renewal in American evangelicalism."

Tish Harrison Warren, Anglican priest and author of *Liturgy of the Ordinary* and *Prayer in the Night*

INALIENABLE

HOW MARGINALIZED KINGDOM VOICES CAN HELP SAVE THE AMERICAN CHURCH

ERIC COSTANZO, DANIEL YANG, AND MATTHEW SOERENS

An imprint of InterVarsity Press
Downers Grove, Illinois

InterVarsity Press
P.O. Box 1400 | Downers Grove, IL 60515-1426
ivpress.com | email@ivpress.com

InterVarsity Press® is the publishing division of InterVarsity Christian Fellowship/USA®. For more information, visit intervarsity.org.

All Scripture quotations, unless otherwise indicated, are taken from The Holy Bible, New International Version®, NIV®. Copyright © 1973, 1978, 1984, 2011 by Biblica, Inc.™ Used by permission of Zondervan. All rights reserved worldwide. www.zondervan.com. The "NIV" and "New International Version" are trademarks registered in the United States Patent and Trademark Office by Biblica, Inc.™

While any stories in this book are true, some names and identifying information may have been changed to protect the privacy of individuals.

The publisher cannot verify the accuracy or functionality of website URLs used in this book beyond the date of publication.

Cover design and image composite: David Fassett
Interior design: Jeanna Wiggins
Images: gemstone closeup: © Daniel Grizelj / Stone / Getty Images
 stone wall: © kamisoka / iStock / Getty Images Plus
 watercolor painting: © philsajonesen / E+ / Getty Images

ISBN 978-1-5140-0304-6 (print) | ISBN 978-1-5140-0305-3 (digital)

Printed in the United States of America ♾

Library of Congress Cataloging-in-Publication Data
Names: Costanzo, Eric, author. | Yang, Daniel, 1979- author. | Soerens,
 Matthew, 1983- author.
Title: Inalienable : how marginalized kingdom voices can help save the
 American church / Eric Costanzo, Daniel Yang, and Matthew Soerens.
Description: Downers Grove, Illinois : InterVarsity Press, [2022] |
 Includes bibliographical references and indexes.
Identifiers: LCCN 2021061342 (print) | LCCN 2021061343 (ebook) | ISBN
 9781514003046 (print) | ISBN 9781514003053 (digital)
Subjects: LCSH: Christianity–United States. | Church. | Poor. | Church
 work with the poor. | Church work with people with social disabilities.
Classification: LCC BR517 .C659 2022 (print) | LCC BR517 (ebook) | DDC
 261.0973–dc23/eng/20220211
LC record available at https://lccn.loc.gov/2021061342
LC ebook record available at https://lccn.loc.gov/2021061343

26 25 24 23 22 | 6 5 4 3 2

FOR OUR WIVES—

Rebecca Costanzo, Linda Yang, and Diana Soerens

CONTENTS

1

WHY THE AMERICAN CHURCH NEEDS SAVING

What good will it be for someone to gain the whole world,
yet forfeit their soul? Or what can anyone
give in exchange for their soul?

MATTHEW 16:26

"IT WAS LIKE A FIRE ALARM going off in the church," reflects Beth Moore, whose Bible studies have influenced tens of millions of Christians. "I've never been naive enough to think that evangelicalism didn't have its problems, but I believed we were a gospel people, that the gospel of Jesus Christ was first and foremost to us." Instead, she says, recent years have seen the "gospel witness of the church" unravel, as many evangelical Christians in the United States have silently tolerated or openly embraced nationalism, sexism, and racism, "compromising our values for power."[1]

Moore is certainly not alone in her soul searching. Many are questioning whether the evangelical commitment to the authority of the Bible as the inspired Word of God has momentarily become—or perhaps has long been—secondary to the pursuit of political power and control. Many outside the church have assumed this for some time, resulting in a significant loss of credibility for the

American church. We've reached the point that just 9 percent of non-Christians have a positive opinion of evangelicals[2]—and, though evangelicals represent only a minority of all American Christians, the conflation of "evangelicalism" with "Christianity" in the minds of many non-Christians has meant that the broader church is viewed with skepticism. In other words, it feels like the American church is often repelling people from, rather than drawing them to, Jesus.

For Moore, the "fire alarm" began sounding in 2016 as her fellow evangelicals seemed indifferent to the admissions of sexual immorality by then–presidential candidate Donald Trump—and followed up soon after with their wholehearted endorsement and unwavering embrace even with no sign of his repentance.

For others, it has been the public fall of once-prominent pastors and ministry leaders caught in sins of hypocrisy and even harmful crimes.

For still others, it has been churches and denominations divided over obscure academic theories of systemic racism—while turning a deaf ear to the experiences of Black brothers and sisters, and seemingly being unbothered by their quiet exodus from their fellowships.

Or it has been revelations of sexual abuse within churches, denominations, and Christian ministries and subsequent coverups and shaming of victims, often rationalized by the belief that these institutions were too big—and doing too much good for God—to fail.

Or images of the Christian flag and "Jesus Saves" signs being waved during an insurrection at the US Capitol that included calls to hang the vice president of the United States, the assault of law enforcement officers, and prayers from self-described "patriots . . . that love Christ" who unlawfully invaded the Senate floor.[3]

Or Christians' susceptibility to and culpability in internet-fueled conspiracy theories that initially downplayed and then exacerbated a global health crisis, putting their own lives and those of their neighbors at risk.

We could go on. It feels like we're in a tailspin, like we may have forfeited our soul.

At the root, we believe, are both a theological and a heart problem. Many in the American church have replaced worship of God with idolatrous pursuits of wealth and power, at the cost of our integrity. White evangelicals have become known for ethnocentrism and for stoking fear of those who are different from them. The American church has developed a reputation for being driven by control, comfort, and security, as opposed to being known by love for one another, as Jesus instructed (Jn 13:35). Our political motivations and nationalistic tendencies have created a syncretism that blurs the lines between true discipleship and mere partisanship. As a result, many have come to see the American Christian emphasis on "family values" as nothing more than words, especially when our leaders and churches flagrantly fail to practice what they preach.

To be clear, however, this is not another book about Donald Trump, nor is it about Jerry Falwell Jr., Ravi Zacharias, Mark Driscoll, or others on a long list of high-profile Christians whose abusive leadership or hypocrisy has been exposed in recent years. It's also not the story of how we got into this mess. In their books that have become bestsellers, historians such as Jemar Tisby and Kristin Kobes Du Mez have already carefully documented the history of how American Christianity (and particularly White evangelicalism) has been complicit with racism, sexism, and nationalism—essentially White patriarchy masquerading as family values.[4]

Instead, this book seeks to answer questions such as, *Where do we go from here? Can and should the American church be saved? Can American evangelicals revive our public witness, and how?*

While we're uninterested in simply resuscitating a damaged religious brand, we believe—because we have seen it—that God is still at work in the American church, and we want to be a part of restoring her gospel witness. To do so, we're going to need to learn to listen to voices that have historically been at the margins of American Christianity.

PERCEPTION AND REALITY

Many within our evangelical world consider an increasingly negative reputation among those outside the church as proof that we are doing something *right*, earning the world's scorn that Jesus promised his followers (Jn 15:18; 1 Jn 3:13). Though there is a real sense in which the church should not be driven by popular opinion, we are also called to earn the respect of those who may never embrace our convictions. Moreover, they should be unable to ignore our "good deeds," which ultimately glorify God (Mt 5:16; 1 Pet 2:12). If reputation is indeed part of gospel witness, our witness is in tatters.

When the people of Israel claimed to bear God's name while simultaneously pursuing idols, God warned through the prophet Ezekiel, "[You have] profaned my holy name" (Ezek 36:20). This is a charge that should chasten us. The reality is that evangelicals are most often despised not because we are Christians, but because of distinctly *unchristian* attitudes and behaviors. As Russell Moore notes, "The culture often does not reject us because they don't believe the church's doctrinal and moral teachings, but because they have evidence that the church doesn't believe its own doctrinal and moral teachings."[5]

If we are actually committed to the work of God's kingdom, the commissions of Christ, the example of the New Testament church, and a biblical social ethic, we should be driven to care deeply for how others perceive our attitudes and actions. We should be known for our love, compassion, humility, and countercultural blessing of our opponents, earning worldly scorn *only* for doing what is right, never for what is wrong (1 Pet 3:8-9, 16-17). When we preach an anemic gospel while blatantly dismissing parts of the biblical witness that do not line up with our personal or partisan interests, we don't just appear to lack self-awareness, but "God's name is blasphemed" among those outside our faith (Rom 2:24).

We are to do what the apostles and the ancient church modeled: "Be wise in the ways you act toward outsiders; make the most of every opportunity" (Col 4:5). We are also to live lives that evoke questions from those on the outside about what fuels our unique hope—because we revere Jesus Christ as Lord (1 Pet 3:15). Right now, however, our public witness is not evoking questions from outsiders about our hope—fewer than one in ten non-Christians describe evangelicals as "hopeful"[6]—but rather about how we have come to compromise our stated convictions in so many ways. As the church emulates Christ, we are called to give ourselves "for the life of the world" (Jn 6:51)—but, as Glenn Packiam laments, "It's hard to be given when the world wants nothing we're giving."[7]

THE SINKING SHIP

Though many American evangelicals fear a looming persecution that might seek to silence the Christian voice in the public square, the reality is we are on the verge of forfeiting it ourselves. Many within our churches are leaving behind the evangelical label—and sometimes Christianity altogether. According to Barna, "The share of practicing Christians has nearly dropped in half since 2000."[8]

Likewise, the last decade has seen more young adults leave organized religion than any time before.[9] By 2020, less than half of Americans said they were members of any church or other house of worship, down from 70 percent as recently as 1999.[10] For a time, evangelicalism was one of the few Christian traditions that had not yet faced steep decline in membership. That no longer seems to be the case.[11] Simply put, while many American evangelicals were focused on gaining influence in a few successive political cycles, we may have lost an entire generation, with ripple effects for Christians of other traditions.

Beyond the statistics, though, this is personal for each of us, as we imagine it is for most reading this. We know and love people who have made the decision in recent years to walk away from the Christian faith. Each story is distinct, but many fit the profile of those who became disenchanted by public hypocrisy and failures in the American church, began to deconstruct the faith they had inherited from others, and ultimately decided it was not worth rebuilding. We're saddened, not because American Christianity is declining in numbers or public influence, but because we still genuinely believe these friends are missing out on the most profound hope possible: Christ and his coming kingdom.

As we watch more believers abandoning their faith and those not within the fold seeming less likely than ever to consider it, we are compelled to act. And we are convinced the most substantial threats to American Christianity are not those from the outside but from within. A story told by Rabbi Shimon bar Yochai nearly fifteen hundred years ago illustrates this well:

> Men were on a ship. One of them took a drill and started drilling underneath him. The others said to him: What are [you] sitting and doing?! He replied: What do you care[?] Is this not underneath my area that I am drilling?! They said to him: But the water will rise and flood us all on this ship.[12]

The ship that is American Christianity is filling up with water, in many cases as a result of holes we've drilled ourselves. The wounds which continue to weaken our effectiveness are self-inflicted and yet all too visible; nevertheless, many deny the existence of the very attitudes and actions for which we collectively need to repent. The solution, we believe, is to return to the inalienable truths revealed to us in Scripture.

RETURNING TO WHAT IS INALIENABLE

That which is *inalienable* is essential and undeniable. That word resonates for some Americans because of its role in the Declaration of Independence, where it is used to describe the rights to "life, liberty and the pursuit of happiness."[13] That commitment was, at best, what Martin Luther King Jr. described as a "promissory note" to be claimed by future generations of Americans, since it clearly was not applied by the founders to *all* men (to say nothing of all women) at the time of the nation's founding.[14]

Our goal is not to examine what's admirable or not in the foundation of our nation, but rather the core, inalienable truths about God that we must recover if the American church is to save our sinking ship: his kingdom, image, word, and mission. These truths are at the very center of the biblical narrative.

Drawn from the Latin word *alius*, meaning "other," to call something inalienable means that *there is no other*: what is inalienable has been established by God and therefore cannot be removed or abolished. For example, there is no other God (Ex 20:3) and thus we must reject idolatry—whether of our nation, our security, or our privileged position in society. Additionally, in God's kingdom, while the beauty of culture and ethnicity remain, there is no "other"— neither Jew nor Gentile; male nor female; citizen nor immigrant; White nor Black, Latina/o, Arab, Asian, nor Indigenous. Instead we "are all one in Christ Jesus" and of equal worth and importance (Gal 3:28). Scripture is clear that "God does not show favoritism" (Acts 10:34; Rom 2:11; Gal 2:6) and that faithful discipleship requires us to emulate our Lord.

We've written this book because we believe American Christians are at a critical crossroad, and the very soul of the American church is at stake. Jesus Christ promised that his church will endure until he returns again (Mt 16:18). He did not make that promise to the American church, however. If we are to stem this tide of decline and decay, it will take all of us—and it will take humility to listen to voices of the church beyond the White American evangelical stream of the faith which has long assumed leadership.

LEARNING FROM THE GLOBAL CHURCH AND THE MARGINS OF THE AMERICAN CHURCH

To the extent they think of them at all, American Christians have far too often made the mistake of viewing Christians from other parts of the world as our "little brothers and sisters,"[15] as if they are less equipped by the Holy Spirit because they have fewer resources and smaller theological libraries. On the contrary, we believe the global church to be among God's greatest and timeliest gifts to the American church, particularly in this season.

In the course of writing this book, we reached out to a number of church leaders in Latin America, Africa, Asia, and Europe whom we've met through our work and travels, asking for their candid perspectives on the state of the American church. One of those conversations was with Pastor Luis Luna of Honduras, who describes what many global Christians feel the more they engage with American evangelicals:

> There is that "go and get it done" mentality that we understand is part of the American entrepreneurial spirit and, in a sense, very much part of the American church. It feels like, "Since we have the money, we have the funds, we have the resources, and we have the structure . . . let's just go and fix these people's problems and then get out of here."[16]

Instead of this approach, throughout this book we have worked to elevate the voices of global Christians who speak prophetically through the Holy Spirit from their own biblical and cultural experiences. Though many of them have yet to be given the chance to significantly influence American evangelical thinking, we have sought out their voices of discipleship by design. We have also worked to lift up the perspectives of American Christians of color, many of whom come from communities which have been marginalized throughout American history. We are convinced that their readings of the Bible, which often come from different social locations than those of most American Christians, provide wisdom and will be a part of the corrective process that reveals our blind spots.

In addition to the voices of Christians from beyond the United States and from historically marginalized communities within, we have also purposefully sought out the voices of women. Whether intentionally or not, most of us are formed primarily by male perspectives on matters of faith. Though women make up the majority (about 55 percent) of US Christians,[17] they have long been on the margins of influence in terms of how Americans think about our faith. Just one-quarter of students in evangelical seminaries in the United States, and an even smaller share of the faculty, are female.[18] We would be enriched if we instead followed the model of Jesus, who, as Jo Saxton demonstrates from the Gospel narratives "saw women, their worth and their value, even when they were unseen by others."[19]

For many of us who are male and who grew up in the White-majority, dominant culture of the United States, it will take humility to look beyond the voices most like our own that have traditionally been the only ones we allow to inform us. We're convinced that the American church desperately needs to heed these fresh voices.

DEEPENING OUR ROOTS WITH THE HISTORIC CHURCH

There's one more set of voices we must listen to as we seek to recover the inalienable foundations of our faith: the dead. Throughout this book, we've sought to amplify the historic church—the voices, stories, and practices of Christians from the past who are often overlooked by contemporary American Christians.

There's a wealth of wisdom to be gained from the careful thinking of Christians of centuries past. Looking to the historic church is a way to, as G. K. Chesterton said, refuse "to submit to the small and arrogant oligarchy of those who merely happen to be walking about."[20]

It is common these days to hear pastors, church planters, and other Christian leaders describe their goal of having a "New Testament church," as if there were a solitary, prescriptive model. With so much distance between our time and culture and those of the first Christians, it is perhaps naive nostalgia to think ancient Christians did it better than we do today. Nevertheless, the witness and wisdom of the church throughout history provides us with a consistent reminder that there has always been a collective longing for a purer and more basic form of the church, and this longing has at times been a part of bringing renewal to prevailing models.

From the book of Acts forward, there has not been one generation of Christ's church that has not seen a movement of God's Holy Spirit. Nevertheless, most American Christians have very little knowledge of the roots of their own church traditions, much less that of any other Christian expressions. Evangelicals in particular often need to be reminded that the church existed for a millennium and a half before the Protestant Reformation, as even some seminaries no longer require pre-Reformation studies of church history.

For most of us, successfully honoring and learning from the history of the church will mean being willing to dig deeper into our backstory than we have before. As Roberta Green Ahmanson writes, "As long as I can remember, I have been looking for footprints left by Christians who lived before me."[21] This practice has enriched our own theological endeavors, and we believe it will enrich yours as well.

Deeper roots and a wider appreciation for diverse Christian expressions will only serve to further solidify our understanding of and commitment to the core truths about God's kingdom and Christ's work through his church.

WHO WE ARE: AMERICAN, MALE, AND EVANGELICAL

Before embarking on this journey together, we want to introduce ourselves. In addition to all being US-born males, we are a pastor, a missiologist, and a parachurch ministry leader, respectively. Each of us has also been educated by evangelical institutions, which we acknowledge gives us a particular, limited perspective on some important themes.

Even more, we are a trio of friends who all care deeply about, and are not ready to give up on, the American church. We want to stop the drilling on the ship and follow God's direction to begin patching some holes—and in some cases replacing entire rotten planks. We have little to offer if we are no longer on board. As James K. A. Smith observes, "You cannot be a prophet on your way out the door. You cannot shake the evangelical dust off your feet and then hope that your criticisms lobbed from elsewhere will somehow *change* things."[22]

Though we've mostly written this book in the first-person plural, we each bring distinct experiences and perspectives. Occasionally, then, as in the following paragraphs, we will break into our singular voices.

Eric. I'm blessed to pastor a great church in which the people care deeply about the gospel, our community, and the vulnerable around the world. If that were not true, I might have dropped the evangelical label by now. That would be a major identity shift for me, since I have spent my entire confessional Christian life, from the age of twelve until now, as an evangelical and specifically as part of the Southern Baptist Convention (SBC). I was baptized and married in an SBC church, all my degrees are from SBC schools, and every vocational ministry position I've ever held has been in an SBC institution or church.

Like many others, however, I've grown frustrated in recent decades watching the word *evangelical* be hijacked by those who would use it only for self-serving purposes, or for those of their tribe or preferred political party. In the last few years in particular, I've also grieved when some of my denomination's best pastors and leaders have exited, feeling misrepresented and unsupported—including many you will find quoted in this book.

All that being said, I am forever grateful for the ways in which God has used my evangelical background and community to help shape me as a follower of Christ. Many faithful men and women have invested in me, and both my academic and church experiences have allowed me to engage in biblical studies and relationships with other Christians from every walk of life and from almost every corner of the earth. My contributions to this book are an outflow of the work Christ has been doing in my life in the last few years to sharpen my focus on prioritizing his good news, his kingdom, and his care for the vulnerable. I remain in the evangelical world for the foreseeable future, and I pray that God will continue to use my family to proclaim Christ as a light to those stumbling in darkness and a refreshment to souls who are weary.

To the pastors reading this book: I get how hard it is to shepherd people these days. We see clearly that if we fail to reach the generations coming behind us who are all but disconnected from the church as it is, our congregations will not survive. At the same time, many of the issues those young people want us to address—such as racism, wealth, poverty, and social justice—are lightning rods for many of our current congregants. Generational and political divides also seem sharper than ever, and no matter how we engage such things we are likely to hear critical comments or receive scathing emails from those who represent one side or another. The global Covid-19 pandemic we've faced has not helped things, of course, as we feel like we must be prepared to pivot in a new direction at a moment's notice. It's a hard time to pastor a church, but I also believe it's an essential time for pastors not to give up. This is our moment to lead better than we ever have in full surrender to Christ and for the glory of his kingdom.

Daniel. Although I'm contributing to this book as a missiologist and church planter, I'll disclose that my underlying motivation for writing is deeply personal. As a Hmong American, my heritage is much different from Eric's and Matt's. In 1979, my family arrived in the United States as refugee immigrants from Laos by way of Thailand. I was born just a few months after my parents landed two hours west of Chicago in East Moline, Illinois. At the risk of being crude, I often tell people I was conceived in a Thailand refugee camp and born in an Illinois cornfield!

Not long after I was born—and after nearly forty years of animism and practicing Hmong folk religion—my parents became Christians through a small Lutheran church that helped sponsor and resettle them. Some might say God sent refugees like us to the United States so that Americans could reach us with the gospel. Others might say we were socialized into a version of American civil religion. I'm starting to wonder if God sent some refugees like us to shake up American civil religion, and to reach Americans with the gospel.

As of the writing of this book, I'm forty-one years old, around the same age my father was when he became a Christian. However, different from him, I had a somewhat typical American church upbringing, which included attending worship services every Sunday, midweek prayer, youth groups, and summer camps. But fifteen years ago, I began exploring how to make sense of—and perhaps even theologize—the existential gap between my parent's early refugee experience as non-Christians and my full immersion into American evangelicalism. I can see with a little more distinction now, compared to when I was younger, that we were socialized into something more complex than what Jesus' disciples started as a Messianic movement in the first century. And while I'm careful not to conflate American nationalism with evangelical Christianity, I am very empathetic toward those who in our day genuinely have a difficult time seeing the distinction.

For some young former Christians, the reputation of American evangelicalism became their excuse for leaving the church. Some never-will-be Christians have reasoned that American evangelicalism is why people should avoid Christianity altogether. This makes me believe even more that marginal communities, the global church, and the ancient church are prophetic reminders to Americans of what biblical Christianity actually stands for. And although I very much identify as an evangelical and an American, I also feel like I am potentially contributing to the problems of American evangelicalism if I hide or downplay my heritage and my family's immigrant narrative. Because there's always that chance that God didn't send us here just to be reached by Americans. It may be that there is a lot of shaking up and reaching out that people like me have to do as well.

Matthew. As a child attending a private evangelical elementary school, I began each morning pledging allegiance to the Bible: "God's holy Word . . . a lamp unto my feet and a light unto my path."

In many ways, that commitment to the authority of the Scriptures as the inspired Word of God is what has defined my faith and what it has meant to me since my earliest childhood—shaped by my Midwestern, nondenominational "Bible church"; my family; my school; and much of the media my parents permitted in our home— to be a Christian.

As I grew—if, like the apostle Paul, I can "go on boasting" (2 Cor 12:1)—I became something of a Sunday school all-star. I memorized hundreds of Bible verses. I've barely missed a daily "quiet time" since I was introduced to the discipline in elementary school. I was trained to view *every* issue—science, literature, history ("*His* story"), and definitely politics—through a biblical worldview.[23]

Even as a kid, I vaguely remember being warned that there were *other*, not-evangelical churches that employed a "potluck" approach to the Bible, trusting the parts they liked and ignoring the teachings they found old-fashioned, embarrassing, or inconvenient, like the resurrection and the virgin birth.[24] Not us: we stood alone on the Word of God: the B-I-B-L-E, as the popular children's song refers to it. God said it. We believed it. That settled it.

Later, as a student at an evangelical college, I began to realize that even those who shared a commitment to the authority of Scripture could disagree in good faith on how particular passages should be interpreted and applied. I encountered Mennonites who took Jesus' words so literally that they believed we should oppose, rather than rally around, the US military incursion into Iraq. I met Presbyterians and Anglicans who looked to entirely different passages to justify baptizing infants than those I used to dismiss the practice as unbiblical. I eventually lived for a season with Nicaraguan Pentecostals whose worship style was so distinct from anything I'd experienced that I wondered if they really belonged in the same religious taxonomy.

I also realized there were Bible verses that, for whatever reason, I'd somehow missed as I read repeatedly through my Bible, and which so far as I can remember were not the subject of sermons I'd heard. This came to a head when I began a career with World Relief focused on serving immigrants.

Until then, I don't think I'd ever thought of immigration as a biblical issue. But it took little more than a basic word search to realize that the Bible actually has *a lot* to say about immigration. In the Old Testament alone, I found ninety-two references to the Hebrew noun *ger*, an immigrant.[25] Soon, I began to notice that nearly every major character in the Bible was a migrant of some sort, from Abraham to Ruth to Daniel to Jesus himself. Now when I read the Bible, it's hard *not* to see migration as what missiologist Sam

George calls "a megatheme of the Bible"[26]—and I've had to ask what other biblical themes I've overlooked.

Having now worked for more than sixteen years with World Relief—which, though a ministry of the National Association of Evangelicals, has recently found itself out of step with the views of most White US evangelicals toward refugees—I've often wondered if the label *evangelical* is worth retaining. But I'm convinced that American evangelicalism's problems—the White evangelical majority's views of immigrants is just the tip of the iceberg—are actually a symptom of placing too *little* emphasis on the Bible, not too much.

WHO IS THIS BOOK FOR?

This book is for Christians who have sensed that the ship of American Christianity is sinking, or at least taking on water, and are wondering what they can do. It has not been written toward those who find the status quo entirely satisfactory, nor for those who feel they already have the answers and have little patience for doubt, mystery, or wonder.

Moreover, this book may not satisfy those whose tendency is to scan a book; look for key names, words, or phrases with which one disagrees; and, upon finding any, immediately dismiss the rest of the book's content. We have purposely drawn from some sources who are lesser-known or who have come from marginalized communities, as well as some who many American evangelicals have been conditioned to devalue or disregard without having actually engaged with them personally. In other words, we choose not to say to anyone, "You have nothing to teach or offer me." Our purpose is not to chase more controversy, but rather to stretch us all toward healthy growth in some areas while keeping our feet on solid ground.

We realize the spectrum of our readers will be wide ranging in the way they relate to American Christianity and to American evangelicalism, in particular. There will likely be some from inside American evangelicalism who think we are overly critical. There may also be others, both insiders and outsiders, who think we are overly optimistic.

But for those of you who have deep concerns about the future of the American church, we see you, and we're with you, and we pray you will find hope alongside us within these pages.

We also see you pastors and leaders who are wrestling with how to follow Jesus faithfully and to disciple those under your care to do the same. We know you are frustrated by the many external, unchristian influences that seem to have more sway on your congregation's beliefs than you do as their pastor.

We see you church members and attenders who suspect that what you hear on Sunday mornings or from other evangelical voices may have more to do with American values than with the inalienable truths of Christianity.

We see those of you whom the pollsters call the *nones*, who have no formal affiliation to any kind of organized religion, yet still have a lingering and sometimes nagging sense that God wants you to experience community with people of Christian faith. We hope this book will help you to not feel alone.

We see those of you who have felt like outsiders and tourists to Christian environments and the evangelical subculture.

And we also see those of you who no longer find evangelicalism or perhaps Christianity of any variety a safe place to call home for your sense of spirituality, including you *exvangelicals*.[27] We acknowledge your individual experience and applaud your courage to speak up and speak out. We see the holes in the ship that caused so many of you to jump. And we are grieved by your departure and by those who continue to drill more holes. Our goal is not necessarily to persuade you to join or stay on the evangelical ship, but rather to call us all to faithful discipleship.

Whoever and wherever you are, we invite you to join us on this journey to discover and rediscover the inalienable truths of God's kingdom with an open heart and mind.

QUESTIONS FOR REFLECTION AND DISCUSSION

▶ Do you resonate with the description of a fire alarm going off in the church? Was there a particular moment when you felt that something was profoundly amiss in American Christianity?

▶ In your assessment, is American Christianity more often rejected by the broader American culture because of doctrinal beliefs or because of a failure by Christians to live up to self-professed convictions?

▶ Can you think of an example of a voice from outside America or one that has been marginalized within America that has been formative to your own spiritual journey?

▶ As you begin this book, think about your current relationship with the church. If you identify as Christian, would you consider yourself evangelical, mainline Protestant, Catholic, associated with a particular denomination, or non-denominational? If you do not identify as Christian, were you formerly Christian, never Christian, or not entirely sure about your beliefs? If you're reading through this book with others, acknowledging your own current view of the church and your personal history could be helpful to them.

ACTION STEPS

▶ As you read, pay attention to the footnotes and develop your own further reading list with perspectives you find compelling or challenging, particularly from authors from beyond America or from marginalized communities within America.

▶ In his personal introduction, Eric talked about his own Christian community within his family and his church. As you begin the journey through this book, identify those key people with whom you feel safe to discuss spiritual things and with whom you can be vulnerable and feel safe. If you cannot identify anyone, ask God to reveal a person(s) in your life who can become that kind of community for you.

▶ Daniel mentioned his unique perspective as a Hmong American child of refugees. If you're unfamiliar with the history of the arrival of Hmong people to America, these resources are a good start: Kao Kalia Yang's memoir *The Latehomecomer: A Hmong Family Memoir* (Minneapolis, MN: Coffee House Press, 2008) or *The Hmong People Movement: Part 1, Part 2,* and *Part 3* (The Alliance, 2005, www.cmalliance.org /video/watch/20061).

▶ Matthew shared how early on he was surprised to find that the Bible speaks frequently to the theme of immigration, which led him to wonder what other biblical blind spots he may have had. If you are not familiar with how the theme of immigration is addressed in the Bible, consider taking up the Evangelical Immigration Table's forty-day "I Was a Stranger" Bible-reading challenge, available at www.EvangelicalImmigrationTable .com/iwasastranger.

PART 1

THE
KINGDOM
OF GOD

2

KINGDOM CENTERED

The LORD reigns, he is robed in majesty;
the LORD is robed in majesty and armed with strength;
indeed, the world is established, firm and secure.
Your throne was established long ago;
you are from all eternity.

PSALM 93:1-2

Blessed is the Kingdom of the Father and of the Son and of
the Holy Spirit, now and forever and unto ages on ages.

OPENING WORDS OF THE DIVINE LITURGY
OF SAINT JOHN CHRYSOSTOM

"THE MOST IMPORTANT ELECTION in our nation's history..."
We've heard this every two to four years of our lifetimes. Moreover, similar language has existed in American elections going back to at least 1805,[1] often accompanied by dire warnings about what will happen if the "other side" wins.

In an ideal world, American Christians would lead the way in countering this political apocalypticism, whether from the right or the left, with a narrative grounded in faith. Instead, we've been complicit in fostering such attitudes within our own echo chambers, where most of the people speaking into our lives look and think like us and only reinforce our existing beliefs.

Is this really what we've been taught to do—to listen to those saying what we want to hear over listening to and being challenged by the Word of God?

We should know better. If the Bible truly is our authority, as we've claimed, we should know that the kingdom of God does not function the same as American politics. We should know that blind partisanship, stirring up endless controversies, and the like are incredibly toxic to our public witness. Even in the face of the most critical of elections and political debates, as many of our recent ones have been, we should know better than to place our hope and trust in a ruler, party, or institution. We should also know that those who do so are never fulfilled, and instead find only disappointment and disillusionment.

None of this is unique to our time. The temptation to sacrifice personal or collective integrity for earthly power and success has plagued God's people since the earliest civilizations. Surely the devil had this in mind when he took Jesus up to a high place and promised him "all the kingdoms of the world" if only Jesus would bow down and worship him (Mt 4:8).

The devil's words betrayed both his great arrogance and ignorance regarding Christ's authority and identity. Satan's empty promises and that which had tempted humankind in the past did not move Jesus. He refused to dishonor God's name or forfeit his mission. Instead, Jesus' response, drawn directly from the Hebrew Scriptures, resounds loudly into our time: "Away from me, Satan! For it is written: 'Worship the Lord your God, and serve him only'" (Deut 6:13; Mt 4:8-10; Lk 4:5-8).

Jesus' rejection of the devil's temptations was like a springboard that launched his personal and public ministry with the words: "The time has come. . . . The kingdom of God has come near. Repent and believe the good news!" (Mk 1:15). From that time forward, Jesus spoke of *his* eternal and unshakable kingdom more than any other topic—more than love, more than sin, more than the Law, more than the church, more than heaven or hell, and even more than death and resurrection. As Russian Orthodox theologian Alexander Schmemann observed, drawing from the liturgy of Saint John Chrysostom, "From the beginning the destination is announced. The journey is to the Kingdom. This is where we are going—and not symbolically, but really. It is the goal, the end of all our desires and interests, of our whole life, the supreme and ultimate value of all that exists."[2]

Instead, we have settled for the fleeting privileges of our little kingdoms on earth, and in such ways lost much precious credibility in our culture. Centering the kingdom of God is our way back.

God's kingdom is a "mystery" (Mk 4:11 NASB), as Jesus said, full of wondrous surprises. As a result, much ink has been spilled to provide definitions of the kingdom of God upon which we could not improve.[3] Our aim in this chapter is to go beyond merely a theological or devotional expression regarding God's kingdom. Using his kingdom as our lens, we can widen our views of where, how, and among whom God is at work—and we can do so joyfully. The countercultural kingdom of God shapes our character, joins us together with the global church in the Spirit and in mission, and pulls us forward in following Jesus.

A COUNTERCULTURAL KINGDOM

The allure of "all the kingdoms of this world" has been the downfall of many. In this wilderness moment for American Christianity, will chasing furiously after cultural and self-serving priorities like wealth, power, control, status, and security bring the death knell of our churches, or will we follow Jesus' example of resistance and refusal for the greater purpose of true kingdom ministry?

Hau Suan Khai is a Burmese Christian whose grandparents converted from Buddhism to Christianity in the 1960s. His children are the fourth generation of his family to be discipled as followers of Christ. Khai and his family came to the United States as refugees in 2014 and immediately planted an evangelical church. Since then, he has become a pillar in his local community and in 2016 received the Lifetime Achievement Award from the United Nations High Commissioner for Refugees. Khai describes the presuppositions he and many other Burmese Christians had about the American church before being resettled to the United States, and the reality they experienced once they arrived:

We did not think America was 99 percent Christian; we thought it was *100 percent Christian*. America has "In God We Trust" on its money, obviously referring to the God of the Bible. We thought every city would have many churches all filled with people of all ages. Yet in all the American churches we first visited we saw mostly elderly people. I remember in the first church where we witnessed this, the question came into my mind: *Where are the younger adults? Are they in a different part of the building?* One of my first surprises was learning they were not in the building at all.

One of the hardest parts of this reality for us is that we are the fruit of the American missionary. We are still in the church because of your mission work. But sometimes it feels like we are two friends, and you told us something and we followed you, but now you are trying to skip away from the things taught to us. We fully committed to follow you and later you tried to escape from that way.[4]

Khai's words are sobering, as is the reality that American churches are indeed facing the growing realities of declining membership. Even more sobering is the fact that historic churches throughout western Europe have been emptying for decades. In eastern Germany, the birthplace of Protestantism, declines have been faster and more widespread, and entire communities have no church attendance.[5] Germany as a whole, according to a recent survey, ranks dead last among all European nations in the percentage of those who "say they believe in God with absolute certainty," with only 10 percent answering affirmatively.[6] In fact, out of formerly Christian places in the world, eastern Germany is one of the least Christian today. As Martin Knispel, a pastor in Berlin, argues, "With the exception of a few small migrant churches that are being planted and enjoying some growth, Berlin is not just 'post-Christian'; it is 'post-post-Christian.' The people have forgotten that they forgot about God."[7]

Certainly, external factors like secularism and religious pluralism have played a major role in Europe's Christian decline, especially among younger people.[8] But the German Protestant church eroded significantly from the inside, as political opportunism within the church indulged ideologies and parties who perpetrated egregious human rights violations, committed genocide, and ultimately divided an entire continent through the heart of Berlin. The German Protestant church may never recover from the disillusionment resulting from its past unholy relationships between the church and political regimes—and this is instructive for American Christians. We cannot possibly be a "pleasing aroma of Christ" (2 Cor 2:15) in any culture when we reek of un-Christlike attitudes, behaviors, and alliances. The kingdom of God is wholly incompatible with such things.

Nevertheless, American Christians are also often enticed by "the kingdoms of this world." As missiologist Lesslie Newbigin noted, for decades we've put excessive amounts of energy into making sure the "right people" are in office, and then displayed a convenient silence regarding accountability for their actions and influence when those people occupy the seats of power.[9] When our preferred candidates win elections we give thanks to God and see the results as his anointed plan. But when non-preferred candidates win we pray only for their downfall, amplify their perceived failures, or simply deny the results of the elections altogether. Such duplicity is not only dishonest; it is idolatrous. When we elevate any human being to a position of authority in our lives such that even the breaking of God's laws is excused, we are ultimately rejecting God himself as our true king (1 Sam 8:7). Moreover, blind partisanship can easily convince us to circumvent our call to work together for the good of God's kingdom regardless of a political administration.

When we center the inalienable qualities of the kingdom of God, however, our identities and priorities consistently flow in a different direction from our own selfish pursuits, and usually from those of culture as well. Consider how King David, imperfect as he was, stood out among others who held power in the ancient world as he prayed before the assembly in Jerusalem during preparations for building the temple. David ascribed all kingly authority to God rather than himself:

> Praise be to you, LORD,
>> the God of our father Israel,
>> from everlasting to everlasting.
>
> Yours, LORD, is the greatness and the power
>> and the glory and the majesty and the splendor,
>> for everything in heaven and earth is yours.
>
> Yours, LORD, is the kingdom;
>> you are exalted as head over all.
>
> Wealth and honor come from you;
>> you are the ruler of all things.
>
> In your hands are strength and power
>> to exalt and give strength to all. (1 Chron 29:10-12)

Unfortunately, Israel did not maintain this prayerful momentum for long, nor did David always. Throughout the stories in 1 and 2 Kings and 1 and 2 Chronicles, God's people continually rejected his leadership and lost sight of his kingdom as their highest priority. They chose instead to place their trust in the false gods and idols of other nations, as well as their own palaces, temples, dynasties, and conquests. Despite countless warnings from God's prophets, Israel courted endless cycles of disobedience in generation after generation, until their walls and temple literally came crashing down and they became captives in their own lands (2 Kings 17; 24:1-21).

In the face of the idolatrous religion and politics of his own day, Jesus centered God's kingdom and made known its countercultural disposition where "those who exalt themselves will be humbled, and those who humble themselves will be exalted" (Mt 23:12). In the Beatitudes, he taught that this kingdom belongs not to the rich, proud, and prominent, but rather to the poor, righteous, and persecuted (Mt 5:3-12). Within this kingdom, Jesus said, the lowest on earth are great (Mt 18:4) and many who are powerful on earth are least (Mt 20:16). The kingdom belongs to children (Mk 10:14), but the rich find it very hard to enter (Mk 10:25).

Despite Jesus' teaching, we often exalt the proud, rich, and powerful while ignoring or even demeaning the humble, poor, and persecuted. We've also been quick to join the cultural trend of classifying people we've never met as our enemies. Christian Smith, in his classic work *American Evangelicalism: Embattled and Thriving*, argues that evangelicalism in particular has found some of its most noteworthy "successes" when it can identify "forces that seem to oppose or threaten it." Evangelicalism "*thrives on distinction*, engagement, tension, conflict, and threat," he adds. "Without these, evangelicalism would lose its identity and purpose and grow languid and aimless."[10]

We've applied this backward thinking to how we vote, who we listen to, and what we share online—often driven by fear that someone or something might jeopardize our comforts or false securities. Empathy and understanding are evaporating in our culture, and many American Christians are not fighting to keep them. In the same way, the exploitation and further marginalization of people and groups within our own communities are ignored or even justified rather than being addressed biblically.

What changes might our communities experience if modern-day disciples—rather than participating in such behavior—were the first to take a listening posture toward those who represent different points of views? What if those same disciples displayed a Christlike empathy and helped foster greater levels of respect and understanding? What if rather than pushing back on discussions related to racism, privilege, and justice, American Christians became the first to dive into such topics using a biblical framework in light of God's kingdom? Mark Shaw and Wanjiru M. Gitau, writing about the importance of engaging the most pressing social issues in Africa through the church, observe that "when the church gets caught up in this vision of the coming kingdom and seeks to witness to it in the present, acts of social justice and economic deliverance are often stressed. The church becomes a counterculture opposing the status quo and working for radical change."[11]

Among the most countercultural things Jesus ever said, no matter the culture, were his commands in the Sermon on the Mount: "But I tell you, do not resist an evil person. If anyone slaps you on the right cheek, turn to them the other cheek also," and "You have heard that it was said, 'Love your neighbor and hate your enemy.' But I tell you, love your enemies and pray for those who persecute you, that you may be children of your Father in heaven" (Mt 5:39, 43-45). Instead of the perpetual "us against them" mentality, Christ gave us a different paradigm for cultural engagement, even in the face of conflict—and especially in the face of conflict. This Christlike way of living is not cultivated in echo chambers, but rather in communities of empathy and understanding where believers are willing to take a listening posture and, when necessary, to forgive and seek forgiveness.

We may indeed be in the wilderness, but in this cultural moment, the American church has a unique opportunity to become "living expressions of the kingdom of God,"[12] in which the perspectives, priorities, goals, and character of our communities of faith reflect a kingdom-centered worldview.

KINGDOM CHARACTER

Within the last decade, American Christians' double standards for their preferred political figures have devalued personal character altogether. Polling suggests that White American evangelicals specifically went from being the religious demographic *most* likely to insist that personal character and integrity mattered in a national leader to the group *least* likely to do so.[13] It should not surprise us then that increasing numbers of people are disheartened with American Christians and the mixed messages we're sending about the relationship between our faith and the power structures of our culture.

D. L. Mayfield is an author and evangelical pastor's daughter who has recently discarded the evangelical label. She notes the grief she and others in her generation felt when their parents and pastors, who had vehemently criticized President Bill Clinton's sexual immorality, had no such response toward (and even excused) credible allegations and recorded admissions of sexual assault by Donald Trump. "I'm so confused," she said. "[They're] the ones who raised me to take the Bible very seriously and yet . . . we seem to be throwing it all away."[14]

While this kind of duplicity might be human nature, it does not represent the character of God's kingdom. The kingdom character that God displays in himself is the same character he expects from his people. His character is seen throughout the Hebrew Scriptures and the New Testament and displayed most clearly in the person of Jesus Christ.

The most common description of God's character throughout the Hebrew Scriptures—in fact, the very words God used to describe himself—is that he is "compassionate and gracious . . . , slow to anger, abounding in love and faithfulness" (Ex 34:6; Num 14:18; Neh 9:17; Ps 86:5, 15; 103:8; Joel 2:13). And God commanded his people to be imitators of him. As he spoke through the prophet Micah,

He has shown you, O mortal, what is good.
And what does the Lord require of you?
To act justly and to love mercy
and to walk humbly with your God. (Mic 6:8)

God's kingdom character was then fully personified in Jesus. Through his life, teaching, and ministry, Jesus Christ became the clearest picture of the kingdom of God in all of Scripture and the created universe. The writer of Hebrews describes this in the opening words of the epistle: "In the past God spoke to our ancestors through the prophets at many times and in various ways, but in these last days he has spoken to us by his Son, whom he appointed heir of all things, and through whom also he made the universe" (Heb 1:1-2).

Using a "Christ Hymn" of the early church, the apostle Paul exhorted Christians to "have the same mindset as Christ Jesus,"

Who, being in very nature God,
did not consider equality with God something
to be used to his own advantage;
rather, he made himself nothing
by taking the very nature of a servant,
being made in human likeness.
And being found in appearance as a man,
he humbled himself
by becoming obedient to death—
even death on a cross! (Phil 2:5-8)

From his arrest through his crucifixion, Jesus displayed unwavering commitment to God's kingdom purposes in speech and action. Though his life being taken from the earth was the ultimate display of depravity and injustice, he did not resist it (Acts 8:33). He even prayed for the forgiveness of his persecutors (Lk 23:34). As Jesus stood before the Roman governor Pontius Pilate with the opportunity to defend his kingdom and kingship, the character and behavior of the Son of David was completely different from that of powerful men like Herod. Nor did he bear any resemblance to certain members of the Sanhedrin whom Pilate had previously accommodated. When Pilate pressed him, Jesus made clear: "My kingdom is not of this world. If it were, my servants would fight to prevent my arrest by the Jewish leaders. But now my kingdom is from another place" (Jn 18:36).

Consider the many implications of Jesus' statement. In a first-century Judean world of competing thrones, sects, and political loyalties all straining under the yoke of the Roman Empire, the kingdom Jesus identifies is both distinctive and transcendent. His is not a kingdom that can be fought for or defended with human strength, armaments, or weaponized ideas. Rather than deploying his disciples to wage a cultural war, he sent them out to make more disciples following his example in word and deed. His kingdom defeated the seemingly invincible powers of sin and death not through revolt or insurrection but rather through his willing sacrifice on the cross.

THE KINGDOM AND THE GLOBAL CHURCH— OUT OF MANY, ONE

In the summer before my senior year in college, I (Eric) was invited to represent my university at Amsterdam 2000, which was the final global, ecumenical evangelism conference under the leadership of Billy Graham. I was twenty-one years old, and the trip to Europe was my first time outside the United States. Among the strengths of Amsterdam 2000 was the decision to emphasize global Christians in each element of the conference, from plenary speakers and music to breakout sessions.

This purposefulness was clear from the first moments, as the opening ceremony was a procession of all the nations represented in the room—211 in total. Representatives from each nation streamed in dancing and waving while also wearing native dress and colors and carrying their nation's flag. Once every seat was taken, we sang in a wondrous chorus that joined together countless languages. Neither before nor after have I ever seen such a full, diverse picture of the body of Christ in one place. It was like a window into the glorious future promised in the book of Revelation: "I looked, and there before me was a great multitude that no one could count, from every nation, tribe, people and language, standing before the throne and before the Lamb" (Rev 7:9).

What happened in that arena was something that no human effort could ever have accomplished. It was not only a display of *diversity*; it was also a demonstration of *unity*—being "one in Christ Jesus" (Gal 3:28). In that moment, we experienced an entirely new community of wholeness that transcended all other communities to which we would later return. This was not the work of the United Nations or a G20 Summit. It was the kingdom of God at work in our midst through the global church. And it was the most complete picture I have ever seen of the primacy of our citizenship in heaven over the ethnic and national markers that tend to divide us (Phil 3:20). It was also the first time I realized how few global Christians and Christians of color had been in my life to that point.

Among the most beautiful aspects of Christ's otherworldly kingdom is its diversity, which, like a threaded tapestry or a mosaic of stones, comes together for the purpose of portraying a unified depiction of Christ himself through his body, the church. Centuries before *e pluribus unum* became the motto of the United States, it could also describe the inalienable character of the New Testament church. The phrase also fits the global church as it continues to grow worldwide—in diversity and in the unity of the Holy Spirit.

In one of his parables, Jesus described the kingdom of God as a vineyard where all the workers are paid the same wage, regardless of the hours worked (Mt 20:1-16). He also said, "People will come from east and west and north and south, and will take their places at the feast in the kingdom of God. Indeed there are those who are last who will be first, and first who will be last" (Lk 13:29-30). Though we often view the world through paradigms of scarcity and fear of those who are different from us, the kingdom of God is a boundless table of welcome, where each person, regardless of origin or status, has a prime seat like an honored guest at a wedding banquet (Mt 22:1-14; Lk 14:16-24).

Nevertheless, many American Christians still struggle to see Christians from other parts of the world as equals—especially from the developing countries in Africa, Latin America, and Asia often referred to as the Global South. As we will discuss more in the next chapter, American Christians have viewed ministry and mission with the global church as being done only *at* or *for* global Christians. Using the example of short-term mission teams, Latin American theologian Ruth Padilla DeBorst identifies ways American Christians unwittingly devalue their brothers and sisters in Christ from the Global South by blowing in and out without consideration for the kingdom work those believers are doing daily in their context.

"The 'missionaries' are doing many things, but how much of this work has been done with the people," she asks, and "to what extent are those people being acknowledged as Christians with equal value in God's Kingdom?"[15]

Jesus modeled something much different. He chose to come to earth from heaven so that he might do all things *with* humanity and specifically with those he called as disciples. Padilla DeBorst's father, missiologist C. René Padilla, described this as Jesus' "incarnational" approach of imparting God's kingdom character and values among people from all cultural, socioeconomic, and political demographics.[16]

Though it took some time, Jesus' first disciples and other early Christians also learned to value the breadth of God's kingdom work among people of different ethnic and cultural backgrounds as Christ modeled. The apostle Peter, who had once resisted such things fiercely, was among the first to experience this shift of heart and mind. "I now realize how true it is that God does not show favoritism," Peter declared, "but accepts from every nation the one who fears him and does what is right. . . . Everyone who believes in him receives forgiveness of sins through his name" (Acts 10:34-35, 43). Several years later, Peter described the global Christian community as an entirely new people unto themselves:

> But you are a chosen people, a royal priesthood, a holy nation, God's special possession, that you may declare the praises of him who called you out of darkness into his wonderful light. Once you were not a people, but now you are the people of God; once you had not received mercy, but now you have received mercy. (1 Pet 2:9-10)

Every Christian is a dual citizen, with responsibilities to both our earthly and heavenly kingdoms. We live within the tension of citizenship in the kingdom of God and our kingdoms of earth as we faithfully "give back to Caesar what is Caesar's, and to God what is God's" (Mt 22:21). Global Christians understand the tension of dual citizenship well, as many live in contexts where the church is a persecuted minority and their personal rights are uncertain. Others live outside of their homeland, whether as immigrants in a foreign context or displaced persons living in camps or refugee communities. In such contexts these Christians look to the future through the lens of the kingdom to participate in the countless ways that God is at work.

THE KINGDOM MOVES FORWARD, NOT BACK

For the last quarter of my (Daniel's) life, I've been on a theological journey of understanding the missional purposes for myself and others in immigrant communities who came to America from war-torn countries. Though my family came to the United States forty years ago seeking refuge from political persecution, we found much more than that. When my dad became the first follower of Jesus in the history of our family, we found the kingdom of God. In my own walk with Christ, I've learned to reimagine my life as part of a promise and answered prayer that grew out of deeply painful circumstances. That which others intended for evil, God intended for good (Gen 50:20).

Nevertheless, when I was invited in 2010 to attend an education conference in Hanoi and visit the growing churches in the mountains of northern Vietnam, I was nervous about what my father would think. When our family was fleeing the communist regimes of Southeast Asia, North Vietnam was considered by many "the head of the snake." I wavered about accepting the invitation to the conference specifically, not wanting to hurt him by helping a government that was partly to blame for the deaths of our family and our people. When I finally shared my hesitation with him, his encouraging response in Hmong was unforgettable: "You should go. All of that is in the past. God taught us to love our enemies. Everything has changed. God brought us to America for a reason—so we can help those who used to be like us."

My father's words filled me with both hope and perspective. In that moment I understood a profound truth in a fresh way: Jesus changes the way we view our past so that even those with the most painful histories can have hope that everything is being made new and moving forward, both for our own good and the good of his kingdom.

Jonathan Edwards called the created universe "a stage upon which the great and wonderful work of redemption should be transacted."[17] The kingdom of God, progressing in a series of acts, is on display in each movement of the Bible and in every generation, culminating in Jesus Christ. As the spool of time unwinds and history progresses, the characteristics, plans, and purposes of God's kingdom become clearer; it moves forward as light that is increasingly overwhelming darkness until all darkness has passed away and only light remains (Jn 1:5; 1 Jn 2:8; Rev 21).

Many modern theologians and teachers have described the kingdom of God as "not yet," in anticipation of Christ's future and triumphant return when the fullness of his kingdom will be realized. But the kingdom can also be described as "already," because Christ is at work on the earth now through the Holy Spirit and the church. Kenyan theologian J. N. K. Mugambi applies the present-tense nature of the kingdom to the work of the gospel in Africa:

> The Good News which Jesus proclaims to the world is not theoretical. It is practical. It is news which in real life rehabilitates individuals and groups that are marginalized by various natural and social circumstances. In contemporary Africa, the Good News understood in this way ought to rehabilitate the afflicted individuals in every region, country and locality. The Gospel ought to help Africans regain their confidence and hope.[18]

As a result, the kingdom of God is not only a destination, but also a *direction*. This is the thrust of Christ's statement in the model prayer:

> Your kingdom come,
> your will be done,
>   on earth as it is in heaven. (Mt 6:10)

This was both how he taught his disciples to pray and the future he promised. The *already* of his kingdom on earth now is headed toward the *not yet* when all things here are as they are in heaven. As Ellen Vaughn writes, "Christ's cross is the intersection of time and eternity."[19]

Jesus also illustrated the forward direction of the kingdom through parables and metaphors about growth and production. In Mark's Gospel, he says the kingdom is like seed scattered across the ground that, as time passes, sprouts into a great harvest (Mk 4:26-29). In Matthew, Jesus compares the kingdom to wheat that sprouts, grows heads, and outlasts the weeds so that it might be brought into the master's barn (Mt 13:24-30); to a mustard seed that starts small but grows into a great tree (Mt 13:31-32); and to yeast working itself through flour to become leavened bread (Mt 13:33). He also describes the immeasurable value of the kingdom, like a matchless treasure that exceeds any other investment (Mt 13:44), or a pearl of great price worth selling all one's possessions to own (Mt 13:45-46).

Jesus' teaching about the kingdom involves active participation on the part of his people. When we put our best energy into his kingdom work around us, the work gives true meaning to our efforts, whenever and wherever they are given. The forward direction of the kingdom also gives meaning to both the past and present, and it ends with the accomplishment of all God's good and redemptive plans for his creation in which all things will be made new in Christ (Rev 21:1-5). In other words, the direction of God's kingdom is a hopeful one. As N. T. Wright observes,

> You are not oiling the wheels of a machine that's about to roll over a cliff. You are not restoring a great painting that's shortly going to be thrown into a fire. You are not planting roses in a garden that's about to be dug up for a building site. You are— strange as it might seem, almost as hard to believe as the resurrection itself—accomplishing something that will become in due course part of God's new world.[20]

What, then, are our primary roles within the kingdom now? First, we must stay in the "flow" of God's kingdom and actively participate in God's work. As Paul proclaimed to the Athenians, "in him we live and move and have our being" (Acts 17:28). Second, we must announce the presence of God's kingdom in every space we enter. Because his kingdom transcends and permeates all that exists, there is no place we can go where he is not already present and at work. The kingdom moves forward through God's strength, not human strength. Counterintuitively, the kingdom often advances through Christlike humility, weakness, and surrender. Therefore, even where poverty, injustice, pain, sickness, and death are present, we can announce with confidence that the kingdom is already there. As Peruvian scholar Vilma "Nina" Balmaceda attests:

> The kingdom of God is wherever the King is present, and the King is present where people are suffering. I have seen the Lord more present in prison, in the walk of migrants trying to cross the border, and with the survivors of political violence in Venezuela, Peru, and Colombia. The King is present in the midst of their suffering giving hope to human beings when circumstances seem completely hopeless.[21]

SEEK FIRST THE KINGDOM

When the devil took Jesus up to the high place and promised him the kingdoms of the world, Jesus resisted and rejected his temptations. Believing the lie that one can gain the whole world comes at the cost of forfeiting the soul.

The truth is, many of those attitudes that currently repel people from the American church or cause them to leave altogether have nothing to do with the kingdom of God. God's kingdom is not self-serving, but rather advances through the humble and devoted. The message of his kingdom is also not only good news for one kind of people or group, but for all who are exposed to the light of Christ. The kingdom of God, as revealed in Jesus Christ, is above all other kingdoms, more powerful than all other thrones, more valuable than any treasure, and more worthy of the commitment of our entire lives than any other endeavor.

Indeed, every Christian is a dual citizen—with residency on earth and in heaven. When there is a conflict, however, our citizenship in God's kingdom always comes first and outranks every other membership and commitment, because only his kingdom "will never end" (Lk 1:33). Contrary to the kingdoms, empires, and thrones of man— which come and go—God's inalienable kingdom is firmly established, permanent, and eternal. As Martin Luther King Jr. wrote, "The great military leaders of the past have gone, their empires have crumbled and burned to ashes. But the empire of Jesus, built solidly and majestically on the foundation of love, is still growing."[22]

QUESTIONS FOR REFLECTION AND DISCUSSION

▶ Based on what you've read in this chapter, how would you define and describe the kingdom of God to someone who is unfamiliar with the idea?

▶ How Christian would you consider America to be—Christian, post-Christian, post-post Christian, or something else?

▶ What do you think the impact on American culture would be if the character and behavior of Christians consistently reflected God's characteristics of being "compassionate and gracious, slow to anger, abounding in love and faithfulness"?

▶ Why do you think Jesus used stories and metaphors about production and growth when describing the kingdom of God?

▶ What does it look like for Christians and churches in America to stay in the "flow" of the kingdom of God?

ACTION STEPS

▶ For the next seven days, take a break from political and cultural commentary from mainstream media/news, social media, and so forth (you may need to remove some apps from your phone to avoid opening them as a matter of habit), and replace that time with reading and meditating on one of these Bible passages each day:

- 1 Chronicles 29:10-20

- Psalm 146

- Matthew 4:1-11

- Matthew 13

- Philippians 2:5-11

- 1 Peter 2:9-25

- Revelation 21

▶ Identify something you are hopeful about right now and where you believe the kingdom of God is present in your life or around you. Take intentional steps to be present in that space and to take an active role in what is happening.

▶ Choose a country you've never heard of and learn more about the church as it exists there. After you've gathered some information, pray for the church or an individual believer in that country. A great resource to help is http://operationworld.org.

3

DECENTERING THE (WHITE) AMERICAN CHURCH

Christianity has become a non-Western religion;
which means, not that Western Christianity has become
irrelevant, but rather that Christianity may now be seen
for what it truly is, a universal religion, and that
what has taken place in Africa has been
a significant part of this process.

KWAME BEDIAKO

THE LAST VISIBLE MARKERS of when my (Matthew's) neighborhood in Aurora, Illinois, was populated primarily by German immigrants are the Wurst Kitchen sausage store and the church where my family and I are members. Constructed by German immigrants more than a century ago, the church building's inscription still reads *Erste Deutsche Ev. Luth. St. Paulus Kirche*. At some point, the services switched entirely to English as many German immigrants abandoned their native language in an effort to demonstrate their loyalty to the United States.

As Mexican immigrants arrived in the 1990s, the demographics of the neighborhood began to change and the church launched a

Spanish language service. Eventually, the English-speaking congregation moved to a new building across town, but the Spanish-speaking congregation stayed. Today we worship primarily in Spanish, with English translations available for those who need it. Most Sundays a couple from Costa Rica leads worship, *hermanos* and *hermanas* from Mexico read the Scriptures, and our pastor, Alex Merlo, originally from Honduras, preaches. Others in the congregation are from Puerto Rico, Guatemala, Cuba, and Venezuela, along with some who were born in the United States. The students of the church's pre-seminary *escuela misionera* theological education program have gone on to plant six other Spanish-speaking churches, advancing the mission of proclaiming the gospel that was started on that street corner by German immigrants more than a century ago.

The history of my church, in many ways, parallels a shift happening nationally and globally. While it was once true that the large majority of Christians in the United States were of European origins, close to four in ten US Christians are now people of color,[1] and that share is likely to continue to increase.

Global Christianity is also becoming less American and European. Whereas in the early twentieth century 82 percent of the world's Christian population lived in the Global North,[2] today nearly 70 percent live in the Global South, and the most common language spoken by Christians is Spanish.[3]

Whether we realize it or not, classical Western Christianity, which has given birth to many church traditions around the world including those of the United States, has been decentered. In other words, the average Christian in the world is not an American and she's definitely not an aging, White male with particular political leanings.[4]

Jehu Hanciles, a historian and theologian born in Sierra Leone, reminds us that "the ultimate achievement of the Western missionary movement was its pivotal role in the dramatic shift in global Christianity's center of gravity, which has witnessed the emergence of the non-Western world as the new heartland of the faith."[5] It is important to understand that the achievement is not about some intentional process of decentering Western Christianity by

Europeans. Hanciles is attesting to the autonomy and agency of non-Western Christians, and how the gospel empowers once it takes root. As Majority World churches have grown in maturity and indigeneity, he adds, they have made tremendous progress in separating out Western culture and structures from biblical Christianity—both of which came partly from colonial missions.[6] This is not to say that indigenous forms of Christianity from the Majority World are more authentic than Western forms or that they are above the need for reproof, but rather that it is no longer (and perhaps never was) the place for Western Christians to police their authenticity or to critique their expressions.

In the same vein, decentering Western Christianity does not mean it is irrelevant, is second-class, or has become obsolete—it just means North America and Europe should no longer define the norms of what it means to be a Christian. Not only is Christianity growing fastest in the Global South, but churches in Africa, Latin America, and Asia are continuing the decolonization process of Christendom,[7] uncovering a more indigenous Christianity with lesser Western influence. As Tish Harrison Warren observes:

> When I think of evangelicals, I think of Singaporeans planting churches in Thailand, or Rwandan families serving refugees in Uganda, or Nigerian seminarians, or the *evangélicos* of South America—a label widely used by Protestant Latinos. We need to keep these voices front and center in any discussion of the church. They are our future and also our present—the ones who make up the majority of evangelicals on earth.[8]

The challenge for American Christians is to be captivated by a picture of the church that is ancient and global, rather than by one that is Western and American. If the American church is to be saved, we must not only understand but also come to desire the influence coming from our historically marginalized communities and other Christians from around the world, which is an inalienable aspect of Christ's commission to his church by design.

CELEBRATING GLOBAL KINGDOM CITIZENS
ARRIVING AT OUR BORDERS

In just a few generations, the faces and demographics of America have changed dramatically. Over forty-four million people residing within the United States are immigrants,[9] and some are quickly moving from the margins to the center of American Christianity. As sociologist Stephen Warner observes, "The new immigrants represent not the de-Christianization of American society but the de-Europeanization of American Christianity."[10]

According to leading demographer Phillip Connor, "about three in four US immigrants have some Christian background, whether it is Catholic, Protestant, or some other Christian heritage,"[11] which means about thirty-three million immigrants came to the United States already identifying as Christians. There is some truth to the idea Christians often suggest that God is bringing the nations to America, with its robust tradition of religious freedom, so we might "reach them." However, the reality is that many have already *been* reached. In fact, some are arriving in America with the intention of reaching Americans.

Hau Suan Khai says this about the immigration of Burmese Christians to America and their growing influence among American churches: "There was no way for us to come to America unless God had a plan. God brought thousands and thousands of us Burmese Christians to America, we believe, to help revitalize American churches."[12] As Khai indicates, the future vitality of American Christianity is closely connected to the arrival of immigrants. Even secular publications such as *The Economist* and the *Atlantic* have reported on immigrant missionaries coming to the United States to evangelize secular Americans.[13]

As many predominantly White Christian denominations are shrinking quickly, racially and ethnically diverse denominations are steady and even growing. According to the General Social Survey, in 1972, almost 28 percent of the US population identified as regular church attendees belonging to a mainline Protestant church. In 2017, that percentage dropped to just over 10 percent.[14] American mainline denominations are predominantly White; one mainline denomination, the Evangelical Lutheran Church of America, is 96 percent White[15]—and is also among the denominations that have experienced the sharpest declines in membership in the past decade.[16] The decline of mainline denominations is not only a story about racial diversity and declining White church membership; it is also a cautionary tale about the failure to integrate immigrant groups into their theology and traditions.

The converse of this can be seen in some evangelical denominations. For example, the largest American evangelical denomination is the Southern Baptist Convention (SBC), which has reported a gradual drop in membership every year since 2006 when it consisted of 16.3 million people. In 2021, the denomination reported a membership of 14.09 million.[17] While this is a significant drop in membership over fifteen years, during that time the denomination also saw significant growth in the number of new non-Anglo congregations. In its 2020 annual report, the SBC reported that nearly 20 percent of its churches are now non-White, with more than 60 percent of its newest churches being started and led by non-White pastors.[18] While the SBC is still largely White, its consistent growth among non-White congregations, in particular new immigrant congregations, has kept it from experiencing even faster decline.

In other cases, the growth of immigrant congregations has led to net denominational growth. The Assemblies of God has reported membership growth almost every year over the last three decades—decades in which many other denominations saw vast decline. Its largest growth has been among Hispanic congregations, which now make up almost a quarter of all churches.[19] Today, it reports that nearly half of its members are "ethnic minorities."[20] While the Assemblies of God has shown no noticeable growth among White members in twenty years (in 2019, the number of White members was 1.85 million, the same as in 2001),[21] it has grown because of non-White members, particularly Latina/os.

These two large evangelical denominations show that a key difference-maker for staving off fast membership decline is the growth of non-White congregations and the arrival of immigrant churches. While growth and decline are nuanced in other ways—such as changing denominational affiliations, birth and death rates, and the rise of nondenominational churches—there is no doubt that the global church has had a great impact on the American church. To put it another way, it seems that over the last thirty years, global Christianity has already been helping to save some streams of American Christianity from an all-out free fall and decline.

CHOOSING LEADERSHIP FROM THE MARGINS AND THE MAJORITY WORLD

Even as Christianity grows in the Global South and declines in the West, and as the US immigrant population continues to grow, many American Christians are still formed almost exclusively by Western, usually White, perspectives. The American church's lack of urgency and intentionality to seek out and elevate diverse voices, including those of global Christians now residing in the United States, will continue to marginalize the unique perspectives of those whom our society has generally not placed at the center of power. As a result, as biblical scholar Dennis Edwards observes, "the voices of a multitude are muted. The body of Christ is distorted and misshapen because many parts of that body are constricted for the sake of a powerful few."[22] One must wonder how many of the challenges currently plaguing the American church could have been mitigated had it properly valued and incorporated leadership from the margins. However, this is not a new challenge faced only by the contemporary American church.

The book of Acts records that in the early days of the church in Jerusalem, "the Hellenistic Jews . . . complained against the Hebraic Jews because their widows were being overlooked in the daily distribution of food" (Acts 6:1). Culturally and linguistically, the Hellenistic Jews were closer to the Greeks of their time than to the Hebraic Jews. In a community that still had high regard for Jewish culture and customs, the Hellenists could have been considered less kosher, causing them to be marginalized by the majority group. Although the motive for what led to the neglect of the food distribution isn't entirely clear, it is very clear that those most affected by it were Hellenistic widows.

The Spirit-led response of the apostles—all of whom were Hebraic Jews—both addressed the immediate problem and also set an important tone that would shape the church's future. Rather than justifying the neglect or allowing the marginalization of others to continue, they appointed seven men from among the Hellenistic group—Stephen, Philip, Procorus, Nicanor, Timon, Parmenas, and Nicolas—to bring equity to the situation (Acts 6:5). The fact that these men were likely best equipped to minister to the Greek-speaking widows, while important, is not all that was happening in that moment. As Kenyan scholar Paul Mumo Kisau observes, the Judean believers were willing to let non-Hebraic believers "control the distribution of good to *everyone*" (emphasis ours),[23] not just the Hellenists. In doing so, believers from the margins, previously unnamed in the New Testament, were elevated to leadership roles in visible spaces.

From the founding of our nation until today, the American church has often neglected marginal communities. Because of the history of being pushed out of White-led spaces by racist policies and biblical misinterpretation,[24] the African American church tradition in particular was developed on a separate track from White Protestantism. Had White churches honored and invited leadership from marginal communities in the way the apostles did in Acts 6, this would not have been the case.

As a result, many White churches today continue to make similar mistakes and still have yet to resolve certain ongoing tensions. For example, Black churches have generally avoided the dichotomies that have divided White evangelicals in the past century, such as an insistence that Christians choose *either* adhering to historic Christian theological beliefs and personal salvation *or* seeking justice and societal transformation. As Esau McCaulley argues, "The call for individual and societal transformation within the context of the historic confessions of Christianity is the mainstream within Black American Christianity." As a result, the Black church has largely rejected the false choice between viewing the Bible as either prioritizing the need for personal salvation *or* demanding liberation from systemic injustice, insisting "they could affirm the one without denying the other."[25]

Likewise, institutions and organizations that have historically and exclusively been led by White Christians must seek leadership from the Majority World. There are some encouraging examples of this, such as the 2018 election of Eddy Alemán, who is Nicaraguan, as the general secretary of the Reformed Church in America; the appointment of El Salvador–born Santiago "Jimmy" Mellado to lead Compassion International; and the election of the most recent president of the National Association of Evangelicals, Walter Kim, who is the son of Korean immigrants. Nevertheless, these individuals remain the exception and not the rule, and the fact that Christianity has grown rapidly outside of North America and Europe is still news to many Americans. Indeed, many still have no functional frame of reference for Christianity without American-born leaders at the center.

If we fail to account for the growth of global Christianity both in numbers and leadership, our understanding of what it means to be a Christian is incomplete. Worse yet, we will only further the perception—both inside and outside the church in America—that Christians are more like Ned Flanders than they are Damares Alves[26] or Joshua Wong.[27] This also means that the increasing number of Americans who are leaving the church are not in fact rejecting biblical Christianity, but rather an American-centric version, while giving little consideration to the global movement of Christianity around the world.

CONVERTING AMERICAN PRIVILEGE INTO GLOBAL PARTNERSHIP

In 1974, Billy Graham gathered 2,300 evangelical leaders from 150 countries for the first International Congress on World Evangelization held in Lausanne, Switzerland. This inaugural meeting produced The Lausanne Covenant, which became a standard agreement among evangelicals for missionary activity in the world. The significance of this gathering was in the globally diverse composition of its attendees and their consensus on the need to see Christian mission both as evangelism and social change. This was done particularly through the lens of the global church, or what they called the "whole church."[28]

This covenant marked an intentional shift to see evangelicalism not primarily as a Western expression of Christianity but to acknowledge and affirm the rise of evangelicalism in the Majority World. The eighth principle of the covenant addresses the need to see churches in global partnership and begins by saying:

> We rejoice that a new missionary era has dawned. The dominant role of western missions is fast disappearing. God is raising up from the younger churches a great new resource for world evangelization, and is thus demonstrating that the responsibility to evangelize belongs to the whole body of Christ. . . . Thus a growing partnership of churches will develop and the universal character of Christ's Church will be more clearly exhibited.[29]

While perhaps easier said than done, this statement, in principle, is a reminder to Western churches that their role in the world is mainly to partner, and never to own. Likewise, it is a reminder to "younger churches" to seize the opportunity to lead both locally and globally. The kingdom of God dignifies all its partners, lifting up those who do not have significant means and humbling those who do. The reliance on God begets a reliance on one another, producing a different attitude and mentality. The history of Christianity has been marked by global relationships that were perhaps more personal than they were organizational. A shift from privilege and self-reliance to partnership and interdependence based on authentic relationship is a return to historic Christianity and a marker of the kingdom of God.

One of the obvious areas in partnership that needs continuous evaluation and innovation is resources—means and money. Ruth Padilla DeBorst points out that "while the map of Christianity has been redrawn, the economic map shows not the slightest change."[30] The ability to do life, church, and theology without daily concerns about poverty and marginalization is a privilege shared by a large number of American Christians, and yet not shared by many other Christians from around the world. Again, this doesn't mean American Christians should operate from a guilt complex because we're living relatively comfortably. It does mean, however, that we should constantly reevaluate our activity in the world, acknowledging privilege and power dynamics that come from comfortable living.

The ancient church of the first century had to learn how to access but not fully rely on the financial power centers of their world, which enabled them to flourish. The churches in Macedonia had little means and little money, for example, and yet they were praised by the apostle Paul for their participation in mission, especially for giving out of their poverty and even beyond their means (2 Cor 8:3). Paul's affirmation and Christlike attitude toward these younger, poorer churches is a model for how American churches should respect partner churches from the Majority World with a sense of mutuality. And this respect also entails an intentional posture of learning from their traditions and experiences, so as to expand our theological imagination and stretch our understanding for how the gospel can bring transformation and healing to the world.

LEARNING ABOUT THE BIGNESS OF THE GOSPEL

The book of Matthew references three distinct times when Jesus specifically uses the phrase "good news of the kingdom" or "gospel of the kingdom" (Mt 4:23; 9:35; 24:14), two of which include him healing sicknesses and diseases. Preaching the nearness of the kingdom as good news (Mk 1:15) accompanied by signs, miracles, and wonders was a regular part of Jesus' earthly ministry. The apostle John tells us that this pattern of ministry was so normative for Jesus that, "if every one of [the things Jesus did] were written down, . . . even the whole world would not have room for the books that would be written" (Jn 21:25). Jesus' proclamation of the gospel of the kingdom led to real and tangible change on earth, even in immediate circumstances. He also commissioned us as his disciples to follow the same pattern of ministry in our kingdom preaching and ministry (Lk 10:9). Looking to the global church for how the gospel of the kingdom is proclaimed and lived out can perhaps help the American church return to Jesus' pattern for ministry.

In those parts of the world where Christianity is fastest growing, at least two common dynamics emerge. First, Western Christianity exported its cultural understanding of the gospel into the world and it has taken root. But second, in many places, these imported versions of the gospel are now being challenged, refined, and held up like a mirror for Americans to see.

One example is the witness of the Latino church. In his book *Brown Church: Five Centuries of Latina/o Social Justice, Theology, and Identity,* Robert Chao Romero describes "Brown Theology" as a unique and consistent body of theology based on the Bible that comes from the Brown Church, which he defines "as a prophetic ecclesial community of Latinas/os that has contested racial and social injustice in Latin America and the United States for the past five hundred years."[31] In his explanations, Romero makes a scathing but warranted assertion as to why it is necessary to delineate Brown Theology from colonial Western theology:

> Brown Theology rejects the narrow presentation of Christianity as eternal "fire insurance" that leaves most of life untouched by God's love and redemption. According to this narrow conception of Christianity, which has been around in Latin America since colonial times, we believe in Jesus so that we can be forgiven and so that we can go to heaven after we die. Notwithstanding the critical importance of heaven and forgiveness, this short-sighted version of Christianity presented during the conquest of the Americas ignores the biblical value of justice and the social dimensions of Jesus' redemption. It thereby allowed for the genocide and dehumanization of native and African communities, and the presentation of a corrupt and distorted gospel.[32]

Romero reminds us that for several hundred years, there were Latina/o theologians who articulated the gospel in a more comprehensive way that was still consistent with evangelical theology of today. Brown Theology recognizes the need for personal salvation and transformation while also acknowledging that the gospel is deeply tied to biblical justice and creation care.

In fact, creation care is a consistent theological theme among many global Christians, but one that has often been downplayed in American theology. While the Bible is filled from cover to cover regarding the connection between creation and stewardship of the land, many American evangelicals view creation care as a minor issue in regard to faith and the efficacy of the gospel. However, global Christians from around the world recognize the need to remove this platonic and dichotomous thinking. "The Cape Town Commitment," framed in 2010 by the Lausanne Movement, provides a basic theology for why creation care is a direct implication of the gospel:

> The earth is created, sustained and redeemed by Christ [Col 1:15-20; Heb 1:2-3]. We cannot claim to love God while abusing what belongs to Christ by right of creation, redemption and inheritance. We care for the earth and responsibly use its abundant resources, not according to the rationale of the secular world, but for the Lord's sake. If Jesus is Lord of all the earth, we cannot separate our relationship to Christ from how we act in relation to the earth. For to proclaim the gospel that says "Jesus is Lord" is to proclaim the gospel that includes the earth, since Christ's Lordship is over all creation. Creation care is thus a gospel issue within the Lordship of Christ.[33]

We can see the tangible effects of how gospel ministry directly affects creation care in countries facing tremendous environmental challenges such as India. Ken Gnanakan was an Indian educator, environmentalist, and theologian who began his career as a chemical engineer and eventually began ministering in his home city of Bangalore. Early in his ministry he prioritized environmentalism because he wanted to improve the living conditions of the people of Bangalore. In 1979, Gnanakan started what eventually became known as ACTS (Agriculture, Crafts, Trades, and Studies) Group. For him, ACTS was not simply a nonprofit or an NGO but rather a holistic Christian mission organization reimagined around the gospel and creation theology. Today, ACTS is committed to total development through projects that revolve around education, environment, and health programs in the slums of India, where many regions are seeing substantial growth in Christianity.[34]

In a commentary on the Psalms, Gnanakan offers a biblical rationale for why it is imperative that we understand our human responsibility in creation through the broader context of the gospel:

> We must do our part, but must also recognize that God has planned the final restoration of this fallen creation. In Romans 8:20-21, the Apostle Paul refers to creation being liberated from its bondage to decay. This is generally understood as a promised reversal of the curse that creation was subjected to as a consequence of human sin (Gen 3:17-19). . . . We are called to be stewards, protecting this intricately planned world God has entrusted to us. Even more, we are called to be "responsible stewards" (Gen 2:15; Mt 25:20-21; 1 Cor 4:2; 1 Pet 4:1). Responsible stewardship demonstrated through God's love will result in practical actions to promote sustainable living as well as right attitudes towards the environment. As Bible-believing Christians, we are called to care for creation in order to protect, conserve and bring healing to our wounded world.[35]

He challenges us to remember that the gospel of the kingdom entails a very important dimension of human responsibility in creation care. And through the voices of Latin American theologians renewed in our time in the work of many like Romero, we are reminded that the gospel and justice have always been coupled together by Christians in colonized societies. They join the cacophony of voices from kingdom citizens from around the world influencing American Christianity to have a greater gospel imagination, and to think more deeply about what it means to be a local church that is truly shaped by the worldwide church.

STRIVING TO BE A LOCAL AND A GLOBAL CHURCH

The last century saw a movement within several sectors, first among city planners and environmentalists, urging us to be "glocal"[36]: to think globally and act locally. Many in America have caught this vision, understanding that globalization is not just about multinational corporations and climate change. In its essence and at its best, the global church was already a grassroots local entity, both decentralized for optimal indigenous expression and centralized to maintain a common and culturally transcendent identity.

This dynamic was also present in the first-century church. Early on, the church in Jerusalem became the authority for what it meant to follow Jesus. It was composed primarily of Jewish followers, and thus its culture, theology, and leadership were Jewish. As the gospel began to spread throughout the Roman world among non-Jewish people, including many who were culturally Greek, the Jerusalem church maintained authority as to what it meant to be a follower of Jesus and what was expected of new believers (Acts 11:19-30; 15). These culturally Jewish deliberations created challenges because they often made little sense to non-Jewish believers. Thankfully, the Jerusalem church began to take the Christians living outside of Judea into consideration, making concessions for them, including those decided at the Jerusalem council (Acts 15:1-35).

In time, the center shifted away from Jerusalem to more multicultural Roman cities such as Antioch, with ramifications for church leadership and even for theology. As people of various cultures in Antioch became followers of Jesus, they began to congregate in ways that were different from Jews but also different from their culture of origin. They formed a new people that was multiethnic and globally minded but still connected to the ancient Jewish Scriptures. It was there in Antioch among that church that "the disciples were called Christians first" (Acts 11:26).

The locally rooted church in Antioch had an authentic global-mindedness that changed its leadership, theology, and ministry. While it's wrong to say that the church in Antioch was a *better* expression than the church in Jerusalem, it's right to say that it was *better situated* to connect with the global stage for which Christianity was being prepared. While first-century skeptics could still argue against this newest expression of the church, they could no longer say that Jesus' followers were merely religious Jews from the periphery of society. On the contrary, it was actually from among the skeptics that new Christians were emerging.

Over the last three decades, Bob Roberts Jr. has led his church in Keller, Texas, to be locally present and globally influenced, training hundreds of pastors and church planters to lead churches in the same way. In the mid-1990s, Roberts started an NGO in northern Vietnam to help local American churches directly partner with Vietnamese governmental organizations to engage different domains of society.[37] This completely changed how he thought about the local church and missions. Instead of just doing religious work (especially doing it poorly) in other countries, he discovered that local churches in America could develop long-term relationships with city leaders of other countries for the transformation of society.[38] Roberts challenges the local American church to break out of its near-sighted mindset:

> The kingdom is a wholistic, viral response to the different infrastructures of society within a connected world. Today, with all of the connections of globalization and the various domains of the world intersecting our lives, it's easier than ever to practice kingdom work because the kingdom itself is a viral, organic response. It's societal, as opposed to religious, skeletal, and institutional.[39]

What Roberts pioneered years ago is becoming part and parcel to American churches, especially to those who understand that American Christianity has been decentered around the world. If the local church is primarily about doing religious work among its homogeneous members, then its actions will favor individuals from its own community over others. While this may have a positive nurturing effect that should not be neglected completely, focusing exclusively on local church work for your own can perpetuate bias and exclusion. Centering local church work can also result in protectionist and preservationist mentalities. But when understood as both a kingdom and a global entity, the local church and its work intersect the public domains of society by necessity, which allows it to meet its purpose as an organic response to the diverse needs of society.

Of course, one church cannot be all things to all people, but in seeing itself beyond its immediate locality, it has a better chance at becoming more things to more people. And as this happens, church leaders will usually seek to grow their membership toward higher levels of racial diversity and multiethnicity. However, in our cultural moment in America, churches are discovering that this cannot—and must not—be achieved through tokenism and mere diversity quota; it can only happen through a deep application of the gospel in community.

SEIZING OUR EPHESIAN MOMENT

The essence of the oneness of God's people amid diversity is a biblical theme expressed throughout both the Old and New Testaments, but the missional vision is perhaps made most explicit in the apostle Paul's epistle to the Ephesians.[40] The British historian and mission scholar Andrew Walls explains that the original Ephesian moment—in reference to the church in Ephesus, which was composed of both Jews and Greeks—was brief, ending in 70 CE with the destruction of the Jewish state, which scattered the Jews and left the church monocultural again. However, Walls maintains that Paul assumed a culturally diverse church when he wrote this epistle:

> The Ephesian letter is not about cultural homogeneity; cultural diversity had already been built into the church by the decision not to enforce the Torah. It is a celebration of the union of irreconcilable entities, the breaking down of the wall of partition, brought about by Christ's death (Eph 2:13-18). Believers from the different communities are different bricks

being used for the construction of a single building—a temple where the One God would live (Eph 2:19-22).[41]

Paul's revelation to the Ephesians was that embedded in their local churches was the revealed mystery that Christ is known to a greater extent, and even perhaps to the fullest stature, when displayed by both Jew and Greek living in unity for the gospel. The eschatological vision of the true Israel had now been made complete in Christ by the uniting of Jews and Gentiles, where congregations like the ones in Ephesus were an instance and an embodiment of this vision. Each member came from a culture that needed to be converted to Christ, and "each was necessary to the other, each was necessary to complete and correct the other; for each was an expression of Christ under certain specific conditions, and Christ is humanity completed."[42] From Walls's theological framing we can deduce that now, in our generation and our day when the levels of diversity are greater than ever, our dedication and response to our own Ephesian moment should also be greater than ever.

In another work, *Missionary Movement in Christian History: Studies in the Transmission of Faith*, Walls puts forth two principles that represent opposing tendencies in cultural engagement and integration that can tend to generate tension, yet both originate in the gospel: the *indigenizing principle* and the *pilgrim principle*. Although he originally formulated these principles in the context of pioneering missions and evangelism, they are easily transferable to the theological and spiritual development of local churches and American Christian institutions.

The *indigenizing principle* comes from understanding that God accepts us "as we are," which includes not just our individual selves but also the cultural context from which we come. The impossibility of separating an individual from their social context leads to the necessity of indigenizing both faith and community. Every believer longs for a place where they can "feel at home" as a Christian. The Jerusalem council in Acts 15 was the process by which a "home" was being created for Gentile Christians and by which their faith was becoming more indigenous.[43]

The *pilgrim principle* challenges one's natural sense of identity and belonging. God, through the person and work of Jesus Christ, not only takes people as they are, but he also transforms them into who he wants them to be. Where the *indigenizing principle* particularizes the faith of the Christian to their culture and group, the *pilgrim principle* universalizes it. The believer is introduced to more than what they have ever known, which includes meeting other members of the family of faith, some of whom are from very different backgrounds.[44]

In her book *Why This New Race: Ethnic Reasoning in Early Christianity*, Denise Buell explains that for the early church, becoming a Christian was an "ethnic reasoning" process where the early believers were not only crossing a religious boundary to become a Christian, but also "a boundary of membership in one race to another."[45] The early Christians, composed of many ethnic groups, underwent a process which led them to become a new *ethnē,* or a new people group. This process included tensions and growing pains not unlike the ones described in Acts 6 or in Galatians 2—and not unlike the ones experienced today in many multiethnic churches across America.

Walls's *indigenizing* and *pilgrim* principles provide a framework to understand the dynamics of the ethnic reasoning process and the tensions that often come along with it. From these two principles, we draw four markers of belonging that can help build American churches and institutions that reflect global Christianity in our modern Ephesian moment.

Marker number one (indigenizing): the congregation fosters ongoing growth in a person's awareness and acceptance of their ethnicity, encouraging them to grow in their uniqueness in Christ. The apostle Paul described the unity of diversity in the church: "In him the whole building is joined together and rises to become a holy temple in the Lord" (Eph 2:21). Often, diversity will bring tension, but the process of being joined together in the Lord brings growth. Growing together in a social unit and learning to share a common language allows people to develop accommodations for one another, which radically diminishes confrontation and conflict.[46] More than just resolving tension, there is something uniquely drawn out of a person that only someone of another culture can evoke. Likewise, there is more to be explored and experienced in one's own culture when shared with someone of another culture. A congregation that values the unity of diversity is more likely to appropriately draw out and meaningfully highlight the cultural contribution of its members.

Marker number two (indigenizing): the congregation accepts a person's ethnic perspective as normative and valuable to its development as a theological and discipleship community. A community of diverse Christians whose doctrinal and practical theology has little input from its minority or marginal members will be one-dimensional in both theology and mission. Such a community may only be capable of regurgitating inherited models rather than creating new and more effective ways of reaching diverse groups of people. As non-Jews, the Ephesians may not have been able to perceive on their own the insight Paul shared with them in chapters two and three. Nonetheless, Gentiles like them were very much a part of Paul's own discovery process of this profound revelation: "This mystery is that through the gospel the Gentiles are heirs together with Israel, members together of one body, and sharers together in the promise in Christ Jesus" (Eph 3:6). This theological development in Paul's life and in the life of God's covenant people proved that Gentiles have an equal stake in the mission of God because of Christ. The inclusion of the Gentiles in the true Israel does not imply that a church's theology is a hodgepodge of ethnic experiences. Instead, this mystery discloses that there is no cultural gatekeeper for the gospel.

Marker number three (pilgrim): the congregation sees the completed work of Christ as the means to regulate a person's ethnic pride, combating ethnocentrism and elitism. The person and work of Christ is the anchor for a believer's primary identity.

Ethnocentrism is incompatible with the one who has been crucified with Christ and whose life is not their own (1 Cor 6:20; Gal 2:20). On the contrary, God has reconciled both Jew and Gentile to himself in one body through the cross, killing the hostility that one may raise over the other (Eph 2:16). Meaningful belonging to the body of Christ will always mean that a fixed ethnicity is not the final destination for a believer. As a result, a healthy multiethnic congregation is a potential safeguard against ethnic superiority. Multiethnic congregations must always be discerning toward the individual regarding what is redeemable about their culture and expose to them what must be put off regarding their former way of life (Eph 4:22). Just as the gospel anchors our identity in Christ, it is also the knife that performs surgery on our hearts, cutting away any excessive ethnic pride.

Marker number four (pilgrim): the congregation challenges a person to regularly give up their preferences in order to live peaceably and to reflect the gospel to the world. Lastly, pilgrims who are becoming more like Christ in a multiethnic and missional congregation find themselves freely contextualizing their life to maximize the exposure of the gospel to an unbelieving world. Paul's versatility in becoming "all things to all people so that by all possible means I might save some" (1 Cor 9:22) speaks not of a compulsion to be like others, but of the freedom to not be enslaved to his own cultural preferences. In Christ, Paul was given many modes and expressions so that he could easily put preference aside if it meant winning someone over with the gospel message.

Not every congregation in America can or should be multiethnic. We believe there are practical considerations and theological reasons why America still needs healthy language-specific or ethnic-specific churches, especially among new immigrants. When a community warrants multiethnic congregations, however, healthy models in which there is meaningful belonging act as a microcosm and a window for others to see how the world can come together in a local church.

American churches that are multiethnic and globally minded are not exempt from criticism. At the same time, if American Christians will discover and prefer their kingdom and global identities over nationalistic ones, our churches might experience repentance and renewal and be better positioned to listen to our critics with greater empathy and humility. To get there, we must recenter the kingdom of God and decenter American cultural expressions of church that have often subtly led us to replace true worship with idolatry.

QUESTIONS FOR REFLECTION AND DISCUSSION

▶ Does your church or surrounding community have a strong bias for or against a particular racial or ethnic group? If so, how does this prevent minorities from feeling like they belong to the community?

▶ What has been your understanding of the gospel? Do you think how Jesus proclaimed the gospel of the kingdom in his time is different from how it is done today by American Christians?

▶ How does Robert Chao Romero's description of Brown Theology challenge you?

▶ Which of the four markers for meaningful belonging resonates with you in your own journey toward understanding your ethnic identity and belonging?

▶ Identify how local American churches can partner with churches from around the world in ways that encourage strong mutuality.

ACTION STEPS

▶ Reflect on what cultural and historical traditions have most influenced your own community and leadership style. Identify the unhealthy or unbiblical habits that should be changed or abandoned altogether in your own personal life. If you journal, consider writing these things down as a way to remind yourself of your commitment.

▶ Study the community and leadership structures of the New Testament, especially from Acts 2:42-47, Acts 6:1-7, and Philippians 2. Consider similarities with some cultures from the Majority World. Compare them to the leadership structures that might be typical in American churches. Examine your own leadership structures to see how collective leadership could benefit your community.

▶ Whether for an occasional visit or even as a long-term shift, consider becoming part of a church where you are under the spiritual teaching and leadership of someone from a different background than your own, particularly one that has been on the margins of influence in the American church.

PART 2

THE IMAGE OF GOD

4

AMERICAN CHRISTIAN IDOLS

In America we have idols,
many—but not of wood or stone—
not in honour of Mercury, Minerva, Apollo, Mars,
Bellona, or Jupiter! No! But, nevertheless, we have idols
that hold the people captive—entrance and spell-bind
them with the witchery of their charms, and wrap
them in the thralls of their enchantments!

REV. J. R. BALME (1864)

WHEN BEN KIRBY posted a picture of a prominent Christian worship leader who was sporting an expensive pair of tennis shoes, he unwittingly launched the Instagram sensation known as PreachersNSneakers. Since that first post, which Kirby describes as "a poorly informed joke for my four hundred followers, delivered with a dose of cynical snark,"[1] PreachersNSneakers has delivered hundreds of images of pastors and others with the going rate of their designer shoes or clothing worn during church services. In addition to exposing the extravagance and sensationalism of some pastors and leaders, PreachersNSneakers also provides a disturbing glimpse into distinct forms of idolatry that exist within the American church.

Idols exist in every culture and have always been a temptation for God's people. Throughout Scripture God consistently forbids all forms of idolatry—because of his holiness, first and foremost, but also for our own good. Idols are destructive and, as Sri Lankan Christian scholar Vinoth Ramachandra notes, those who worship them "call up invisible forces that eventually dominate them. When what is meant to be a servant is treated as a master, it quickly becomes a tyrant."[2] The psalmist expresses this very thing after decrying the futility of idols:

> But their idols are silver and gold,
>   made by human hands.
> They have mouths, but cannot speak,
>   eyes, but cannot see.
> They have ears, but cannot hear,
>   noses, but cannot smell.
> They have hands, but cannot feel,
>   feet, but cannot walk,
>   nor can they utter a sound with their throats.
> Those who make them will be like them,
>   and so will all who trust in them. (Ps 115:4-8)[3]

The idols of today, like their ancient counterparts, make promises they cannot fulfill. They also demand sacrifices we cannot afford to give, including the most valuable thing we have to offer God: true worship. And they present a distorted view of the divine image. The church, as God's people in this age (Jn 1:10-13), must submit ourselves to God completely, that his Spirit might empower us to root out our idols and replace them with only that which evokes true worship of him alone and stirs us to action for the advancement of his inalienable kingdom.

That American Christians are known among many not for our primary allegiance to God's kingdom, but rather for our allegiance to wealth, power, and voting blocs suggests that the very fabric of our churches has become idolatrous. Thus the idols plaguing the American church are not made of wood, metal, or stone, but instead lie in ideas, passions, pursuits, and relationships that continually demand more of our hearts and lives. And like every idol that humans have ever worshiped and served, they will destroy our soul. The goal of this chapter is not only to identify common forms of American Christian idolatry, but also to call each of us to lay down our own idols in repentance so that we might prayerfully see new life and reinvigorated kingdom ministry in our churches again.

IDOLS AS OLD AS THE BIBLE

Ramachandra describes how idols both distort true worship and enslave us as human beings: "Idols are creation substitutes for the God of creation. They elevate some aspect of the created order to the central place that the Creator alone occupies."[4] This is precisely how the apostle Paul characterized the rampant idolatry among the nations in the Roman world of the first century, as people "exchanged the glory of the immortal God for images" and the truth of God "for a lie, and worshiped and served created things rather than the Creator—who is forever praised" (Rom 1:23, 25). Far more dangerous than the idols of various cultures, however, are those idols fashioned, nurtured, and protected by God's people inside the community of faith.

God's warnings about idolatry among his people are a theme throughout the Hebrew Scriptures. When God gave the Ten Commandments to his people via Moses, he addressed idolatry first: "You shall have no other gods before me," and "You shall not make for yourself an image in the form of anything in heaven above or on the earth beneath or in the waters below. You shall not bow down to them or worship them" (Ex 20:3-5). And as Israel was being established as a nation, God warned his people through the prophet Samuel: "Do not turn away after useless idols. They can do you no good, nor can they rescue you, because they are useless" (1 Sam 12:21).

Accordingly, the primary confession of faith of the Hebrew people, the Shema passage in Deuteronomy 6:4-9, begins with the foundational belief that God alone is worthy of worship: "Hear,

O Israel: The LORD our God, the LORD is one," followed by that which Jesus called the first and greatest commandment (Mt 22:37-38): "Love the LORD your God with all your heart and with all your soul and with all your strength."

Idolatry among God's people, therefore, is more than just "the principal crime of the human race," as Tertullian of Carthage defined it.[5] Idolatry inside the community of faith is a rejection of God's explicit love for his people, and a blatant form of infidelity (Is 54:5-8; 62:5; Jer 2:1–4:4).[6] As the prophet Jonah prayed from the belly of a great fish:

> Those who cling to worthless idols
>   turn away from God's love for them. (Jon 2:8)

Nevertheless, nearly every Israelite generation was inclined to worship idols—some from the nations around them and some that they fashioned themselves. Throughout the Hebrew Bible, which has a relatively small selection of words in its vocabulary, there are more than twenty unique words for various idols. These words populate literally hundreds of verses related to idolatry in ancient Israel.[7] Time and again, as Isaiah wrote, the people of God bowed down in worship to things fashioned by the hands of human beings and prayed, "Save me! You are my God!" (Is 44:10-20).

So too did idols imperil the first Christians. In the book of Acts, Paul challenged cultural idolatry in at least three prominent Greek cities. In Thessalonica, he was run out of town for proclaiming Christ amid their widespread idolatry (Acts 17:1-10). In Athens, a city full of idols made of gold, silver, and stone, Paul preached at the renowned Areopagus about the one true God of the Bible, his creation of all that exists, and the salvation, lordship, and resurrection of Jesus Christ (Acts 17:16-34). And in Ephesus, Paul's proclamation of salvation in Christ alone greatly disrupted the idol-making business of a group of craftsmen who fashioned idols for the city's patron goddess, Artemis. The idol-makers accosted Paul and brought the entire city into an uproar as they testified: "you see and hear how this fellow Paul has convinced and led astray large numbers of people here in Ephesus and in practically the whole province of Asia. He says that gods made by human hands are no gods at all" (Acts 19:23-41).

Several of the apostles also confronted idolatry inside the church—as displayed in ideas, attitudes, and lifestyles. Paul called sexual immorality, impurity, and evil desires antithetical to the kingdom of God, and classified greed specifically as idolatry (Eph 5:5; Col 3:5). Peter instructed displaced Christians in many places to resist the "detestable idolatry" in which they used to live, including "debauchery, lust, drunkenness, orgies, carousing and . . . reckless, wild living" (1 Pet 4:1-4). And John, in the final words of his first epistle, implored the church plainly: "Dear children, keep yourselves from idols" (1 Jn 5:21).

FACING OUR OWN IDOLS

Anything becomes an idol when we seek peace, comfort, or security through it rather than in God. As we turn to the American idols that have infiltrated the church, consider some of the major areas in which Americans prioritize time and money: entertainment, politics, sports, technology, personal improvement, and productivity. These massive industries are not necessarily idols themselves, but their foundations are frequently idolatrous ideas and attitudes that influence the American church as much as any other part of our culture.

Tim Keller and Ed Stetzer offer helpful insight by narrowing down common American idols into overarching categories, including personal idols like greed, power, and sex; intellectual idols based on ideologies of the political right or left, philosophies, and value systems; and cultural idols like economic prosperity, military power, and technological progress.[8] Within these categories are common American cultural ideas, attitudes, and behaviors that create fertile ground for idol production—both outside and inside the church.

Individualism. American Christianity, especially within evangelicalism, has traditionally emphasized the need for personal faith.

Undoubtedly this comes in part from the American spirit of individualism, which greatly values a strong work ethic and personal responsibility. Such things complement the Bible's teaching on personal confession and repentance demonstrated by good works. At the same time, an exclusively individualistic approach to biblical interpretation and ecclesiology is a misunderstanding of what is the majority context of the Bible: people living in community. That's why, as Catherine McNiel observes, most of the New Testament is written in the second-person plural, to "y'all," not just to "you," a nuance our English translations tend to obscure.[9]

This is an area where our global brothers and sisters in Christ have much to offer us. In fact, in all the interviews of global Christians we conducted for this book, each person mentioned American individualism at some point. Those from the Global South describe a church culture in which an individual is only as important as his or her contribution to the shared life of others in the community. Joseph Bataille, for example, says: "In the Haitian church there is a sense of interdependence; we count on each other; we recognize our need for each other. It's a collectiveness that builds a greater social health."[10]

In his book *The Next Evangelicalism*, Soong-Chan Rah commits an entire chapter to individualism, explaining, "The American church, in taking its cues from Western, White culture, has placed at the center of its theology and ecclesiology the primacy of the individual . . . [rather] than the value of community found in Scripture."[11] Such an environment readily manufactures the most pervasive and perhaps deadliest idol of all—the worship of self.

The American Christian tendency to elevate the individual above the community has produced in many areas a "Christian" subculture isolated unto itself. We have our own schools, media outlets, music and film industries, streaming services, dating sites, and retail outlets, to name a few. We've developed alternative methods of science, carved out our own sections of academia, and even encouraged our church members to patronize Christian-owned businesses as much as possible. Though these are not all bad things, they create an illusion for many that true Christian community can exist unto itself without engagement with larger society. But as missiologist David Bosch reminded us, "The Spirit is not held hostage by the church, as if his sole tasks were to maintain it and protect it from the outside world. The church exists only as an organic and integral part of the entire human community."[12]

The kinds of isolationism that grow out of an individualistic church culture often create blind spots that result in unchecked, unhealthy expressions of the church. When believers turn to isolationism, secular ideas and attitudes are more likely to be seen as a threat than those labeled "Christian." What better way for idolatry to infiltrate the church unnoticed than when the idols themselves have been labeled "Christian" within our own subcultures?

One of the most common blind spots related to individualism among American Christians is the failure to acknowledge the existence of corporate sin, such as racism or sexual abuse at the institutional and denominational levels.[13] Even in the face of some of the American church's most shameful attitudes and actions, calls for corporate repentance are met with responses like, "Why should we apologize for things said or done before we were born?" or "Why can't we stop dwelling on the past and just focus on preaching the gospel?" If we are to be leaders in racial conciliation as opposed to bystanders or even antagonists, we must own our sins as individuals, personally, and as communities of faith, collectively.

As the body of Christ, all of us in the church bear some responsibility for both past and present sins inside the community of faith even in cases when we might not have been personally culpable or even present. We must take care not to use our propensity for addressing personal sin and repentance as an excuse to not address the needs of others and the systemic and structural flaws of our institutions. The community of faith is interconnected in ways that transcend even time and space, as Paul reminded the Corinthian church: "if one part [of the body] suffers, every part suffers with it" (1 Cor 12:26).

What might the American church look like if we replaced our individualism with a biblical model of community?

Materialism and consumerism. It is no secret that American culture continues to grow more materialistic and consumer driven, and valuing profits over people has become commonplace. When Milton Bradley introduced The Game of LIFE in 1860, just before the Civil War, the goals of the board game were to attain virtues like honesty, honor, and bravery and to avoid vices such as crime, disgrace, and idleness. Since rebranding in the 1960s, the goal has been simply to get rich by amassing houses, cars, and perhaps a family along the way, with personal character and morality playing no role whatsoever toward winning the game.

We live in a "sensate society," as Christian ethicist J. Daryl Charles observes, in which our habits, goals, and technologies are aimed largely at increasing physical comfort.[14] The desire to have "what we want, when we want it" is the mantra of the day, and yet what we want never seems to be enough. American Christians also face the constant temptation to keep building bigger barns to store up things that make us rich in possessions but poor toward God (Lk 12:13-21).

In some cases, the tireless American drive for greater productivity is a real benefit to the world—such as the cooperation of manufacturing companies to multiply ventilators near the beginning of the Covid-19 pandemic in 2020 or the unprecedented expediency with which vaccines were developed a few months later. Often, however, we promote productivity as a competition rather than something done for the good of the community. The desire to "make something of oneself" through economic and social advancement resonates with our individualism and is also driven by our materialism. As a result, we measure ourselves and others by what we produce and how fast we produce it rather than by the intrinsic value God applies simply to our humanity.

At the heart of our materialistic and consumer-driven culture is a formidable idol: greed. As the fourth-century Cappadocian theologian Gregory of Nazianzus wrote, the sickness of greed grows like "a tumor which, when it bursts, releases a discharge of licentiousness that eats its way further into the skin."[15] As idols are prone to do, greed continually metastasizes and is never satisfied. To the churches in both Ephesus (Eph 5:5) and Colossae (Col 3:5), Paul defined the idol of greed as "an insatiable desire for more,"[16] and instructed them in no uncertain terms: "put [it] to death."

Jesus used the word *mammon*, a personification of money, to describe the servitude greed subjugates human beings to: "No one can serve two masters. Either you will hate the one and love the other, or you will be devoted to the one and despise the other. You cannot serve both God and [*mammon*]" (Mt 6:24). As Ramachandra explains, mammon is an idol which seeks "to re-create us in its image. . . . Instead of men and women controlling money, now money controls men and women."[17]

Greed is a destructive idol on both the personal and communal levels. In the New Testament era, greed was the major reason the wealthy among the Jews and Gentiles enjoyed abundance and excess while the sick and poor were neglected. Such disparity has also existed throughout the history of the church. In 1797, the British abolitionist William Wilberforce confronted the church on its materialism by contrasting what he called "real Christianity" with the prevailing, idolatrous systems he perceived among professing Christians of the upper and middle classes in England. Wilberforce wrote, "It is now no less acknowledged than heretofore, that prosperity hardens the heart. . . . Prosperity and luxury, gradually extinguishing sympathy and puffing up with pride, harden and debase the soul."[18]

On my first Sunday as pastor of my current church, I (Eric) promised never to prioritize buildings and budgets. I've since learned how hard this kind of pietism is to live out. Buildings wear out or no longer complement current ministry goals, while budgets, much like costs of living, tend to increase rather than decrease. Yet when buildings, budgets, or models are elevated above faithfulness in worship and service, they cease to be tools for ministry and instead become paths to idolatry. As Miroslav Volf observes, when our resources move from "means to ends themselves . . . we are like those among frustrated painters who are so obsessed with the quality of their tools that they never actually get to painting."[19]

In the Global South, where most churches reside among the poorest people, the luxuries and excesses of many American churches are unimaginable. This is not altogether a bad thing, as Ruth Padilla DeBorst observes, because in such settings Christians do not have "an imagined personal immunity" that many Americans associate with acquiring more wealth and possessions. Instead, "those in the Global South experience life much differently. They are more honest about the fact that life is messy and that, even if you attempt to, you can't distance yourself from pain, brokenness, injustice, and death."[20]

If not constantly examined, the attractional church models, brands, and franchising strategies of the American church can become more driven by pleasing consumers than being faithful to sound New Testament ecclesiology. We must remember that if *mammon* rules our hearts, God does not. In the same way, if the consumer is king, then Christ is not. Like the rich young man who chose his wealth over becoming Christ's disciple (Mt 19:16-22), we must resist and reject the idol of greed if we are to follow Christ faithfully.

What might the American church look like if we replaced our materialism and consumerism with kingdom-focused investments and extravagant generosity?

Celebritism. The celebrity culture of the United States is like no other culture and is much older than many realize. Our infatuation with the rich and famous began long before Hollywood. It was in the eighteenth century in Europe, followed soon after by the United States, when words like *celebrity* and *star* became popular in the theaters and other entertainment venues.[21] With the ubiquity of the internet and social media in the twenty-first century, the sensationalism of American celebrity culture has spread to every corner of the earth. Just as The Game of LIFE morphed into valuing wealth and success above virtuous living, so too Americans have grown to equate fame and fortune with significance. And American Christians are certainly not exempt from promoting such falsehoods.

Americans explicitly call our celebrities *idols*, and much of the celebritism we create within our Christian subcultures is another symptom of idolatry within the American church. Transient sensations like PreachersNSneakers put the idol of celebritism, along with greed and materialism, on full display. Moreover, many Christian celebrities or self-proclaimed influencers are propped up as spokespeople for the American church at large, even if they do not accurately represent the perspective of most American Christians or even speak in our best interests. In an individualistic and consuming culture that overvalues celebrity, people are drawn to those who can accumulate a lot of anything—including followers.

Vilma "Nina" Balmaceda explains how perplexing it is to Christians in the Global South when they see American Christians "taking their cues from people with a big name in the world of arts, or sports, or with many followers on social media . . . even though they don't have any virtue on their own that's worth following."[22] Yet when one celebrity's lack of virtue results in an inability to platform them further, we desperately seek out the next athlete, actor, musician, or billionaire who will claim the Christian label.

Likewise, World Relief Rwanda director Moses Ndahiro identifies an American dream culture within the American church that appears to value a person's credentials and level of income above the guidance of the Holy Spirit.[23] Nevertheless, their interpretations, opinions, and preferences are treated as exclusive by some, and any who question or challenge them are deemed disloyal or even heretical. Elevating any person or their views to a place where they cannot be questioned is idolatry, and this idolatrous loyalty also creates a vicious cycle: we begin to view *our* ways as exclusive and seek out only voices who reinforce our views, as they beckon us to do the same.

The American Christian idol of celebritism is perhaps most destructive when our celebrities become the center of public scandal, shame, and hypocrisy. When someone deemed a spokesperson manipulates people or resources for personal gain, commits or covers up abuse, or facilitates toxic or abusive church environments, the entire American church and its witness bear the effects.

As we face the many challenges that currently exist and those that lie ahead, American Christians desperately need Spirit-filled, faithful, and humble leaders. For many of us this will mean being less enamored with our own preferred celebrities, and widening the range of voices who influence us and in whom we invest. For the American church, resisting the idol of celebritism will also require cultivating new voices that better represent the actual composition and priorities of an increasingly diverse American Christian culture.

What might the American church look like if we replaced our celebritism with a fresh vision for diverse, genuine servant leadership?

Christian nationalism. In the early nineteenth century, the French diplomat Alexis de Tocqueville observed: "The Americans combine the notions of Christianity and of liberty so intimately in their minds that it is impossible to make them conceive the one without the other."[24] Since the earliest days of our nation, it would seem, the American church has struggled to demonstrate a healthy relationship between faith and patriotism, and faith and politics. To be sure, patriotism and nationalism are common in cultures worldwide, and not all that comes with them is intrinsically sinful. Like any other created thing or idea, however, when elevated above our commitment to the living God and his kingdom, both patriotism and nationalism become idolatrous.

Recently, Christian nationalism—a fusion of Christian and American identities, often promoted through political effort—has reemerged as an issue of much theological debate. Far more than a recent phenomenon, Christian nationalism has reared its head in many American generations. Historian Stewart Davenport describes the struggle of White American Christians in the period just before the American Civil War "trying to understand themselves and their world with the Bible in one hand and John Locke in the other."[25] In the next century, as Kristin Kobes Du Mez describes, militant forms of Christian nationalism advanced in response to the perceived threats of communism during the Cold War and jihadism after 9/11. The promises to "keep America Christian, American families strong, and the nation secure" blended the language of faith with efforts to invigorate America-centric patriotic and masculine power.[26]

Shortly after 9/11, when many Americans were rallying around the flag, my (Matthew's) church at the time canceled its traditional Easter cantata in favor of a patriotic concert. Instead of focusing on what is rightly the center of the church calendar, Christ's victory over death, the choir and congregation sang about God's love for and blessing of America. What is perhaps most troubling is that, at the time, I do not recall being concerned at all by the idea that we might substitute a sole focus on Christ's resurrection with a focus on America.[27]

In 1941, C. S. Lewis wrote about the dangers of a so-called Christian Party as a political strategy, which was being considered among Londoners and which would combine the religious and political preferences of an elite few:

> Whatever [the Christian Party] calls itself, it will represent, not Christendom, but a part of Christendom. The principle which divides it from its brethren and unites it to its political allies will not be theological. . . . By the mere act of calling itself the Christian Party it implicitly accuses all Christians who do not join it of apostasy and betrayal. It will be exposed, in an aggravated degree, to that temptation which the Devil spares none of us at any time—the temptation of claiming for our favorite opinions that kind and degree of certainty and authority which really belongs only to our Faith.[28]

Lewis went on to warn Christians that such efforts would inevitably result in both religious and political leaders adding "'thus said the Lord' to merely human utterances . . . pretending that God has spoken when He has not spoken."[29]

We must not forget that Christian nationalism also has a history of being rooted in the idea that God has a unique love and preference for the United States over other nations, similar to (or even replacing) his covenant relationship with the people of Israel. Native American Christians have often warned that such "conflation of Old Testament Israel with US history" leads to a dysfunctional theology that has been used to justify dehumanizing rhetoric and sinful treatment of Indigenous populations throughout US history.[30]

Christian nationalism inherently blurs the lines between God and country, such that we fail to distinguish between our primary allegiance to Christ—and his transnational and transcultural kingdom—and what should be an incomparably lesser allegiance to our earthly nation. By presupposing "an idealized national exceptionalism of God's chosenness, blessing and approval of America," warned the late Richard Twiss, we end up with "a unique Americanized version of Christianity that directs attention away from identity in Christ and his kingdom."[31]

Christian nationalism commonly merges with a "persecution complex"[32]—a lingering sense that certain forces are continually at work, intending to strip away liberties from individuals or churches precisely because they represent Christian beliefs and ideals. This American Christian complex it shortsighted at best, especially when compared to global Christians and other religious groups around the world who are in fact persecuted minorities. This mindset also leads to characterizing national or political opponents as a threat and as enemies of God and church, as if they are at the same time treasonous and blasphemous. American Christians must ask ourselves honestly if our concerns are truly about persecution and protecting the liberty to practice our faith, or rather about a fear of losing purely American ways of life.

Christian nationalism is often nothing more than syncretism, a subtle yet common way that idolatry pollutes Christian faith and practice by blending or equating Christianity with cultural beliefs, ideas, or institutions. Many Western Christians think of syncretism as a "mission field" problem, as seen when new believers confess Christ as Savior and Lord but still mix in worship of traditional gods, offer prayers to dead ancestors, or continue to pray in mosques, temples, or shrines dedicated to their previous religion. Yet according to Padilla DeBorst, Christians in the Global South are used to seeing "Christianity and Americanism coming in the same cultural packaging,"[33] in mission contexts *and* inside the American church. The results of syncretism are just as disastrous for the American church as in foreign contexts, because in both cases, the distinctive natures of biblical faith and the Christ-centered gospel are cheapened and reduced in their effectiveness.

What might the American church look like if our patriotism and nationalism were overshadowed by a bold, renewed allegiance to God's inalienable kingdom?

Tribalism and partisanship. Much like Americans fight for individualism, we also fight for our tribe. We all have tribes, whether ethnic, religious, social, political, or economic. The more we associate only with people like us, the more likely we are to overinflate the perspectives of our own tribe while judging the opinions and perspectives not from our tribe as invalid. Such a mindset is at best prideful and at worst becomes idolatrous when our tribe becomes our utmost identity.

While there is certainly biblical precedent for protecting and providing for our loved ones (Neh 4:13-14; John 15:9-17; 1 Tim 5:8), tribalism easily develops into ethnocentrism, through which we view people like us as favored and superior. Ethnocentrism intensifies the blindness induced by the idolatry of tribalism and frequently produces bias and prejudice that is detrimental to others outside the group. Ethnocentrism and tribalism also tend to embolden us to decry the speck in the eye of others while ignoring or even justifying the plank in our own (Mt 7:3-5).

Throughout US history, ethnocentrism among White Christians has often degenerated into racism—in both people and structures. Historian Randall Balmer argues that it was not concern for the dignity of preborn lives and changing abortion policies that motivated American evangelicals (especially of the fundamentalist persuasion) to become more politically active in the 1960s and '70s, but rather a desire to retain segregation in schools.[34] The rise of private Christian schools throughout the US beginning in those decades, populated mostly by White families, is evidence of this.

Half a decade later, White American Christians still have the reputation of enabling racist leaders, systems, and structures. Sadly, recent polling suggests that the number of American Christians willing to engage these indictments is decreasing, rather than increasing.[35] Many have doubled down on their resistance to dialogue about past and present racial injustices, and some even demonize all anti-racism movements.[36] The presence of these attitudes and actions among American Christians has led to a crisis of faith among many Christians in the Global South who ask, "Was the US ever really 'Christian' at all?"[37]

Ethnocentrism reveals itself in the ethnic makeup of our churches as well, which usually do not reflect the beauty and diversity of God's kingdom and the global church. Instead, most White churches in the United States remain rigidly ethnically homogeneous, and grow mostly through transfer of membership and the baptizing of our own children.

Many US churches once intentionally focused on a particular ethnic group as a growth strategy, following the Homogeneous Unit Principle (HUP).[38] Some churches derived overly pragmatic strategies from the HUP that played to people's ethnocentric tendency to feel more comfortable among others who are like them, which occasionally produced numerical surges. In the process, however, as Alejandro Mandes notes, "the strategy legitimized the very thing Jesus spoke against in John 4, when the disciples balked at him for speaking to a Samaritan woman."[39] Jesus renounced the idolatrous ethnocentrism of his day in word and deed, and he calls us to do the same in ours.

On a positive note, a growing number of younger Christians, regardless of race, have expressed their desire to work toward racial justice and reconciliation.[40] This gives us hope that the idol of racism will not be ignored in the next generations, and could even be confronted more determinedly. If this becomes the case, we must take care that other idols related to tribe or party do not rise in its place. If we elevate religiosity, ideology, or social improvement above right relationships between ourselves, God, and neighbor, we will be, as Ramachandra warns, "exchanging one set of idols for another . . . [by] confronting idolatry with idolatry."[41]

Political partisanship is another form of tribalism that often becomes idolatrous, energized by the idols related to greed and nationalism, and inflamed by many of our preferred "celebrities." Hau Suan Khai has seen this in his home country of Burma (also known as Myanmar), where some who fall out of line with their party are swiftly excluded from leadership and still others have their voices extinguished. Khai adds, "The last few years have revealed lots of dirty things in politics in both Burma and the United States. In all places we must be motivated by our Christian convictions and influenced by policy not popularity."[42]

Political partisanship frequently comes with its own kind of religious fervor. As Volf notes, we live in a cultural moment in which the gap between knowledge and opinion is widening, different moral universes are colliding, and political strategies are akin to tactics of war. As a result, he observes, "nationalisms are burgeoning everywhere; bridges between communities and nations are collapsing and walls are going up, all in the name of cultural, ethnic, or national identities defined in highly oppositional terms."[43] When Christians enter faith and politics as if into war, our beliefs, opinions, and preferences wind up in constant conflict even with one another, resulting in a never-ending tug-of-war match in which there is no winner.

Idolatrous forms of tribalism, including ethnocentrism and partisanship, result in attitudes and actions that are both incompatible with Scripture and incapable of achieving God's kingdom purposes. In yet another countercultural way, the church becomes a "global family" and a place of belonging that transcends any biological, racial, national, or sociopolitical identities.[44] Khai describes this sense of belonging among Burmese Christian refugees who engage regularly in American churches: "We have been pleasantly surprised at how many American Christians are friendly to us and treat us like they've known us for many years. It gives us comfort and confidence in a new place."

What might the American church look like as a place where walls based on ethnicity, gender, party, and social location are torn down rather than built up, resulting in a community of God's people unified through faith in Christ (Gal 3:26-29; Eph 2:11-22; Col 3:11; 1 Pet 2:9-10)?

IDOL REPENTANCE THAT IS NOT IDLE REPENTANCE

In the twelfth century, a small French parish became widely known for its wooden Jesus figure on a cross next to the altar that would mystify worshipers and pilgrims when it "came to life"—as its head, eyes, and tongue would move—during high points of services. This relic of the past can now be viewed in the Cluny Museum in Paris, along with the pedal, iron rod, and springs the village priests used to operate it.[45]

When we trade authentic worship and devotion for a manufactured religious product, we too present an idolatrous Christianity in which Jesus is a caricature rather than the Christ. We may implement the best models and methods and put on great shows with bright lights, loud music, and engaging content, but when idols are present our worship is misdirected and ultimately devoid of true substance. As Ramachandra adds, "When 'God' is co-opted to bless our private or national projects, when pastors compete for bigger and richer churches, or when worship is evaluated by 'how it makes me feel,' rather than how we are transformed into Christ-like service to the world, we are practicing idolatry."[46]

Though many of the idols we've discussed are firmly entrenched in some of our churches, they are not invincible. God's power has toppled the most formidable idols and temples to false gods that ever existed. No one worships Dagon, Molek, Baal, or Asherah today. The temples to the Greek and Roman gods are in ruins and benefit only the tourism industry. For millennia, countless people who once suffocated in the bondage of idolatry have, like Paul wrote regarding the Thessalonians, "turned to God from idols to serve the living and true God" (1 Thess 1:9).

We believe God can deliver the American church from her idols as well. Indeed, nothing and no one else can bring true healing to the brokenness of our communities and societal structures except the living God, revealed most clearly in the gospel of the risen Christ. "The only effective antidote," Ramachandra explains, "is a vision of the One who having all power at his command, humbled himself, and embraced the role of a lowly servant to unmask and dethrone the powers that have ravaged his world."[47]

The only way forward, therefore, is the wholly transformative process God has always required from his people who have become idolatrous: repentance. Repentance begins by asking God to search, know, and test our hearts and minds (Ps 139:23). Such divinely infused self-examination will certainly reveal the ways we have elevated our idols over faithfulness to God and sought security where it cannot be found. Through the prophet Jeremiah, God gave his people a specific prayer of repentance that is both for confession on the part of the individual believer and a call to repentance for the entire community of faith.

> We acknowledge our wickedness, LORD,
>   and the guilt of our ancestors;
>   we have indeed sinned against you.
> For the sake of your name do not despise us;
>   do not dishonor your glorious throne.
> Remember your covenant with us
>   and do not break it.
> Do any of the worthless idols of the nations bring rain?
>   Do the skies themselves send down showers?
> No, it is you, LORD our God.
>   Therefore our hope is in you,
>   for you are the one who does all this. (Jer 14:20-22)

Repenting from and rejecting our idols has been an ongoing process for each of the three of us, and we've encountered many others on this same journey. D. L. Mayfield is one of them. In her book *The Myth of the American Dream*, she recounts a process of realizing that many of the long-held values she gained while growing up as an American evangelical were not advancing God's inalienable kingdom, but rather were aimed at pursuing "a dream life for ourselves . . . in the opposite direction of Jesus." As she too continues laying down her American idols, she confesses, "The circumstances that felt to me like a crumbling of my worldview were actually moving me toward a more biblical one."[48]

We've also encountered churches, both big and small, that have taken steps to counteract American Christian idolatry through intentional actions. Some have elected to use their budget to pay off medical or school debts in the community rather than to construct larger buildings. Others have invested in immigrant and refugee communities around them, teaching and demonstrating that the good news of God's inalienable kingdom has no borders. Many churches have begun empowering the gifts of those previously overlooked—whether women, students, minorities, or immigrants—so that more than a few can display their gifts for kingdom purposes. There are White and Black churches who rise above ethnic, tribal, and political divisions to partner in service and shared discourse. The same has happened with American-born churches and churches made up mostly of immigrant Christians.

In this cultural moment, it is vital for the American church to be clear about the central, biblical truths of our faith and fully committed to God's kingdom priorities. We live in this world but are not "of the world" (Jn 15:19) nor are we to "conform to the pattern of this world" (Rom 12:2). Rather, we are to live "as foreigners and exiles" (1 Pet 2:11) who "do not love the world or anything in the world" (1 Jn 2:15), because partnership with this world and its idols is "enmity against God" (Jas 4:4).

Instead of fighting for our idols when they are threatened, we must lay them down willingly. In their place, the same Holy Spirit who produces the fruit of God's kingdom character in the life of the believer—namely, love, joy, peace, patience, kindness, goodness, faithfulness, gentleness, and self-control (Gal 5:20-23)—can empower the American church to be "an alternative and prophetic community" in the face of the particularly American idols always surrounding us.[49] To become this kind of community, we must also restore our commitment to affirming the true image of God in every human life and relearn to see every person as our neighbor, both of which we turn to in our next chapter.

QUESTIONS FOR REFLECTION AND DISCUSSION

▸ In your opinion, how did American Christianity get to a place where a phenomenon like PreachersNSneakers is even possible?

▸ What are some uniquely American idolatrous ideas, attitudes, and behaviors that you see in churches today? What categories of American Christian idols would you add to those listed and discussed in this chapter?

▸ What potential idols do you see in your own church? In your own life?

▸ How do we learn to value and empower genuine Christian leadership over the temptation to create and promote our own celebrities?

▸ How can we resist divisions and tear down walls related to race, gender, and sociopolitical issues in a culture where such issues are highly polarized and driven by agendas?

ACTION STEPS

▸ Take the lists and categories of idols you've identified and name them out loud one more time. Then write them down and choose a symbolic way to lay them down—perhaps in a worship service, in a personal or small group time of prayer, or maybe even by destroying them in some creative way (just don't accidentally damage anything else in the process!).

▶ With your church small group or a trusted group of Christian friends, plan to have a time of prayerful lament regarding the idols plaguing the church. After your time of lament, plan a separate time where only thankful and celebratory words about God and his church are allowed. Consider taking Communion as part of this time.

▶ Praying Scripture is always a good practice. Take Jeremiah's prayer at the end of this chapter and make it your own. You might use it as an individual prayer for your own heart and life, or as a corporate prayer in your community of faith, whether in a small group or worship setting.

5

IMAGO DEI AND NEIGHBOR

The way we talk about other human beings
has become a crisis of the soul.

SAMI DIPASQUALE

IT WAS ONE OF THE COLDEST NIGHTS of my (Eric's) life as I faced the hardest question I've ever been asked. I was with a small group of friends in northeast Poland supporting church-planting efforts. That evening we were hosting the first of several public discussions about God in a local coffee shop. Our plan for each night was for me to raise a few theological questions, address them from Scripture, and then open the floor for dialogue with our entire team and those in the audience.

To this day, none of us can even mention that trip without bringing up the very first question asked on the first night at that coffee shop. To provide a clear picture of what happened, it's important to understand the larger context of where we were. In 1939, nearly five million Jews lived in Eastern Europe, whereas today, there are less than eighty thousand.[1] In almost every Polish city, large or small, streets and buildings bear plaques remembering well-established Jewish families who are no longer there, most of whom were snatched up by soldiers and later killed. Having visited many of the same Polish cities over a period of several years, we came to know a number of people who could remember the names of the Jewish families who had once been their neighbors.

In that coffee shop on that very cold night, a sense of dread came over the room as an elderly Polish woman with a scarf around her neck and a heavy coat on her lap asked her question. As every face in the room slowly turned from her and back toward me with widened eyes, I had already guessed what she had asked. Nevertheless, time slowed down in that moment as we waited for our translator to interpret. He closed his eyes, took a deep breath, and then repeated her question in English: "Why did God allow the Holocaust to happen?"

Like many people, I had wrestled with the same question many times myself, though certainly not to the same degree. Having visited many Holocaust sites throughout Poland, Yad Vashem in Jerusalem, and Holocaust museums in the United States, I can attest that not much shakes one's view of theodicy—the justice and goodness of God despite the existence of evil—like ethnic cleansing and genocide. To hear that question asked by that precious elderly woman in that setting, however, left a mark on all who were there.

Soong-Chan Rah recounts how researching the role of the German church in Nazism led to a period of deep sorrow in his own life:

> I saw images of Christian pastors doing the "Heil Hitler" salute alongside SS officers. I saw an image of a German Christian academic who had grown a mustache to look exactly like Adolf Hitler's. I read about the horrific apathy and even participation of the German church that gave justification to genocide. The historical failure of the German church compelled me to reflect on the ongoing failures of the American church in the twentieth and twenty-first centuries.[2]

How *could* God, not to mention millions of human beings who claimed to believe *in* God and his Scriptures, allow something like the Holocaust to happen? Dietrich Bonhoeffer addressed such questions as he also courageously confronted the evils of Nazism, including the German church's complicity in it. He described the process of dehumanization, among Christians in particular, as desensitizing one's thinking about human dignity through one justification after another, to the point that a numb *nothingness* is all that remains. "People surrender everything in the face of nothingness: their own judgment, their humanity, their neighbors," Bonhoeffer wrote. "Where this fear is exploited without scruple, there are no limits to what can be achieved."[3]

I wish I could tell you that I came up with a profound answer to that dear lady's question—one I can only assume she's been asking nearly all her life. Instead, I can only pray now as I did then that the words through which I stumbled were used by the Holy Spirit and in some way gave her comfort that God is good and that he comes near to the brokenhearted (Ps 34:8, 18). Nevertheless, her question remains a haunting reminder of the horrors that human beings—even Christians—are capable of when we devalue the life of any person, and especially an entire ethnicity.

The Bible is consistent that each human life, without exception or qualification, is imbued with value by God, having been made in his image, and each person is a neighbor whom Jesus commanded us to love. Just as our idolatrous worship is an affront to the nature of God, so also are many of our idolatrous attitudes and actions an affront to the image of God in human beings. As in the previous chapter, we must address the idols of our hearts and lives that transgress the first great commandment of Christ—to love God with every part of our being—and the second—to love our neighbors as ourselves.

WHAT DOES IT MEAN TO BE MADE IN THE IMAGE OF GOD?

What are the origins of the belief that "all men are created equal" and "endowed by their Creator with certain inalienable rights"? Or, as the United Nations' document "The International Covenant on Civil and Political Rights" asserts, that the "recognition of the inherent dignity and of the equal and inalienable rights of all members of the human family is the foundation of freedom, justice, and peace in the world," and that "these rights derive from the inherent dignity of the human person"?[4] Though such language is present in Greek philosophy and other historical documents like the Magna Carta, its deepest roots are in the book of Genesis.

For nearly two millennia, the Latin phrase *imago Dei*, or "image of God," has been the most common description of what sets humanity apart from everything else in creation. The high point of Genesis 1 occurred when God altered both the rhythm and function of his creative work by calling the last day "very good," rather than simply "good," with the creation of human beings. Imago Dei is drawn from God's own words in Genesis 1:27 (emphasis ours):

So God created mankind in his own *image*,
in the *image* of God he created them;
male and female he created them.

When God fashioned creation's final piece, humanity, it was clear that we were different. God spoke everything he created into existence, and all he created moved and functioned upon his word. But when God spoke to the human beings, they could speak back. This differentiation between us and all other creatures became an important marker for much of the Western Christian tradition,[5] culminating in Thomas Aquinas. Aquinas argued that God endowed human beings with authority and responsibility over other created things because of our God-given intellect and abilities to reason and perceive right and wrong.[6]

The fundamental worldviews and ideologies of most ancient cultures did not ascribe this kind of worth to human beings in general. Some ancient people saw the image of the divine in human rulers, sages, or priests. Others looked to created things like the sun, mountains, or the sea. Many also worshiped images of gods, goddesses, or created things. In the Hebrew Scriptures, however, we find the image of God imprinted on human beings, with no differentiation of status between them. In doing so, God has woven inherent dignity and indelible value into the material, intellectual, and spiritual fabric of every single human life. Humanity is set apart as caretakers and proxies of God, which dignifies, rather than devalues, the rest of creation.

This worldview remained unique to the Hebrews even to the time of Jesus. During a period when many viewed emperors and kings, like Caesar, as gods, while classifying most people as insignificant, the first Christians proclaimed the imago Dei. An anonymous fifth-century Christian expressed the church's countercultural teaching beautifully:

> The image of God is not depicted on gold but is imaged in humanity. The coin of Caesar is gold; that of God, humanity. . . . God imprints His image neither by hammer nor by chisel but through his original divine intention. For Caesar required his image on every coin, but God has chosen man, whom He has created, to reflect His glory.[7]

Every human being carries the full dignity and potential of God's image in their whole being, as does all of humanity. Our dignity as human beings is grounded not in our attributes or capacity, but rather in God's relationship to us. As Martin Luther argued, God gave to human beings not only intellect and a will to know *about* God, but also to know God and to seek that which he desires.[8] The closer we grow to God and seek his will wholeheartedly, the more we reflect his image and character faithfully.

WHERE IT ALL WENT WRONG AND HOW GOD MADE IT RIGHT

Much like our idolatry results in an incomplete and distorted view of the divine, so we often acquire a flawed view of the image of God in people. This began with the first sins of the first human beings, the consequences of which resulted in divisions between people and peoples that had not existed before.[9] In subsequent generations the sinful hearts of human beings led to hostility, competition for resources, and a perpetual disparity between rich and poor, all of which also had not existed before sin. Yet even as God was announcing the consequences for sin, he introduced good news for humanity. In the Garden of Eden, God promised that someday, a woman would give birth to a son who would suffer, but eventually "crush [the] head" of evil (Gen 3:15).

The appointed time came when God sent his son, Jesus, to the earth to be born from a human mother, with completely human flesh and blood (Gal 4:4). This moment that we call the incarnation, when "the Word became flesh" (Jn 1:14), is extolled by the monk John of Damascus in an eighth-century song:

> He whose throne is heaven and whose footstool is the earth shall be held in the womb of a woman. . . . Wonder! God is come among humanity; he who cannot be contained is contained in a womb; the timeless enters time, and great mystery. . . . God empties himself, takes flesh and is fashioned as a creature.[10]

The incarnation of Christ changed the very method by which we measure time—as eventually the calendar of Europe, and ultimately that of the Western world, was altered in recognition that history's most pivotal turning point occurred in Bethlehem.[11] More importantly, the incarnation finally provided the clearest image of God in the flesh and blood of a human being—including his kingdom character (Heb 1:3).[12] As Simon Chan observes, "Human dignity is predicated on the incarnation, which reveals God's ultimate goal for humanity in Christ."[13]

God's kingdom came to earth in a human body and was encountered through human features. Jesus' eyes rested gently on outcasts. His arms welcomed children. His fingers touched lepers and the eyes of the blind. His feet were made dirty and calloused as he walked through cities, towns, and remote villages. His vocal cords proclaimed justice for the poor, oppressed, and captive. Eventually his hands bore the signs of divine sacrifice, as he atoned for the sins of the very people he created.

It is in the incarnation, therefore, that the imago Dei meets the *missio Dei*. At all times Jesus prioritized the mission of God, expressing even as a twelve-year-old boy at the temple, "I must be about My Father's business" (Lk 2:49 NKJV). A key part of his mission was to reframe the way God's people view the image of God and divine purpose given to every human being, especially those whose inherent dignity is maligned by others. As Howard Thurman argues in his book *Jesus and the Disinherited*, the incarnate Christ identified more with the marginalized and those who had "no place to lay their heads" (see Lk 9:58) than he did the distinguished and powerful.[14]

This was God's plan for humanity from the very beginning: that just as Christ would come to ransom people from their sins, he would also redeem God's image. In his person and ministry, Jesus gave humanity the clearest picture of God's kingdom character by living in absolute conformity to God's standards and glorifying God in all he said and did. In his humanity, Christ modeled the intention and purpose for the image of God in each of us, so that we might also reflect God's kingdom character in ways that point to his goodness and salvation. Just as Christ perfectly embodied the imago Dei in word and deed as a man, so he also commissioned his church to carry forward the missio Dei including from among the marginalized.

WHEN THINGS GET COMPLICATED

American Christians are well known for applying imago Dei to defending the sanctity of life for the preborn. Without question, defending the inalienable human dignity of a life inside the womb is a God-honoring thing. At the same time, a growing number of Christians recognize that being "pro-life," though it cannot mean *less* than protecting preborn children from abortion, must also mean much more. This is a necessary return to what is a deeper understanding of the imago Dei, especially considering criticisms often levied against American Christians that, though we fight hard for the life in the womb (especially in election seasons), we fail to fight for the quality of that life once the child is born.

It's one thing to affirm the sanctity and dignity of all human life when speaking in generalities or broad categories. It's quite another to do so regarding specific people who occupy the same spaces as us and whose choices may positively or negatively affect us. They might need to draw from the same resources we use. Someday they might subscribe to a different belief system than us, hold differing opinions than us, or even side with our opponents or enemies. If any of those things come true, our encounters with them could be unpleasant or even threatening. When things are complicated in this manner, we might not always affirm human dignity in the absolute terms we used before they were born.

There is a subtle yet powerful moment in Tolstoy's *Anna Karenina* when Levin, a main character, sees the conspicuously beautiful Anna standing next to a painting of herself from a noteworthy Russian artist. Levin is spellbound by her portrait and thinks to himself how Anna herself could never be as beautiful as the idealized version painted on canvas. At the same time, he realizes the painting is not nearly as beautiful as the real Anna, because it could never capture completely the essence and complexities of her true self.[15] Her personhood displayed more worth and beauty than any painted portrayal of her physical appearance ever could.

Tolstoy's story is also a reminder that we sin against the image of God when we objectify others. Objectification is a form of idolatry, a cheapening of personhood, and a gateway to full-fledged dehumanization. Nowhere is this more prevalent than in the pornography industry, which is a global epidemic of a different kind. While all forms of objectification demean the image of God in people, pornography profanes human dignity and often leads to other destructive sins. It thrives on more than lust and envy—it is rife with degradation. Much of the porn industry is also accompanied by human trafficking of children and adults who are often subjected to slavery and sexual abuse, which we will discuss more in chapter seven.[16]

Objectification and dehumanization invite a new classification into our worldview for all whose appearance, lifestyles, and cultural views differ from our own: the "other." The way many American

Christians have spoken about immigrants in recent years is a fitting example. As Christian ethicist William Barbieri Jr. notes, these Christians describe the sanctity and dignity of human life with objective terms like "innate," "God-given," and "inseparable," but use subjective language for immigrants as if dignity can somehow be lowered or raised based on one's documented status or choices.[17] Narratives from mainstream and social media often inflame such ways of thinking into an unfounded fear of the "other," though in the vast majority of cases no personal threat exists.[18]

Stereotyping a person or group as "other" commonly leads to racism, marginalization, hostility, or looking the other way when such things are present. The "other" mentality pairs naturally with idolatrous tribalism, to the point that we become known more for who we're against than who we're for.[19] Such attitudes are clearly incompatible with the image, person, work, and example of Christ Jesus. When we view others through the lens of his kingdom, there is no "other"; there is only neighbor.

NEIGHBOR

Imago Dei is a fundamental starting place for understanding the unique relationship God initiated with human beings and the indescribable impact of the person and ministry of Jesus Christ. But it is not the finish line. When Jesus addressed issues related to human dignity and the purposes of God's people, he consistently turned to the second great command and the word *neighbor* (Mt 5:43; 19:19; 22:39; Mk 12:31-33; Lk 10:27). The apostles Paul, James, and Peter also referred to the second great command as the highest of God's laws of love toward people (Rom 13:10; Gal 5:14, Jas 2:8, 1 Pet 4:8).

Though we often think of a neighbor in smaller terms, as someone who resides near us, the Hebrew understanding of the word was much bigger. In Leviticus 19, the chapter from which Jesus establishes the second great command, neighbors whom God's people are to love as they love themselves include the poor (Lev 19:10), a day laborer (Lev 19:13), the deaf and blind (Lev 19:14), the rich (Lev 19:15), their people (Lev 19:16), a fellow Israelite (Lev 19:17), one who has wronged them (Lev 19:18), and the foreigner who resides in their land (Lev 19:33-37). The Hebrew word *rea,* often used for "neighbor," is also the root of the name *Ruth*—given to the poor, widowed, Moabite woman who became a resident alien in Bethlehem and ended up in the bloodline of David and Jesus (Ruth 1:1-22; 4:13-22; Mt 1:5). Thus, when Jesus chose the word *neighbor* to define how God expects his people to love others, he chose perhaps the biggest word possible. Neighbor is bigger than nation, bigger than tribe, bigger than family, and certainly bigger than self.

According to Miroslav Volf, the scope of the word *neighbor* does not change even when we are persecuted. Volf was born into a context of severe religious persecution in Croatia, in which his father, a Pentecostal pastor, was detained for months in a concentration camp where he nearly starved to death without ever having been given a fair trial. Nevertheless, Volf's father, like the apostle Peter, believed it to be our Christian responsibility to "honor everyone" (1 Pet 2:17 ESV), even those who persecute the church. Volf recounts how his father faithfully followed the instructions of Peter's epistle, which "demands nothing of others, but much of the Christian communities themselves. Instead of insisting that the persecuting non-Christians tolerate Christians, it commands the persecuted Christians to honor non-Christians!"[20]

The most descriptive teaching on the second great command came on an occasion when Jesus was asked a difficult question. Luke 10:25-29 records the exchange:

> On one occasion an expert in the law stood up to test Jesus. "Teacher," he asked, "what must I do to inherit eternal life?"
>
> "What is written in the Law?" he replied. "How do you read it?"
>
> He answered, "'Love the Lord your God with all your heart and with all your soul and with all your strength and with all your mind'; and, 'Love your neighbor as yourself.'"
>
> "You have answered correctly," Jesus replied. "Do this and you will live."
>
> But he wanted to justify himself, so he asked Jesus, "And who is my neighbor?"

What follows is perhaps Jesus' most well-known story, the parable of the Good Samaritan (Lk 10:30-37). Jesus illustrates the second great command in the parable through the virtuous deeds of an anonymous Samaritan traveler who went out of his way to care for a Jewish traveler who had been robbed, beaten, and left for dead on the side of a road. The Samaritan acted after two important Jewish religious figures, a priest and a Levite, deliberately passed by the injured man, crossing to the opposite side of the road. Because of Jesus' teaching, the term *Samaritan* today is synonymous with aiding strangers.

In the Jewish world in which Jesus taught, the idea of a good Samaritan was oxymoronic. By the time of Jesus' ministry, the deep-seated hatred between Jews and Samaritans was palpable. When Jesus used the Samaritan in the parable, he inserted a character his audience not only would have considered to be "other," but more so would have assumed to be the last to offer compassion or assistance, if not a villain who would only make matters worse.

THE GOOD SAMARITAN IN
THE MIDDLE EAST AND AFRICA

Although American Christians have produced a myriad of books and sermons about the Good Samaritan parable, in many ways our Western worldview limits our understanding of this kind of teaching. Here again the perspectives and insights of global Christians prove this parable still has much to teach us.

Andrea Zaki Stephanous is an evangelical Coptic scholar and prominent community leader in Cairo who has written extensively on the Middle Eastern context of the Bible. Comparing contemporary clashes between Arabs and Jews in the Middle East and Muslims and Serbs in Bosnia to the struggles between first-century Jews and Samaritans, Zaki argues that Jesus' parable is a model for overcoming even the most deep-seated "hatred, malice, and fear." He writes:

> In this complex religious and nationalist context, Jesus tells
> the parable of the good Samaritan which declares that faith

transcends belief and nationalism. The man who was injured and abandoned on the road was a Jew. Two clergymen who shared his faith and nationality saw him but ignored him. The one person who did come to help him was different from him in his nationality and faith. However, he helped the man and cared for him with love and kindness, expressing his belief in the one God and in a human brotherhood that transcends faith and nationalism.[21]

Kenyan philosopher John S. Mbiti offers us a similarly rich perspective in his proliferation of the Christian use of *ubuntu*, a word found in several African languages and commonly expressed as: "I am because we are; and since we are, therefore I am."[22] The African church, much like the ancient church, has a continual sense that the imago Dei is sometimes most clearly seen within the context of community, because the idea of "neighbor" is always present so long as we "remain in touch with others."[23] Nowhere should this be experienced more fully than in the church itself, which Christ has called his own body.

At the same time, *ubuntu* reminds us that the imago Dei is also seen in the total human community, for whom Christ commissioned the work of the missio Dei. South African theologian Mojalefa L. J. Koenane compares *ubuntu* to the New Testament word *philoxenia*, which is often translated "hospitality" but literally means "love for the other" or "love of the stranger." In repudiating all forms of xenophobia, Jesus' parable of the Good Samaritan makes instead *ubuntu* (*philoxenia*) the spiritual and moral obligation of every disciple.[24]

Namibian missiologist and scholar Paul John Isaak uses *ubuntu* when comparing the racial and ethnic division addressed in Jesus' parable to modern African settings like Namibia, South Africa, Rwanda, and Burundi, and also in the United States:

> The story of the travelers deals with racial harmony and what it means to be human and humane, or to be someone with *ubuntu*, that is, someone who is welcoming, hospitable, warm

and generous, with a servant spirit that affirms others. . . . The Samaritan was moved with compassion that overcame religious and racial animosity and he treated the Jew with a sense of *ubuntu*.[25]

In the same way, Jesus said, "Go and do likewise" (Lk 10:37).

WORDS MATTER

In many ways, we can trace atrocities like the Holocaust back to words. As Vinoth Ramachandra contends, "Words and images are more powerful instruments of domination than armies, machines, or bureaucrats."[26] What begins with "they're only words" can quickly spiral downward into dehumanization.

Using one recent, offensive example of messaging related to Central American migrants traveling in caravans, let's consider how a path into dehumanization might look today, with social media and other platforms allowing mostly unrestricted sharing of alternative facts and misinformation thousands—if not millions—of times over, including content that is intended to provoke conflict or even violence:

1. Scrolling through social media, I pause on words, images, or memes that communicate something like, "This is not a migration, this is an invasion!" to describe Central American men, women, and children traveling through Mexico toward the US border, most of whom intend to request asylum under the terms of US law.

2. I move from observer to participant by "liking" or sharing the content; I am now a source of the messaging myself.

3. Soon, generally through algorithms I don't control, the volume of messaging I see that reinforces negative ideas about migrants increases. By this point I no longer question the "facts" or claims presented.

4. The more I engage such content, the more forceful the messaging becomes. It may become vulgar or even violent, such

as a meme we've seen circulated that includes the phrase "shoot to kill." Though I might recoil somewhat at first, I fail to reject or call attention to the sinfulness or dangers of this kind of messaging.

5. After a while, I develop a sense, whether consciously or subconsciously, that Central American migrants are of lesser value than I am.

6. I become quick to point out perceived or alleged faults of Central American migrants (and others like them), while at the same time failing to hold those who show hatred for or perpetrate violence against migrants responsible for their words and actions.

7. I blame the migrants themselves for the hatred or violence they endure.

8. I find myself encouraging or even participating in hatred or violence toward migrants.

9. I no longer recognize the image of God in migrants.

Words indeed matter, and they influence our obedience to the second great commandment. Moreover, word environments that dehumanize others breed very dangerous potential outcomes. As Dennis Mwangwela from Malawi observes, when American Christians endorse cultural narratives that frame people made in God's image as subhuman, we not only fail to be pro-life—we embolden attitudes and scenarios that lead to death.[27]

The apostle James characterized evil words spoken of others as if they are idolatry—they are both an affront to God's image in human beings and antithetical to true worship of God himself (Jas 3:9). Paul added that we should not only refrain from using words to tear others down, but also we should intentionally use them to build up. Our words should be filled with the Holy Spirit, be kind and compassionate, and "give grace to those who hear" (Eph 4:29-32). The path to repentance for the ways in which we have transgressed the image of God and rejected the second great command will likely take us through some necessary processes to heal our hearts and relationships.

REHUMANIZATION AND RECONCILIATION

In her book *Disunity in Christ*, Christena Cleveland discusses "contact theory," a twentieth-century concept that argues that people from vastly different backgrounds who are also separated by distance often have negative emotions about each other based on inaccurate perceptions. Among the various methods tested to bridge such divides, none were as successful in reversing misconceptions as personal, crosscultural contact between the people or groups in question. As Cleveland concludes, "Crosscultural contact has often been described as an exercise in error reduction. . . . Contact creates a context in which errors can be challenged and corrected."[28]

Early Christians exemplified this for us. The good news of Jesus Christ united Jew and Gentile, Jew and Samaritan, and many others from different social strata like opposing particles fused together. In the generation after Paul, an Athenian philosopher named Aristides called Christians a "third race"[29] because the Hebrew Christians were no longer exclusively Jewish, and the Gentile Christians no longer worshiped the pagan gods of their ancestors and cultures. As Paul had written, the hostility they once had for each other was put to death and peace now defined them (Eph 2:14-16)—not a superficial peace like that of the *Pax Romana*, but rather that of God-given *shalom* through the Holy Spirit in the name of Christ Jesus.

One of my (Eric's) favorite things to watch in our church is that moment when one of our American-born congregants realizes that the owner of their favorite restaurant, their next-door neighbor, or their child's soccer teammate are part of our growing refugee community. The new awareness is life-changing because it comes in the form of living, breathing people.

This happened when Nik and Yana from Ukraine enrolled in our church's ESL classes and then started attending worship services and a young adult small group. As their English improved and they started contributing more to the Bible study discussions, young men and women from their small group came to me weekly to express amazement at Nik and Yana's spiritual depth. Time and again when I informed someone that Nik, Yana, and their children were refugees who fled persecution for their faith, presuppositions were replaced with a new reality. Yana now often reads Scripture in up to three languages during our worship services and has become a teacher in one of our local schools. Nik was recently nominated for deacon service in our church. Like many of the dozens of refugee families who have become an active part of our church in recent years, Nik and Yana have redefined the word *refugee* for those who had been inundated with incorrect or incomplete information.

When we forge personal connections like these, we can never go back to old ways of thinking. Sometimes, our new awareness leads us to more closely examine attitudes and even policies that may be harmful to these families, their livelihood, and their future. This too is a part of the process of repentance and may also reveal the need to initiate steps toward reconciliation with those we've wronged or failed to defend.

REPENTANCE AND RECONCILIATION

We sin against the first great command to love God with our entire being when, through idolatry, our hearts wander outside of a faithful commitment to him. We sin against the second great command when we demean the image of God in any person or narrow our definition of neighbor. Just as recognizing and rejecting our idols leads to repentance through faithful worship of God alone, so also repentance is necessary when we sin against our neighbors. Repentance starts in the heart, transforms the mind, and results in obedient action in the life of the true disciple of Jesus Christ.

South African theologian Allan Boesak uses the story of Zacchaeus (Lk 19:1-10) to demonstrate the ways in which active reconciliation is initiated through genuine repentance. As Zacchaeus modeled, reconciliation requires both a clear acknowledgment of wrongdoing, and restitution and recompense where needed. Sometimes reconciliation requires such a drastic response that, like Zacchaeus, a person forges a new identity by rejecting attitudes and lifestyles of their past related to being an oppressor. Now they stand alongside the oppressed. It was Jesus who gave Zacchaeus his new identity, no longer calling him "the tax collector" but rather "a son of Abraham" (Lk 19:9).[30]

In addition, repenting of sin against our neighbors must be addressed at the communal level, which often goes against the grain of our strong sense of individualism related to personal repentance. Communal repentance is also difficult because it typically requires acute evaluation of structures and systems, as true reconciliation seeks to heal broken relationships and to transform any form of inequality into integrity and wholeness on all sides.

The symbol of baptism in the ancient church illustrated personal and communal repentance all at once. The first Christian baptisms drew from the Hebrew tradition of the *mikveh*, a purification rite in which Jews would walk into a pure, natural water source and be immersed. Among Christians, the new believer would come to similar baptismal waters wearing old and dirty clothes, which were removed as the person entered the water so that she or he was completely unclothed or wearing only an undergarment. After being baptized, the believer would then be given new, clean clothes made of white materials to symbolize being clothed with Christ.[31]

Baptism also became a communal symbol representing the equal status of each believer in the body of Christ—the church. Each person enters the community of faith in the same way: through a new birth (Jn 3:1-5; 2 Cor 5:17; 1 Pet 1:23). The new birth gives each person a new identity because each is a new creation in Christ Jesus (2 Cor 5:17; Gal 6:15; Eph 2:15). And each person is dressed alike, clothed with Christ in new, pure garments (Gal 3:26-27; Eph 4:22-24; Rev 3:5), and growing toward being dressed like Christ in "compassion, kindness, humility, gentleness and patience" (Col 3:12). In a world where so many simply do what "seems right in their own eyes" (Judg 21:25, CSB), Catherine McDowell argues that the church has a unique opportunity to display a radiant, countercultural unity in affirming the imago Dei and modeling love for neighbor.

> Imagine companies, corporations, studios, public schools, law firms, real estate agencies, small businesses and artist communities inhabited by God's people who are living out a right understanding of their identity as images. Imagine a world in which people live as "sons of God," who faithfully represent him in the world. By doing so, they proclaim and demonstrate in every sphere of life God's original creational intent, his redemptive plan and his eschatological goal for humanity.[32]

We can also imagine how renewing our commitments to imago Dei and neighbor, with no exceptions or qualifications so that there is no "other," will reshape many of the ways we read the Bible. Much as our American-centric focus and idolatry has failed to represent God faithfully in the world, we also have failed to faithfully represent his Word, which we turn to next.

QUESTIONS FOR REFLECTION AND DISCUSSION

▶ What kinds of people groups are often dehumanized in American culture today? What are some of the tactics used by people and/or information sources to dehumanize others?

▶ On a personal level, who or what kind of person might you consider to be "other"?

▶ What from the Middle Eastern and African perspectives on the Good Samaritan parable stands out to you?

▶ What are some examples of words from culture, media, or social media that are dangerous and destructive to specific people groups?

▶ Describe a time in your life when your ways of thinking about a person, type of person, or group were changed through personal contact.

ACTION STEPS

▶ Think of a person or kind of person whom you struggle to love or empathize with. Say their name out loud as part of this declaration: "_____ is made in the image of God."

▶ Read through Leviticus 19 and circle or note every person, kind of person, or group associated with the word *neighbor*.

▶ Make a conscious effort to clean up your social media pages from anything that might dehumanize others or does not demonstrate love for your neighbor. Make sure you look for things posted, shared, or "liked." Do so as far back as you can in your account(s) history, and make a commitment to not post, like, or share such things in the future.

▶ Take the lead in your church small group or with a group of friends in correcting misinformation or false narratives about people or groups who might normally be considered "other."

PART 3

THE
WORD
OF GOD

6

THE BIBLE WITH EYES
TO SEE AND EARS TO HEAR

I'm not asking you to listen to me,
I'm asking you to listen with me.

AUGUSTINE

AS A TEENAGER, I (Daniel) often heard missionary stories of how persecuted Christians were more eager to learn the Bible when compared to Americans. The stories portrayed these believers as willing to stop at nothing in order to study the Bible for themselves. I have to admit, the cynic in me thought the stories were tall tales. But years later I would visit one of these places and discover for myself the remarkable hunger for the Bible that truly persecuted global Christians have compared to many American Christians.

My wife and I visited a region where, the year before, a number of Christian communities had experienced tremendous persecution. As we traveled through several of these places, our guide, who was a Christian woman, was careful not to reveal our identity as Christians because of the risks of being noticed by the local authorities. She eventually brought us to the home of a young man who she explained was a pastor overseeing several house churches throughout the nearby area. Within the privacy of his home, our guide felt safe to disclose that we were Christians. When she added that I was a pastor from the United States, the young pastor (who was also a farmer) smiled at me with tremendous relief and immediately asked me to help him with a problem he'd been having. His question was not related to persecution or economic difficulties, but rather about understanding the differences between the books of Exodus and Deuteronomy.

This caught me completely off-guard. Though the answer to his question was simple enough to explain from an exegetical perspective, until I met this young pastor, I had never considered why it was important to know the difference for my own personal faith. We discussed his question for a while, but spent even more time talking about his desire to know the Bible better so he could be more effective in helping those house churches persevere when persecution came again. In addition to being challenged by his deep hunger for Scripture, I also realized a fundamental difference between many American Christians like me and persecuted global Christians like him: some attain a surplus of biblical knowledge beyond what they actually practice, while others obey the little they already know wholeheartedly.

We three authors all come from evangelical backgrounds where, for our entire lives, the Bible's authority as God's special revelation has been proclaimed to the utmost degree. The Southern Baptist Convention's primary confessional statement, for example, addresses beliefs about Scripture even before beliefs about God.[1]

To be clear, we each have a "high view" of the inalienable authority of Scripture and believe the Bible's original words are the very words of God. We also believe this "high view" is worth very little if we come to the Bible with the wrong posture, because there is a significant difference between vocalizing a belief in Scripture's authority and actually submitting one's life faithfully to *him* who endows *all* authority. If our approaches to the Bible result in us walking away "puffed up," feeling superior to others, or emboldened to overpower others with our perceived theological knowledge, we have not read it correctly (1 Cor 4).

Having addressed some much-needed course corrections regarding the two great commands through the lens of God's kingdom, we turn now specifically to what it means to both read the Bible *and* be read *by* it. American Christians have more access to biblical materials and resources than any other people in history. In many ways we have used and shared them faithfully, with global impact. In other ways we have misused them, or at the very least taken them for granted.

The idols we have discussed have played a major role in this. Just as idols pollute our worship and deaden our spiritual and intellectual senses, so also do idolatrous approaches to the Bible produce lifeless interpretations and applications of God's Word. If we fail to engage God's Word without confronting and rejecting all forms of idolatry, we are no different from many of the best-trained religious leaders of Jesus' day, about whom he said:

> Though seeing, they do not see;
> though hearing, they do not hear or understand.

In them is fulfilled the prophecy of Isaiah:

> "You will be ever hearing but never understanding;
> you will be ever seeing but never perceiving.
> For this people's heart has become calloused;
> they hardly hear with their ears,
> and they have closed their eyes.
> Otherwise they might see with their eyes,
> hear with their ears,
> understand with their hearts
> and turn, and I would heal them." (Mt 13:13-15)[2]

In the very next verse, however, Jesus said to his own disciples: "Blessed are your eyes because they see, and your ears because they hear" (Mt 13:16).[3] The purpose of this chapter is to help us reshape our approaches and methods to biblical interpretation and application, so that we might think, speak, and act like true disciples whose spiritual eyes and ears are wide open.

GOD SPEAKS THROUGH THE BIBLE
LIKE NOTHING ELSE

The Bible describes itself as being literally "breathed" into existence by God as his words to humanity (2 Tim 3:16). Within the
Scriptures is an assortment of nearly every genre of writing imag-
inable, yet the Bible is so much more than an unparalleled literary
work. Since God first passed on his words to human beings who
would eventually retell, chisel, and write them down, he has spoken
through the Scriptures like nothing else in all of creation.

I (Eric) saw the transformative work of God's Word firsthand
while serving in a downtown church context with a large population
experiencing homelessness. Among our main ministry goals were
to help those battling chronic homelessness find a safe and secure
place to live while also developing healthier lifestyles and habits.
We spent years employing several different strategies including a
"housing first" model, personal financial counseling, and a job prep-
aration/referral program. Each of these were costly and saw very
limited success. Even when a person made some positive changes,
within a few months we would learn she or he was back on the streets.

Through much frustration and lots of prayer, the Holy Spirit
began moving in our ministry in a fresh way. We paused many of
those programs and started a weekday lunchtime Bible study for
men experiencing homelessness. The first group was remarkably
open to the gospel and to discipleship, in no small part because the
circumstances of their lives had dramatically humbled them. Each
of them also contributed to our discussions with a radical and often
uncomfortable honesty. After several months and many hard
lessons learned, the study began to grow. The men took the Bible
study so seriously that they would ask others to leave if they were
a distraction or only appeared to be interested in a free lunch. There
were even times that our discussions of Scripture became so impassioned that a fight broke out (perhaps not altogether different from
some business meetings in a typical suburban church). Nevertheless, it was amazing to watch men who had once felt threatened
by one another on the streets breaking bread together as

inseparable brothers in Christ, not unlike Jews and Gentiles in the early church.

As God continued to work through the Scripture in their lives, we saw one man after another come off the streets and stay housed. Their physical and mental health improved, and many found and kept gainful employment. Men who had formerly kept mostly to themselves began inviting new faces to join the group. Lonnell, a tall African American man with a sweet spirit, was one of those new faces who came about a year into the group's existence. He still had the chiseled look of the professional boxer he was as a youth. He also had visible brokenness from years of struggling with addiction and from having lived on the street and in shelters for several months before attending our Bible study.

It did not take long for Lonnell to fit in with the group, not only because everyone wanted him on their side, but also because he was hungry to learn the Bible. After a few weeks he entered our re-vamped housing and job training programs and found success. Even when he was working, he found a way to attend Bible study most weeks and established himself as a key leader. Sadly, after attending the group for five years, Lonnell had an unexpected heart episode and ended up in a coma. We were able to contact several of his es-tranged family members who then came to the hospital. Many had not known about the drastic improvements in Lonnell's life, and though they were saddened by his health condition, they were in-credibly thankful he had gained a renewed dignity. Lonnell never woke up from the coma, but instead entered heaven as a man housed, free from addiction, and with a transformed life in which he displayed kingdom character.

Building on the successes of our men's group, we started a Bible study for women experiencing homelessness using the same strategy, and several had similar life changes. As I look back on those groups, which continue to meet to this day, I can say without question that it was primarily through the study of Scripture that the Holy Spirit transformed hearts and lives. This kind of life change does not happen by reducing the Bible to a tool or a weapon for defending one's tightly held opinions and preferences. Instead, it comes through full submission to the Holy Spirit as our biblical illuminator, and from both widening and deepening our views of the myriad ways the Bible can be read, understood, and applied.

READING THE BIBLE WITH HUMILITY AND HONESTY

Whenever I (Eric) visit New York City I make time to visit the Metropolitan Museum of Art. Though the Met is a world-class museum with countless treasures to see, I never skip the galleries of my favorite painter, Rembrandt. On a recent trip, I noticed a group gathered around what I would consider one of his more obscure paintings, *Aristotle with a Bust of Homer*. As I approached, I realized they were university students whose professor was asking them questions about Rembrandt's use of light, symbolism, and clothing styles. I subtly inserted myself into the group, and even contributed a thought into the conversation. After a while, I became aware we were no longer focused on the painting itself, but rather on our own insights. We had ceased praising the artist and enjoying his masterpiece and had settled for drawing all the attention to ourselves. A question occurred to me: *If we could invite Rembrandt himself into this discussion, how many, if any, of our insights would even relate to his artistic intent?*

My question can easily be applied to how we commonly relate to the Scriptures. We love to discuss and systematize our preferred views of God's Word without inviting the Holy Spirit into the discussion. As the apostle Paul made clear in his first epistle to the Corinthians, no one can understand "the deep things of God" without the Holy Spirit and the "mind of Christ" (1 Cor 2:9-16)— which God has given to women and men regardless of culture or ethnicity.

To be sure, the limits of our understanding make biblical interpretation a challenge for all of us. More frequently, however, it is our sinful and prideful hearts that stand between our minds and the Bible's teaching. As Augustine warned, pride closes our hearts toward true revelation much like a "blind person who is in the presence of light but does not truly experience it."[4] And Paul warned the Ephesians that the same Holy Spirit who guides our reading of Scripture can be "grieved" through harmful attitudes, speech, and actions, which also do damage to the community of faith (Eph 4:30).

Nevertheless, we are often quick to idealize our own explanations or those of the spokespeople of our tribe, especially as we become further entrenched in a particular tradition or obtain more theological education—which happens in mostly homogeneous environments. Consequently, we find ourselves discussing the masterpiece without enjoying its beauty. We draw attention to ourselves rather than Scripture's Artist himself. This has been a constant critique of American seminaries, theological education, and biblical training in our churches—the more we learn the more we elevate our own interpretations as if they are as inspired as God's own words.

On the contrary, a posture of humility, honesty, and self-surrender creates fertile soil for the Word of God to take root, grow, and produce fruit. Anabaptists of the sixteenth century described this posture with one word, which they held in common: *Gelassenheit*. Though *Gelassenheit* has no direct equivalent word in English, it is commonly rendered as "yieldedness." *Gelassenheit* is a yielding surrender to God and his work, but also a yielding unto God of those things onto which we hold too tightly, such as our idols, opinions, or preferences. Hans Denck, a key Anabaptist leader, described *Gelassenheit* as both the way we approach Scripture and also that which Scripture produces and matures within us.[5] This is the attitude the true disciple must take to approach Scripture with an open heart, mind, and hands, surrendered to its authority in order to walk in it.[6] Such a posture becomes the identity of the community of faith itself, unified in their surrender to God's direction and the work of his kingdom.

Another way to describe this perspective is giving equal weight to both *orthodoxy*, right belief, and *orthopraxy*, right practice. Many evangelical institutions push their students to pursue excellence in all things related to doctrine, and rightly so. At the same time, doctrine is developed through the interpretation of God's Word; it is not God's Word itself. As such, sound doctrine is a useful servant but an inadequate master, because it must always remain dependent on and teachable by the Holy Spirit. This also means that orthodoxy is never something at which we arrive completely this side of heaven, but rather is always being shaped and formed in us. It is only when Christ returns that we will finally see all clearly and fully, and no longer only "in part" as "a reflection . . . in a mirror" (1 Cor 13:12).

Orthopraxy, on the other hand, is demonstrated in relationship to God, his Word, and people who are made in his image. Becoming an expert in doctrine does not make one a disciple. On the contrary, Jesus taught that the clearest evidence that we are truly his disciples is when we "love one another" as he has loved us (Jn 13:34-35). As was seen in many of the most religious people of Jesus' day, it is possible to become fully versed in a theological tradition or excel in theological education and still have a hardened heart that never truly surrenders to the Word of God.

Today, we need not look far to find examples of men boasting of a high level of theological education whose words lack grace and are often downright spiteful toward others online, in their preaching, or in their writing. There are also others who greatly emphasize kindness and compassion while eliminating the uniqueness of Christ's salvation from their message or even practicing syncretism. Having all the "right answers" is insufficient if it is not matched in loving attitudes and actions toward God and others (Mt 23:1-3), and the fullness of love must be centered in the grace and truth that come only through Jesus Christ (Jn 1:17).

Right belief and right practice must travel together, side by side on the same path in the flow of the kingdom of God, displayed faithfully in the life of every disciple of Jesus Christ. There is no sound doctrine that omits justice, mercy, and faithfulness (Mt 23:23), and there is no true praise, prophecy, or piety without love (1 Cor 13:1-3). Thus, the teaching of the Holy Spirit must always be accompanied by the fruit of the Holy Spirit (Gal 5:22-23). As Paul wrote to Titus, sound doctrine flows out of salvation and grace, and teaches us "to live self-controlled, upright and godly lives in this present age" (Titus 2:12).

READING THE BIBLE WITH A FRESH AWARENESS

Though much of the Bible is told from the perspective of the people of southern Israel (Judea), it also weaves in a great deal of diversity from other nations and cultures. From the Mesopotamian Bronze Age to the Hellenistic world at the apex of the Roman Empire, the Bible was composed over the course of many different civilizations. Instead of using a single author, God chose to use dozens of contributors, both male and female, in multiple languages, from varied walks of life, spanning several centuries and civilizations, to bring the written Scriptures to human beings. These unique strengths of the Bible bolster its ability to speak into countless cultures and contexts.

Within the Bible itself, however, we see conflicts emerge between worldviews. The prophet Jonah is an example of the struggles among the Hebrew people to understand and accept God's work among the nations. Though Jews and Gentiles came together in Christ in the early church, they had to remain diligent as challenges related to their cultural differences persisted and they sought to remain both hospitable toward and unified with one another. Similar to these groups, being aware of our often narrow ethnic and cultural worldviews is an important step toward engaging the Bible with life-giving freedom that also values the diverse contributions of others.

Soong-Chan Rah describes the exclusivity of White, Western perspectives in the formation of American Christian thought as the "Western, white cultural captivity of the church." This majority worldview of the American church imposes several limits on engaging with the Scriptures and creates echo chambers in biblical interpretation where non-White and non-Western perspectives are neither sought nor equally valued. Rah describes this tendency among evangelicals specifically using a contentious yet convicting term with regard to biblical interpretation: *White privilege.*

White evangelicals have the privilege of not engaging with stories outside of their experience. White evangelicals have the privilege of having their experience lifted up as the example of Christian faith. White evangelicals have the privilege of being able to see leaders of their one ethnicity dominate every conference they attend. The reality of white privilege is that very little needs to be done to maintain this position of privilege. . . . In order to break that captivity, there needs to be an intentional relinquishing of power and privilege.[7]

The Western, White captivity of the American church is also evident in the racial homogeneity of our leadership. Pastor Daniel Hill, who is White, describes his realization of the fact that, while most of his life and ministry has been "shaped by exclusively white voices," people on the other side of America's major racial divide experience things very differently: "When you're a person of color, it doesn't matter if you prefer to be under a leader from your own cultural group; you still have to learn to adapt to white leaders. But when you're white, you can choose to stay under the leadership of white people your entire life."[8]

What Hill describes—a White person coming under the leadership of a person of color—rarely ends up happening in American churches. Likewise, it remains far more common for Black people to attend churches led by White people than the other way around. Sociologist Korie Little Edwards notes that even among churches classified as multiethnic or multiracial, only 16 percent are led by Black pastors. From a positive standpoint, this percentage has increased steadily in the last two decades. At the same time, Edwards argues, most multiethnic churches still tend to mimic the culture and theology of White churches, because White people are far less comfortable discussing race itself. She adds, "Multiracial churches often celebrate being diverse for diversity's sake. They aren't challenging racial attitudes that reinforce systemic inequality."[9] As a result, the perception remains among many that White Christians have more to offer than receive from their sisters and brothers of color.

In a sermon at a conference, pastor Charlie Dates lamented this shortcoming even with regard to multiethnic congregations:

> I think that one of the most prophetic witnesses that the gospel can bear in America are some of our authentically multiethnic churches, and even our almost one-hundred-year-old Black church on the southside [Chicago] has a growing number of regular non-Black attendees. . . . I submit, however, that if the Black church goes extinct in our cities, Black people are in real trouble. I'm not saying that we should not have more multiethnic churches, but rather than inviting Black people to leave the historic churches where they are and join your church, why don't you leave your church and join theirs? Why don't you make a different kind of multiethnic church? One that says you can sit under a Black pastor, you can worship where Black music has been sung. . . . That's what it means for the church to be prophetic, not for the church to become like yours, but to step out of its comfort zones.[10]

When White Christians are willing to "unmute" voices of color in our lives and churches, we are welcoming fresh and innovative ways to interpret and apply the Scriptures in an endless variety of contexts. To do so, we must become teachable, place ourselves under the leadership of new voices, and at times step aside to let others be the primary voices.

READING THE BIBLE WITH INDIGENOUS AND GLOBAL CHRISTIANS

Finnish theologian Veli-Matti Kärkkäinen observed nearly two decades ago that it is long past time for classical Western theology to "benefit in an unprecedented way from . . . contextual and global voices."[11] Indeed, the American church is long overdue in refreshing our understanding of Scripture by listening to the voices of Christians and cultural traditions from around the world.

Pivoting from traditional mission models, we authors have learned the incredible benefit of reading the Scriptures *with* global Christians from various traditions, as opposed to reading *at* them. Just as many around the world have received interpretations of Scripture from American voices, global Christians are interpreting God's Word in rich and powerful ways by which we must be shaped.

The GlobalChurch Project's Graham Hill argues that biblical interpretation among global Christians is not only the future of the worldwide church, including in the West, it is also the present:

> Western cultures no longer define how Christians should understand and believe and interpret the Bible. Interpretive approaches in the West are now part of a global conversation. . . . [Majority World and Indigenous Christians] believe in the absolute authority of Scripture. They passionately apply the Bible to everyday life. They put their interpretations into a living conversation with their cultures. And they identify personally with the biblical text and its stories.[12]

Interpreting and applying Scripture with global Christians. The geographic and social locations of many global Christians, along with their wide array of experiences, allow for innovative interpretations and applications of Scripture that many American Christians are unlikely to perceive on their own.

First, global Christians model reading the Bible in community, which the Holy Spirit uses to sharpen them and improve kingdom effectiveness. K. K. Yeo, a Chinese Christian who was born and raised in Malaysia, argues that it is only when we accept the invitation to "engage with one another in *our* interpretations of the Bible [that] we come to appreciate the inexhaustible meaning of the same biblical text that different regions and peoples have to offer— even though the interpretations may look different or even conflict with one another."[13]

The experience of many immigrant Christians in the United States has been one of both learning from and contributing to a largely White, Western context from a minority perspective. Just as they learned the importance of interdependence among believers in the context of their home country, so they have had no choice but to engage in biblical interpretation from a shared perspective in the United States.

Peter T. Cha of Trinity Evangelical Divinity School writes about intercultural biblical interpretation within an American context from both a theological and personal point of view. Cha is a Korean American who received the entirety of his official academic education from American universities and theological institutions. As almost all immigrants do, Cha learned to maintain his ethnic identity and heritage while navigating the large currents of White American culture. He writes about how every disciple, no matter his or her background or culture, benefits from the bringing together of multiple perspectives to more richly mine the depths of Scripture:

If the Church is to be engaged in a biblical ministry that is both pastoral and prophetic, her leaders and members need to first acknowledge that social location does influence how one reads and understands God's word. Such an acknowledgement would enable one to approach the study of God's Word with a level of epistemological humility that confesses the need for the work of God's Spirit. Furthermore, such an awareness of one's own culturally-shaped blind spots would motivate one to seek out the perspectives of "others" who come from different social locations, to see the task of doing Biblical and theological reflections as a communal and collaborative work of God's people.[14]

Second, the worldviews of global Christians offer American Christians different lenses through which we can reimagine the full narrative of Scripture. Many Christians in the Global South, for example, live in cultures with aspects that echo those of the Bible. They can imagine details in biblical narratives from a nearly first-person perspective, with much less cultural distance between themselves and the text than most Western Christians. As Guatemalan author Francisco Goldman writes:

Guatemala certainly feels biblical. Sheep, swine, donkeys, serpents—these are everywhere, as are centurions, all manner of wandering false prophets, Pharisees, lepers and whores. The poor, rural, mainly Mayan landscape has an aura of the miraculous; as a setting it is the perfect backdrop for religious parables about fields both barren and fertile, fruits and harvest, hunger and plenty.[15]

Consider the interpretive edge a Latina/o Christian who has experienced displacement or forced migration holds when reading the book of Acts. She or he can identify personally with the first Christian diaspora, those who were forced out of Jerusalem and its surrounding areas into various contexts all around the Mediterranean in which they were minorities. M. Daniel Carroll (Rodas) argues that Latina/o people commonly have "a principled solidarity" with those seen as "strangers" in a culture—whether socially, economically, or politically—who experience feelings of "alienation and otherness." This sense of solidarity creates a unique kind of unity and bond among Christians—even Christians from diverse places. Carroll discusses his own experiences within Protestant communities throughout Latin America, many of which, he argues, have become places of "refuge and encouragement" for those separated from family and loved ones, with the Bible playing a central role in all that occurs.[16]

Third, many global Christians delve into matters related to the spiritual realm in ways most American churches rarely discuss. Arab Christians throughout the Middle East, for example, speak frequently of dreams and visions. Numerous surveys and interviews done in recent decades have established that a significant percentage of former Muslims report experiencing some form of dream that led to their new birth as a follower of Christ.[17] As their Christian growth continues through discipleship and the practice of spiritual disciplines, they do not discount the metaphysical and subconscious ways that God has spoken to his people throughout biblical and church history.

Many other Asian Christians also come from worldviews that see the work of the "spirit world" in many dimensions of life. Their churches teach about morality, wealth versus poverty, health, and natural disasters as challenges of spiritual warfare in which God's intervention is sought. In rural China, for example, Christians study the biblical text closely but also post its content on their doorposts (Deut 6:9) to guard their homes from evil spirits. Throughout India, believers and churches use the Bible to proclaim freedom in Christ among the *Dalits*, the "untouchable" caste of people who are classified lower than slaves. Rather than seeking the help of false gods and idols, which only perpetuates the paradoxically oppressive worldview of a "just cosmic order," they employ the Bible's teaching on the supernatural power of God to break the curse of oppression.[18]

I (Daniel) think about how Hmong Christians, who first came to Christ only a few generations ago and who have largely understood the physical world in animistic categories, read certain passages of the Bible differently than some American evangelicals. Consider this text: "If my people, who are called by my name, will humble themselves and pray and seek my face and turn from their wicked ways, then I will hear from heaven, and I will forgive their sin and will heal their land" (2 Chron 7:14). American evangelicals in particular often employ this verse as a call to national prayer and repentance, in order to bring about "revival" and blessing for "the land of the free and the home of the brave." But a Hmong believer is more likely to apply this promise to actually healing the physical land. Observance of this passage could mean discovering how disunity among a community might be linked to a failed harvest, which is closer to the original context (see the references to drought and locusts in 2 Chron 7:13). And the act of humbling oneself and praying would be done in preparation for casting folk spirits out of a haunted forest or a water supply. Their application, in some ways, would be much more literal but not any less biblical.

Fourth, many global Christians are the poor, outsiders, or marginalized within their cultures. As a result, they demonstrate a heightened propensity for sound biblical interpretation that results directly in application. Put another way, they not only value hard work, but they also tend to be disinterested in any teaching or philosophy that does not improve their daily activities and output. Wa Christians from Burma and southwest China express this with a traditional saying of their people group: "It is smart to buy a water buffalo, but using it to plow your fields is smarter."[19] These interpretations are not an alternative to biblical teaching but rather are employed in submission to the Bible's authority over all matters of faith and real-life issues among both urban and rural peoples, and for those who face marginalization, oppression, injustice, or severe illness.

Consider also the millions of African Christians who have faced extreme difficulties and dangers related to displacement because of famine and war. Millions of others who remain in their ancestral villages have become exemplary in avoiding syncretism and overcoming strongholds of ancient practices with sound biblical principles. For decades, many of these ancient African traditions seemed impenetrable, especially to foreign missionaries. Indigenous African Christian movements, on the other hand, have made significant strides forward in their own methods of biblical interpretation, drawing on local resources and experiences that parallel biblical narratives and teaching.[20]

I (Matthew) got to witness a powerful example of this on a recent visit to Kajiado, Kenya, a Maasai community in which my Kenyan World Relief colleagues have brought together church leaders of various denominations to care for the most vulnerable in their community. That process began with the pastors examining Scripture together, and then identifying for themselves underlying beliefs that are inconsistent with biblical truth and have created or exacerbated hardships for impoverished neighbors. One church leader whom I met, Beatrice, now works through the various churches to challenge the cultural practice of female genital mutilation—an excruciating practice that she experienced herself and that, though now illegal, remains quite common in parts of Kenya. She roots her brave advocacy in the biblical teaching that women are of equal worth to men in the eyes of God, who made both in his image (Gen 1:27).

So also Middle Eastern Christians have a significant advantage over many others in terms of applying biblical truths to cultural divisions and violence. Through personal experience and/or ancestral tradition, Arab Christians in particular understand well the deep-seated conflicts that exist between Muslims, Christians, and Jews. To this day, Arab Christians also continually face the challenges brought on by the mixing of religion with politics, including extreme forms of fundamentalism that justify atrocious acts of violence.[21]

The content and methods of biblical interpretation among global Christians are of immense value to our American church contexts. Their communal approaches counter our American individualism and challenge us not to forsake the interdependent and participatory aspects of reading the Bible together. Their nearly first-person perspectives of many cultural aspects of biblical narratives help us see Scripture in full color and with fresh insights. Their awareness of spiritual realities that tend to get lost in the fast-paced and material focus of American culture reminds us that God is always at work in ways we cannot see. And their identification with ethnic tensions and power struggles between rich and poor are of tremendous value for the racial and sociopolitical struggles with which we constantly grapple in our North American contexts.

Broadening our use of global and Indigenous Christian interpretations of Scripture in the American church. For the American church to experience a greater global influence at the highest levels will necessitate a thorough examination of our institutions by people of various backgrounds to identify the cultural biases that perpetuate unhelpful and even harmful theology and ministry practices. This is likely to include, at the very least, a diversification of resources and curriculum to train Christian leaders toward a more culturally intelligent study of the Bible. Any sustainable, shared, educational, and formative growth in these areas will not be possible without the intentional development of diversity in scholarship and training.

At the local church level and for individual Christians, interpretive diversity will mean developing meaningful relationships and ongoing interaction with disciples from various backgrounds. These brothers and sisters in Christ can act as a sort of live commentary for how to understand both the plain meaning of the biblical text along with the many alternative and equally valuable ways others find to live it out. For pastors and leaders who do not yet have global or Indigenous Christians ready to participate in worship or teaching, utilizing resources such as The Global Church Project[22] or the *First Nations Version* of the New Testament is important.[23] We also hope that the contributions from global and Indigenous Christians within this book will be useful for teaching and training in faith communities.

Even if the American church fails to open the doors of our minds and congregations to the global church, they intend to remain open to us. As Hau Suan Khai expresses beautifully regarding Burmese Christians who now worship in the United States: "If we cannot influence [American] churches from your pulpits and leadership positions in this generation, for now we can do it with our character—how we live in our workplaces and neighborhoods."[24]

A BASELINE FOR UNITY

American Christians will often cite theological or doctrinal concerns over things like the gifts of the Holy Spirit, liberation theology, the prosperity gospel, and syncretism as reasons we are reluctant to read the Bible with Christians outside our cultural groups. Or we might point to traditional differences such as worship styles, views on Communion, or baptism methods. Or it might be that differences in the practice or application of Scripture make us uncomfortable regarding political or social issues. Or, if we are honest, we might still wrestle with that feeling of cultural superiority because of our wealth, education, and a perceived further-developed church structure.

Acknowledging that certain differences might bring legitimate doctrinal and practical concerns, is there a common theological center to be found and to which all of us might return when problems arise? Many today continue to affirm the Nicene Creed,[25] composed in 325 CE, as solid and fertile ground for articulating the essential tenets of Christian faith and mission and finding a place of unity among the many diverse Christian expressions around the world. In recent years, the term *Nicene Christians* has gained widespread acceptance among many, and in some cases has become preferable to the term *evangelical* or any specific denominational marker.[26]

Far more recently than the First Ecumenical Council in Nicaea, Christians of the semi-nomadic Maasai tribe of Kenya and northern Tanzania composed their own version of the Creed in collaboration with Western missionaries in 1960. The Maasai Creed is a confession rooted in the core beliefs of the Christian faith expressed within the daily life of the Maasai context.[27] The English translation reads:

> We believe in the one High God, who out of love created the beautiful world and everything good in it. He created man and wanted man to be happy in the world. God loves the world and every nation and tribe on the earth. We have known this High God in the darkness, and now we know him in the light. God promised in the book of his word, the Bible, that he would save the world and all nations and tribes.
>
> We believe that God made good his promise by sending his son, Jesus Christ, a man in the flesh, a Jew by tribe, born poor in a little village, who left his home and was always on safari doing good, curing people by the power of God, teaching about God and man, showing that the meaning of religion is love. He was rejected by his people, tortured and nailed hands and feet to a cross, and died. He was buried in the grave, but the hyenas did not touch him, and on the third day, he rose from that grave. He ascended to the skies. He is the Lord.

We believe that all our sins are forgiven through him. All who have faith in him must be sorry for their sins, be baptized in the Holy Spirit of God, live the rules of love, and share the bread together in love, to announce the good news to others until Jesus comes again. We are waiting for him. He is alive. He lives. This we believe.

AMEN

When sung or chanted in its original language, the Maasai Creed uniquely and masterfully incorporates the written confession of the ancient church while also providing a cultural expression from the Global South of today. Its incomparable phrasing such as "Jesus Christ, . . . who left his home and was always on safari doing good," and "all who have faith in him must . . . live the rules of love, and share the bread together in love" present beautiful propositions that could revitalize the American church today. The Maasai Creed, like the Nicene Creed and the Christian faith itself, has the person of Jesus Christ as its center.

The latter part of the creed also points to the unifying symbols observed in nearly every Christian expression around the globe: the bread and cup. Like we said of baptism in the previous chapter, the bread and cup reflect both our personal and communal identity in Christ and symbolize our unity of faith and practice. One might encounter these symbols in a house church in China, a mud hut in Djibouti, or an auditorium in the United States. Whether one's tradition calls the ordinance Communion, the Lord's Supper, or the Eucharist, the biblical truths about Christ and his salvation to which the symbols point are the same no matter the language or culture. As Vinoth Ramachandra proclaims, "Whenever we celebrate the Eucharist, we enact a counter-narrative of globalization that builds the global Body of Christ in every local assembly. It is the *whole* Christ, not some part of him, that is given to us in every local gathering that meets in his name (Mt 18:20)."[28]

WITHOUT AN AXE TO GRIND

Approaching the Bible with eyes to see and ears to hear means having the emotional and intellectual honesty to acknowledge the limits and shortcomings we all have. Such a posture also includes teachability and a willingness to admit when we are wrong. Or, as the iconic preacher and commentator of the Bible G. Campbell Morgan described as his goal: we should examine the biblical text "with no axes to grind."[29]

For those of us who still struggle with blind spots from the White, Western captivity of the American church, voices of color—including those of Indigenous and global Christians—have much to offer us. As God's kingdom advances so that things on earth might continue to become as they are in heaven, so God's Word continues to take root and transform lives in contexts all over the world. As we turn now to the world's poor and most vulnerable, we will see that our global situation is as in need of the living hope of Christ and God's Word as it ever has been.

QUESTIONS FOR REFLECTION AND DISCUSSION

- ▶ Can you tell a story of someone who, like Lonnell, saw his or her life transformed primarily by the reading and applying of Scripture? Is that your story?

- ▶ In what ways do we talk about the painting with little regard for the Artist? In what ways do we draw attention to ourselves and our interpretations as opposed to God himself?

- ▶ What ways do your worldview and the perspective from which you study Scripture limit fair and honest interpretations?

- ▶ What does it mean to read the Bible in community in ways that demonstrate interdependence on one another as the body of Christ?

- ▶ Which of the innovative ways that global Christians interpret and apply Scripture stood out to you most? What else should be added to our list?

ACTION STEPS

▸ When you read your Bible this week, pause as long as you need to beforehand and ask God to center your heart, mind, and attitudes into a posture of *Gelassenheit*.

▸ Also this week: buy a book, read an article, or listen to a podcast written by or featuring a Christian who is a different ethnicity than you or is from a different part of the world.

▸ Listen to an audio version of the Maasai Creed.[30]

▸ Search online for a video example of global Christians observing the ordinance of Communion in a different cultural context and language from your own.

▸ Take the courageous and likely uncomfortable step to place yourself under the teaching or leadership of someone who looks and thinks much differently than you.

7

GOD'S INCLINATION TOWARD THE POOR, OPPRESSED, AND VULNERABLE

If anyone has material possessions and sees
a brother or sister in need but has no pity on them,
how can the love of God be in that person?
Dear children, let us not love with words
or speech but with actions and in truth.

1 JOHN 3:17-18

RECENTLY, I (MATTHEW) was invited to guest preach at a church.[1] Because my role at World Relief and my past writing have primarily been focused on thinking biblically about immigration and refugee issues, I had a well-packaged sermon ready to share on that topic. Instead, they requested I preach on a specific passage as a part of their sermon series on verses that are often misunderstood. I was assigned Jesus' words in Matthew 26:11: "The poor you will always have with you."

That is my least favorite verse.

More precisely, I'm troubled by the way that verse gets misappropriated, especially by those constantly looking for a biblical counterpoint to Christ's inalienable prioritization of the poor, oppressed, and vulnerable. Some have argued that Jesus was calling poverty an unsolvable problem and thus devaluing ministry to the poor. Others have taken Jesus' words as a description of God's sovereign choice that some would always be poor, such that we should not seek to change what he has ordained. Still others might argue that focusing too much on caring for physical needs distracts us from the priority of addressing spiritual needs.

In reality, the Bible makes clear that God is deeply concerned with the well-being of the poor. By better understanding the plight of the poor around the world, we can also better understand God's promises for them from Scripture.

UNDERSTANDING THE GLOBAL SITUATION

The world's poor, oppressed, and vulnerable, in both the Global South and North, are nearly always marginalized in some form. As English theologian Elaine Storkey explains eloquently:

> Most societies also have people on the margins. We can tell who they are straightaway if we visit a heavily indebted, poor country. They're the ones who must live off less than two dollars a day. They're the ones who are most affected by climate change, drought, famines, and malnutrition. They're the ones who suffer from a wealth of diseases, and whose children die very early in life. They're people who wear threadbare clothes, have little education, poor access to fresh water, are vulnerable to epidemics and natural disasters, and whose life expectancy is very short.
>
> But affluent countries also have people on the margins. They're those with little power or influence, no real say in the key decisions that affect their livelihood. . . . They're often people with disabilities, poor health, or long-term illness. They can also be unemployed, the elderly, children, newborn babies,

or single parents. The lives of those on the margins are greatly affected by the decisions made by people who are a long way from the margins and very often don't know much about them.[2]

Those of us who are closer to the center of a culture or society, who have access and means that those on the margins live without, bear a responsibility to those on the margins. Missionally, this is true on a local, national, and global scale. If we are to be faithful stewards of the blessings and privileges God has bestowed on us, we must relearn how to live with empathy and by the Golden Rule (Mt 7:12). If we simply imagine our roles are reversed and we are the ones on the margins, would we not hope and pray that someone closer to the center would be mindful of us?

Today nearly half of the world's population—some 3.3 billion people—face significant poverty and struggle to meet basic needs, a number which has increased dramatically in recent years as a result of Covid-19.[3] For many in the world, especially children, poverty leads to death. In Africa, for example, for every one thousand children born, seventy-four will die before they turn five years old because of deficiencies in basic nutrition or lack of medical care for treatable diseases.[4] Child mortality is just one of many common characteristics of poverty in the developing world, where there is often limited or no access to clean water, prolonged food shortages, and rampant disease. Global numbers like these, while sobering, can also seem impossible to address with any real solutions. If we are paying attention, however, we won't have to look far to realize that there is also poverty in our own backyard.

One of the most effective ways to identify the most perilous forms of poverty in any circumstance is to ask: "Where are people hungry?" Throughout the United States, *food deserts*—communities without nearby access to affordable, nutritious food—exist in both urban and rural areas. Millions of children experience food insecurity and are hungry as a result of living in poverty.

Both in the United States and globally, poverty is often tied to severe oppression. Though slavery has been *legally* abolished nearly everywhere in the world, there are more slaves in the world right now than at any other time in history.[5] Millions are trafficked for things like sexual exploitation, forced marriage, forced labor, and domestic servitude. The vast majority of victims are from contexts of extreme poverty in which they are continually vulnerable. Many are women and children who have their identities and appearances altered and are sold and traded multiple times over. They often come from families and communities with little to no resources available to be put toward rescuing them. David Platt writes about seeing a group of young girls in Asia whom missionaries identified as being exploited in these ways, and yet himself feeling helpless in that moment to do anything for them: "There's really only one thing worse than being lost. What's worse is being lost when no one is trying to find you."[6]

Trafficking and modern slavery are also not just an international problem. Each year tens of thousands of human trafficking victims are identified in the United States.[7] Among those trafficked for labor, undocumented immigrants are the most exploited.[8] Traffickers often use both unfamiliarity with US law and threats of deportation as weapons to keep people in bondage. Pulcherie Kindoho, who was trafficked from West Africa to Paris to Atlanta where she worked without pay braiding hair for four years before finally escaping, describes the layers of vulnerability that kept her trapped:

> I'm often asked why I didn't escape sooner. But I was in a strange new country where I knew no one. I didn't speak the language, and I had no legal paperwork. I had nowhere to go, no one to tell and no way to explain what was happening to me. Trafficking was not even a word that was in my vocabulary, even in my native language.[9]

While a growing number of Christians are raising awareness about these evils, few consider how American and European consumption is one of the largest driving factors. Our addictions to money, sex, and drugs, as well as our habits, including the places we shop, the products we use, and things we *must* have, are actually fueling the slave market—a large portion of which is tied directly to forced and child labor.[10]

American evangelicals have been well known for calling for boycotts over a company's stance on things like sexuality and politics. Are we willing to display the same zeal about whether or not a company or brand is ethically sourcing its products? As Ruth Padilla DeBorst asks,

> Could engaged response[s] to the cries of lives broken by poverty, injustice, and oppression in its many forms—at the hand of unscrupulous employers, of sexual aggressors, of corrupt landowners, of immigration officials, of invading armies, of drugs and alcohol—be directly related to the layers of comfort, satiation, and excess insulating us from those in need, whether we live in the North or the South? . . . How long can Christians in the North simply go about their business, untouched by the plight of fellow human beings—including millions of brothers and sisters in Christ—when that plight is avoidable and depends at least partially on their lifestyle choices?[11]

GOD OF THE VULNERABLE

If I (Eric) close my eyes, I can still feel her tiny tap on my knee. I was sitting in a motorized rickshaw stopped at a light at one of the busiest intersections in New Delhi. All around us were at least five traffic lanes filled with cars, trucks, motorcycles, and other vehicles lined up several deep. I looked down to see a barefoot girl, not more than five or six years old, standing in the middle of the street right next to us. She had tapped my outer knee and was now holding her hand up toward my face, cupped in a begging gesture. I reached into my backpack, pulled out a granola bar, and placed it in her open hand. She quickly tucked it away and reached her open hand right back up toward me. As she grew more aggressive, our cab driver shifted his weight hard toward her and lifted his arm as if to backhand her. I threw my own arm across him, held him back, and gave him a stern shake of the head, and then I looked back at the little girl and refused her second request. As the light turned, we drove away and I watched as she, along with more than a dozen children around her same age, scurried back to the curb once the traffic cleared.

Sadly, as anyone who has spent time in major cities in India will tell you, this little girl is not a unique case. She is one of millions of small children who beg for money in the middle of busy traffic not by choice, but by force. Having had children come up to me in other cities far too many times, I've learned that giving money is not the best thing to do. Of course, doing nothing does not feel right either. But this encounter was different. This was the first time one of those children dodging the cars had touched me. Her tiny tap broke something loose in my heart and life that remains unsettled to this day. There we were, doing "God's work" in cities, villages, and homes all over the Indian subcontinent, and yet we could do nothing for her. Upon returning to our lodging that night I wrote this question in my journal: *If the gospel I believe is not good news for that little girl, for whom is it really good?*

Thanks be to God that all who have ever been poor, oppressed, and vulnerable like that little girl are both seen and deeply loved by God. Likewise, the Bible consistently displays an inclination toward the poor from God's perspective, so much so that many have said that God has a "preferential option" for them.[12] Some American Christians bristle at this kind of language, in part because Scripture teaches in several places that God does not show favoritism based on economic or social rank and also forbids his people to do so.[13] Not showing favoritism is indeed part of God's kingdom character and what he expects from his people. Yet the Bible continually reveals many ways in which God is uniquely present where the poor and vulnerable are found; where people are suffering rather than secure. This is indeed hopeful, especially in the face of suffering among the most vulnerable.

Nicholas Wolterstorff, in his book *Justice*, coined the well-known term "the quartet of the vulnerable" to describe the notable frequency with which the Bible groups together the poor, widows, orphans, and foreigners as those most often "trampled on" by the rich and powerful.[14] God sets himself up as their true defender, lifts them up, and commands his people also to defend their cause and demonstrate generosity to them. In Zechariah 7:9-10, for example, God reminds his people of his consistent commands regarding the "quartet," which they had failed to obey: "Administer true justice; show mercy and compassion to one another. Do not oppress the widow or the fatherless, the foreigner or the poor. Do not plot evil against each other."

In the book of Ruth, Naomi's family experienced the full gamut of the "quartet" within a short period of time. A famine in Israel caused Elimelek and Naomi, along with their sons, to fall deep into poverty (Ruth 1:1). As a result, the family was forced to seek refuge in the neighboring country of Moab, where they would be foreigners. Soon after arriving, Elimelek died, leaving Naomi a widow, and her two sons, Mahlon and Kilion, orphans (Ruth 1:3). Mahlon and Kilion married two Moabite women—Orpah and Ruth—and continued living with them in Moab for ten years. Then, astonishingly, Mahlon and Kilion died, leaving Orpah and Ruth also as widows (Ruth 1:5).

This group of three women, all widowed and without a man between them in a very paternalistic world, had difficult choices to make. Orpah eventually went back to her family's home, but Ruth traveled back to Israel with Naomi, where Ruth would be the foreigner (Ruth 1:11-19). In every circumstance, God showed incredible grace to the women in this story, including the non-Israelite Ruth. As Margo Schlanger observes, "Ruth the Moabite went first from Gentile to Jew, and then from widow to wife, stranger to citizen, gleaner to matriarch, childless to the (great) grandmother of a king."[15]

The "quartet" also appears in the words of the prophet Jeremiah, through whom God exhorts his people: "This is what the LORD says: Do what is just and right. Rescue from the hand of the oppressor the one who has been robbed. Do no wrong or violence to the foreigner, the fatherless or the widow, and do not shed innocent blood in this place" (Jer 22:3). But God does not stop at positive commands. He also rebukes and sets himself up against those who oppress or ignore the poor. Through Jeremiah, he specifically addresses a king who, unlike his virtuous father, was focusing on aggrandizing his palace, resulting in further exploitation of the vulnerable:

"Woe to him who builds his palace by unrighteousness,
    his upper rooms by injustice,
making his own people work for nothing,
    not paying them for their labor.
He says, 'I will build myself a great palace
    with spacious upper rooms.'
So he makes large windows in it,
    panels it with cedar
    and decorates it in red.

"Does it make you a king
    to have more and more cedar?
Did not your father have food and drink?
    He did what was right and just,
    so all went well with him.
He defended the cause of the poor and needy,
    and so all went well.
Is that not what it means to know me?"
    declares the LORD. (Jer 22:13-16)

If we are not defending the cause of the poor and oppressed and actively lifting them up, it is possible that we could be building on their backs and contributing to their exploitation, even if unwittingly. As we become more aware of these realities, we ought to be spurred to action. If we are not, we must ask ourselves, as this passage suggests, if we really know God.

CHRIST OF THE VULNERABLE

We do not have to look far into the teaching and ministry of Jesus to see the many ways in which he identified with, cared for, and elevated the poor and vulnerable. Jesus was announcing the arrival of God's kingdom from place to place when Luke's Gospel records a pivotal moment in Nazareth. As Jesus stood to offer the daily reading in his hometown synagogue, he was handed the scroll of Isaiah and read these words, saying, "Today this scripture is fulfilled in your hearing":

> The Spirit of the Lord is on me,
>   because he has anointed me
>   to proclaim good news to the poor.
> He has sent me to proclaim freedom for the prisoners
>   and recovery of sight for the blind,
> to set the oppressed free,
>   to proclaim the year of the Lord's favor. (Lk 4:18-19, 21)

Of all the words Jesus could have chosen to inaugurate his ministry in Nazareth and beyond, he declared:

- good news for the *poor*
- freedom for the *oppressed*
- hope for the *vulnerable*
- the Lord's favor and generosity for all who need forgiveness, relief, and restoration[16]

Given that this was the start of his public ministry, we must ask ourselves: *Is our version of the gospel we proclaim actually good news for the poor, oppressed, and vulnerable? Or is it mostly good news for people like us?*

Moreover, in his two most well-known collected sermons, Jesus said unequivocally that God's kingdom belongs to the poor (Mt 5:3; Lk 6:20). The poor and vulnerable have primacy in God's kingdom not only because of their circumstances, but because Jesus himself has identified with them. This was demonstrated even in God's choice of the woman who would give birth to Jesus, and the adoptive father who would join her in nurturing him. After all, Mary and Joseph did not appear to be people of much influence in either Nazareth or Bethlehem. When they dedicated Jesus as an infant, they brought the "poor offering" prescribed by God for those who could not afford a lamb (Lev 12:8; Lk 2:22-24). And Jesus lived his entire adolescent and adult life as yet another marginalized Galilean. Howard Thurman wrote,

> Jesus was not a Roman citizen. He was not protected by the normal guarantees of citizenship—that quiet sense of security which comes from knowing that you belong and the general climate of confidence which it inspires. If a Roman soldier pushed Jesus into a ditch, he could not appeal to Caesar; he would just be another Jew in the ditch.[17]

Jesus' social class set an appropriate stage for his ministry. His poverty was tied to both his message and his mission, as he called men and women from all walks of life to follow him. Later in the New Testament, the apostle Paul illuminated the significance of this for followers of Jesus: "For you know the grace of our Lord Jesus Christ, that though he was rich, yet for your sake he became poor, so that you through his poverty might become rich" (2 Cor 8:9). As such, Jesus became the model for all incarnational, Christian mission among the poor and vulnerable. As Ethiopian evangelist and scholar Bekele Deboch Anshiso observes, Jesus intentionally self-identified with those

> on the margin or the periphery . . . of the social scale [who] were regarded as unimportant in society, and Jesus unexpectedly brought to them liberation from their plight and afflictions. He also revealed his divine identity to them and was declared by them as the divine Son of God as well as made them part of his kingdom-of-God's mission on earth.[18]

Given Jesus' radical self-identification with the poor, he was clearly not distancing himself from the poor when he said, "The poor you will always have with you" (Mt 26:11)—the passage on which I (Matthew) was asked to preach. Instead, he was referencing a Hebrew text about generosity: "There will always be poor people in the land. Therefore I command you to be openhanded toward your fellow Israelites who are poor and needy in your land" (Deut 15:11). Furthermore, when we look at Matthew 26:11 in context, we find that Jesus made this statement in response to a disciple's indignation that a woman had used expensive perfume from an alabaster jar to anoint Jesus, rather than monetizing it "for a large sum [to be] given to the poor" (Mt 26:6-9 ESV). The particular disciple who raised this concern was Judas, who "did not say this because he cared about the poor but because he was a thief; as keeper of the money bag, he used to help himself to what was put into it" (Jn 12:6).

Thus, Jesus was not commenting on how to treat the poor but rather was defending the woman's extravagant act of worship that prophetically prepared him for his imminent death. Within a few days of this statement, Jesus was dead, and then, not long after his resurrection, he ascended into heaven. The opportunity to extravagantly worship Jesus in bodily form was fleeting, and the woman had done well to seize it.

The poor and vulnerable are indeed still among us, as Jesus promised. We must take care not to display a Judas-like disingenuity that uses the persistence of poverty—or even Jesus' words, out of context—as an excuse to be indifferent toward real human needs, and that is motivated not by honoring God but by protecting our own financial interests.

Moreover, though Jesus is no longer physically present with us, his words in Matthew 26 are recorded just after he explained in Matthew 25 that we *do* still have the opportunity to demonstrate extravagant love and care for Jesus himself—by caring for "one of the least of these" whom we encounter in a vulnerable situation of being hungry, thirsty, a stranger, unclothed, sick, or imprisoned (Mt 25:40). Jesus, observes Liz Theoharis, "is reminding the disciples that the poor are a stand-in for him. . . . God is not only aligned with the poor but is, in fact, present in (and is of) the poor."[19]

THE CHURCH OF THE VULNERABLE

American Christians are not yet known for our openness to honest dialogue on issues related to poverty, privilege, and justice. White evangelicals, in particular, rather than addressing these things from a biblical point of view that is both comprehensive and authentic, often do little more than debate their finer points or theologize poverty. Many resist even discussing these themes, perhaps realizing that confronting wrongful attitudes and behaviors will likely also require sacrifices and adjustments in lifestyles.

What might it take for American Christians to stop spinning our wheels in the mud and canceling others out over these issues while the world's poor, oppressed, and vulnerable languish in their suffering? We believe that prioritizing the proclamation of the gospel and announcing God's kingdom does not downgrade the importance of faithful action toward and alongside the poor, oppressed, and vulnerable. In order to do both, however, we must first be willing to acknowledge the reality that many of the comforts and privileges we enjoy come at the expense of others. We must then be willing to lean heavily on the biblical insights and perspectives of those who have actually experienced these realities.

C. René Padilla referred to centering the experiences of the marginalized as the "Galilean Option," where life, ministry, and mission happen *from* the margins. Galilee was not the center for Jewish worship and culture nor were its people pro-Roman government. It was a marginalized region from which several rebellions and revolts were launched. It was also the place where Jesus grew up and spent a large portion of his ministry. "Jesus' Galilean Option was not a circumstantial matter," Padilla argued. "It reflected his vision of the Messiah."[20] In other words, the divine initiative to focus on Galilee was not happenstance—it was integral to the ministry of Jesus and how he trained the apostles to eventually engage the rest of the world. The Galilean Option was not just about ministry at the margins or even among the margins—it was about ministry *from* the margins. From Galilee, God embedded a model for the American church to embrace: gospel-centered life and ministry are incomplete unless all, including all who are on the margins, are integrated fully into and enabled to contribute to the mission.

A key measure of true health in our churches—of far greater importance than the quality of our programming—is the meaningful belonging of a socially and economically diverse membership.

There are encouraging models of how to do this well in some parts of American Christianity, but overall we have a lot of work to do. Derwin Gray, a pastor of a multiethnic church, notes that many American Christians who work in diverse environments throughout the week "worship in monocolored, monoclass churches on the weekend."[21] As we continue to yield to God and the priorities of his kingdom, to pursue dignity for all and love our neighbors, we must be willing to confront these issues—starting in our own hearts. At times it may be unpleasant, but it cannot be unwelcomed for the true disciple of Christ.

Many American Christians have indeed expanded their view of pro-life to stress the importance of defending human dignity at every stage of life—as some say "from the womb to the tomb." Both the earliest and last phases of life provide clear examples of those whose condition defines vulnerability: unborn children and the elderly. Though the commitments of many in these areas have been admirable, there are many other groups of people who are often unprotected and whose circumstances are largely ignored or even despised by American Christians.

Among the most obvious examples are refugees and asylum seekers displaced around the world, millions of whom are children.[22] Many are defenseless and in such a condition because of things outside their control like war or state-sponsored persecution. Since the beginning of the US refugee resettlement program, churches and other faith-based organizations have played a central role in welcoming refugees. As my (Daniel's) family experienced, many American Christians have historically walked alongside refugees, immigrants, and their families as they adjust to life in a new country, learn a new language, and become economically self-sufficient. In the last few years, however, many American Christians—especially evangelicals—have changed their tune, falling prey to the politicization of words like *refugee*. In a recent poll, more than two out of three evangelicals (68 percent) surveyed believed the United States should no longer be seen as responsible to accept refugees,[23] even though a plurality of refugees resettled to the United States in recent years have been persecuted Christians.[24]

Despite this troubling trend in public opinion, there are still many American Christians, including many evangelicals, leading the way in welcoming refugees. Despite historically low levels of refugee resettlement in recent years, World Relief has partnered with nearly 4,000 volunteers and more than 1,100 local churches annually to welcome and serve refugees and other immigrants during that time.[25]

In addition, in retirement communities, nursing homes, and rehab centers, churches are often the most present to encourage and care for the elderly. Many Christians and churches also remain the most likely to be seen working with pregnancy centers, promoting foster care and adoption, and supporting families who have children with developmental disabilities.

A beautiful example of this is Morna, whose pro-life convictions regarding the unborn collided with her heart for refugees in dramatic fashion. Morna had been volunteering faithfully in a local apartment complex filled mostly with refugee families who had been resettled by World Relief. She helped lead a children's ministry with kids from Burma, Somalia, Liberia, Burundi, the Democratic Republic of Congo, and various other countries. One newly resettled family from Burma included a pregnant woman, Lah.[26] Shortly after resettling in the United States and meeting Morna, she shared her dilemma: she'd just learned her baby was facing very serious and possibly lifelong health problems, and her obstetrician recommended she have an abortion.

Though Lah was against abortion, she was also afraid she would not be able to provide for her child's needs with her limited financial resources and the stress of dealing with all of the challenges of living in a new, foreign culture. Morna, wanting to help this mother, didn't merely advise her to choose life for her child; she also committed to walk alongside the family and give of herself and her time on their behalf. She transported them to countless doctors' appointments, helped them navigate complicated health insurance questions, and gave of her own limited resources to make sure the child had what he needed, while praying for them constantly.

Another example is Jose, who regularly travels down from his home in Orange County, California, to the US-Mexico border to serve people who have no status in either country. Most are asylum seekers who have been waiting for months in local churches on the Mexican side of the border, praying for the opportunity to make their case under US law that they should not be returned to situations where many fear they will be persecuted or killed. Driven out of their own countries and largely unwanted in ours, Jose brings along his knowledge of the intricacies of US immigration law to help the families understand their options, art supplies for kids, and prayers that God would protect them in the midst of a dangerous situation. The small Mexican congregations that he visits are modeling sacrificial hospitality in remarkable ways, literally converting their sanctuaries, Sunday school rooms, and—in one memorable case—the pastor's office into sleeping areas for dozens of asylum-seeking families. They continue to serve, putting their own health at risk, even when the US government determined that the Covid-19 pandemic made it necessary to indefinitely halt asylum processing altogether. Both Morna and Jose demonstrate bright spots of American Christianity.

Undoubtedly, throughout the last two millennia, it is hard to imagine any enduring institution other than Christ's church that has done more to provide food for the poor, drink for the thirsty, clothes for the unclothed, shelter for the stranger, hospitals for the sick, and hope to the imprisoned (Mt 25:35-36). So also has his church pioneered highly effective work in the fields of education, healthcare, housing, social work, and care for the outsider.[27] Despite some of our struggles, the American church is still known among millions around the world for its compassionate action in times of need. Indeed, God has used the plight of the poor, oppressed, and vulnerable to put his kingdom character on display through the church, and to draw his church near to those with whom he is present and with whom he suffers.

JESUS TOLD A DIFFERENT STORY

Nearly every encounter Jesus had with the religious leaders as recorded in the four Gospels was one of conflict. He continually confronted their attitudes and practices toward the poor, oppressed, and vulnerable, and he challenged their systems as well. Luke 16 records one of these conflicts, just after Jesus had finished teaching about the perils of great wealth and the importance of wise and proper stewardship of resources. "The Pharisees, who loved money," Luke writes, "heard all this and were sneering at Jesus" (Lk 16:14).

Jesus replied, "You are the ones who justify yourselves in the eyes of others, but God knows your hearts. What people value highly is detestable in God's sight" (Lk 16:15).

Then he told them a story (see Luke 16:19-31).

There was a rich man, Jesus taught, who lived in the highest levels of luxury and extravagance. There was also a poor man named Lazarus, who was terminally ill and had been laid outside the gate of the rich man's estate. Lazarus's illness caused painful sores to develop on his body. As he lay outside the gate suffering each day, he longed for even scraps of food from the rich man's table to be thrown in his direction. His only friends were mongrel dogs who licked his sores.

Jesus' story resonates deeply with readers in the developing world. Researcher and theologian Esa Autero interviewed members of a church in a socioeconomically marginalized community in Bolivia and asked them to reflect on this particular passage. A member named Daniel noted several ways in which the rich man's perspective was altogether different from any of his own experiences:

[The rich man] ate every day the best. . . . We can only eat let's say on Sunday a festive meal. . . . He wore extra fine clothing. . . . I have had nice clothes only because I have bought used clothes, right? . . . He had fine clothes to wear of purple and fine linen . . . something that I am never going to be able to buy.[28]

Jesus' story then moves from this life to the next, as both men died and made their journeys to the afterlife. The rich man landed in Hades while Lazarus was given an angelic escort to a place called "Abraham's side." Though a great chasm existed between them, the two men could see each other from their respective final destinations. A dialogue ensued between the rich man and Abraham, through which Jesus was plainly speaking to the Pharisees who were still among the crowd. It is here that several important points emerge.

First, the rich man knew Lazarus by name, but he failed to treat him as a person. As John Chrysostom preached to his wealthy parishioners on one occasion, "If he did not show mercy to this man whom he had to see several times a day as he went in and out of his gate, lying in such suffering and serious illness, what person that he encountered would he ever have pitied?"[29] In the same way, the Pharisees failed to act on behalf of the poor, whom they also saw daily on the streets, in the marketplaces, and in their synagogues.

Second, even after death the rich man still viewed Lazarus as beneath him, speaking to the formerly poor man as if he were his servant. Abraham clarified that in the afterlife, God had set things right: "Son, remember that in your lifetime you received your good things, while Lazarus received bad things, but now he is comforted here and you are in agony" (Lk 16:25). Just as the postmortem destination of each man in Jesus' story was a direct result of his life and experiences on earth, so also the Pharisees were in danger of receiving their full reward in this life (Mt 6:1, 5), followed by punishment in the life to come (Mt 16:26).

Third, and perhaps most revealing of all, was that the rich man and his brothers had been warned of such consequences through their study of Moses and the Prophets but refused to repent (Lk 16:27-29). In the same way, the Pharisees, self-proclaimed experts in the Hebrew Law and Prophets, had failed to put their words into practice. Furthermore, in what some have called foreshadowing but is better described as prophecy, Jesus' story concludes with Abraham making plain that fact that the rich man's brothers (the Pharisees) would not even believe a man who rises from the dead (Lk 16:30-31).

Jesus' story is a direct challenge to our own Pharisaical tendencies as American Christians. Like Lazarus before the rich man's palatial estate, the world's poor, oppressed, and vulnerable have been laid before our own gates—before the gates of our eyes, hearts, and truly our nation. Will our posture toward them be one of compassion and empathy, along with hands open to serve and feet ready to walk beside them? If our posture remains closed to them, how can we truly say we believe in Moses, the prophets, or the risen Christ?

God cares deeply for the millions of people throughout the world, who are not merely on the farthest edges of their social structures, but are a step away from falling off the edge. As God's people, caring for the poor, oppressed, and vulnerable is not an optional add-on to our faith. It is a mandate from God, rooted in his particular concern for them revealed throughout the Bible and modeled perfectly by Christ himself. Christian psychologist Diane Langberg writes about how Jesus identifies most with those who suffer because of his own suffering:

> If you enter into the suffering of people, you enter into darkness. Such darkness would lead to despair were there not a treasure there. The treasure in the darkness is the Crucified Christ. He who can sympathize is there. He who knows anguish is there. He who has felt tormented, abandoned, unheard, and crushed, waits there in the darkness. To enter into the fellowship of his sufferings is to find Him.[30]

Following Christ's example, American Christians can prayerfully give of ourselves even more incarnationally, including our time, resources, and relationships. That might mean choosing to live well below our means so as to be able to support churches and ministries financially who are serving, equipping, and doing life with those on the margins. It may mean prioritizing the time necessary to invest in cultivating reciprocal friendships with those on the margins, even when that means experiencing the discomfort inherent in crosscultural relationships.

Ultimately, demonstrating Christlike love among the poor, oppressed, and vulnerable may also include leveraging our advantages to advocate for and alongside those who are trapped in unjust systems—even when that means engaging in the political process, a theme to which we turn in the next chapter. In doing all of these things in Christ's name, we continue to be faithful to announce the presence and work of his kingdom in their midst.

QUESTIONS FOR REFLECTION AND DISCUSSION

▶ Are there any Scriptures related to the poor, oppressed, and vulnerable with which you struggle?

▶ Have you ever encountered a person whose situation seemed hopeless and you felt powerless to help?

▶ Why do you think the Bible so often groups together the "quartet of the vulnerable": the poor, widows, orphans, and foreigners?

▶ In Jesus' story of the rich man and Lazarus, with which character do you most identify?

▶ What are some tangible ways that Christ's church can be his hands and feet to the poor, oppressed, and vulnerable in your community? Among the nations?

ACTION STEPS

▶ Read some books that will help you to understand the plight of refugees, victims of human trafficking, or the poor. Some suggestions include Abdi Nor Iftin's *Call Me American,* Clementine Wamariya's *The Girl Who Smiled Beads: A Story of War and What Comes After,* Dina Nayeri's *The Ungrateful Refugee: What Immigrants Never Tell You*, or the stories of Mu Naw and Hasna in Jessica Goudeau's *After the Last Border: Two Families and the Story of Refuge in America.*

▶ Reach out to a ministry, organization, or church actively serving the poor, refugees or other immigrants, victims of human trafficking, or women facing crisis pregnancies, and consider opportunities to volunteer. For example, you can find a list of local World Relief offices at http://worldrelief.org/us and a list of all refugee resettlement local offices at www.acf .hhs.gov/orr/map/find-resources-and-contacts-your-state.

▸ Track your consumption patterns for a month: what do you spend money on, and what might you be able to sacrifice in order to give on a monthly basis to a ministry that you trust that cares for those who are vulnerable either in the United States or globally? One option would be to join World Relief's monthly giving community, The Path (www.worldrelief.org /thepath).

PART 4

THE MISSION OF GOD

8

ADVOCACY AND DISCIPLESHIP FREED FROM PARTISANSHIP

On the one hand we are called to play
the Good Samaritan on life's roadside,
but that will be only an initial act. One day
we must come to see that the whole Jericho Road
must be transformed so that men and women
will not be constantly beaten and robbed as
they make their journey on life's highway.

MARTIN LUTHER KING JR.

"TO EVANGELICALS, faith comes first," write longtime National Association of Evangelicals leaders Leith Anderson and Galen Carey. "Taking the Bible seriously and believing in Jesus as Savior and Lord is more important than any politics. Politics and everything else flow out of faith and come much later in priority."[1]

As we have experienced on many occasions, Anderson learned personally that our reputation for "faith first" no longer precedes us. He describes a conversation he had while on a cruise vacation with his wife:

The first night aboard the ship, we went to an assigned dinner table, and someone asked for everyone at the table to introduce themselves and tell why they were on this trip. The woman next to us said she took the trip to get some rest because she had spent the past year as a political activist trying to stop evangelicals from taking over the country. She said, "All those evangelicals really scare me." Then it was my turn. It just didn't seem like a good idea to introduce myself as "President of the National Association of Evangelicals." The problem was that she saw evangelicals totally in terms of politics and not in terms of faith.[2]

Of course, we agree that our faith *should* come first. But if we're honest, politics often do. Partisan politics, in particular, are among the most prevalent American Christian idols that divert our primary allegiance away from Christ and the inalienable priorities of his kingdom. As research by political scientist Michele Margolis suggests, political beliefs have come to shape religious identities for many rather than vice versa, such that someone embraces the values of the Republican Party first, and then feels most comfortable identifying as an evangelical. "Partisanship influences religious decision-making at a certain life stage," she explains, "and the partisan-driven religious choices are evident for many years to come."[3]

NEITHER BLIND PARTISANSHIP NOR APOLITICALITY

Absolute partisanship does great damage to our credibility because it often affects our willingness to be honest and fair and to hold members of our party to the same level of accountability as our opponents. Even worse, as World Relief's Jenny Yang notes, is "hyperpartisanship, a blind allegiance that neglects the values Christians historically hold. We give a blank check to our 'tribe,' and that ends up harming the very people God calls us to love and serve."[4]

On the other hand, the response to hyperpoliticized Christianity for many believers has been to abstain from politics altogether, lest we be tainted or alienate partisans of one side or the other from the message of the gospel. These are noble intentions, but in practice such an approach actually requires us to outsource our political formation entirely to sources other than the Bible and the church. If we declare all "political" issues off-limits for the church—and by that we mean any aspect of our personal or societal lives that might be affected by government, from personal finances to voting decisions to interactions with neighbors whose lives and livelihoods are affected by public policies—we leave many Christians without the tools to think in critical, biblically informed ways about broad swaths of their lives.

I (Matthew) see this in my role with World Relief, where a significant element of my job is to preach at local churches, encouraging congregations to emulate God's love for the immigrants in their community. Often, I'll be asked if I can do so without "getting political."

It's very easy for me to speak to how the Bible talks about immigration without ever endorsing one political party or candidate, so in that sense I'm not even tempted to "get political." But if getting political means mentioning the systemic dynamics of a topic that, rightly or wrongly, most Americans view primarily as a *political* issue, then I cannot avoid it. At the end of the day, politics cannot be eschewed altogether because, as Eugene Cho notes, "politics inform policies that ultimately impact people," and, biblically, "*people matter to God.*"[5]

The idea that we *could* altogether forgo any convergence of our faith and politics tends to be plausibly sustainable only for those whom public policies have generally benefited. African American Christians, for example, who were enslaved, who were not allowed to vote, who endured Jim Crow laws, and who still face both personal and systemic racism, "have never had the luxury of separating our faith from political action," observes Esau McCaulley.[6]

This is yet another area where our American tendencies toward individualism influence our attitudes and opinions. World Relief's Dennis Mwangwela contrasts the perspective of American evangelicals to that of Christians in his home of Malawi: "In the US there is a lot of focus on one's nuclear family—me and maybe my wife and kids—whereas here, the church is broader."[7] If our focus remains only on ourselves, our household, and those who experience life in most of the same ways as us, we may indeed be able to avoid engaging questions of public policy.

The Bible challenges this view on multiple fronts. Consider the *peah* laws of the Hebrew Scriptures, which required God's people to refrain from collecting the entire harvest of their fields or vineyards for their own households, and to leave the edges and corners for the poor and foreigners (Lev 19:9-10). Now, as then, our property and other resources are not ultimately *ours*, because everything belongs to God (Lev 25:23; Ps 24:1), and we are to emulate his concern for the vulnerable—not just express concern for ourselves and our closest relatives. In a mostly nonagrarian society, this might mean reserving a separate bank account into which a share of our income is automatically deposited, to be withdrawn only for giving to others beyond our own family facing financial needs or ministries that serve the poor and the foreigner.

Moreover, the Scriptures dramatically expand the definition of family. As Mark and Luke Glanville document throughout the biblical narrative, "God's people are urged again and again to extend kinship to those who are marginalized."[8] The apostle Paul described the entire church as those who have been adopted as God's children (Eph 1:5), such that we are now united together—even across the ethnic and geographic lines that marked societal divisions—as "members of his household" (Eph 2:19).[9]

Many of us likely would say that if *my* daughter couldn't access a decent education, or *my* son could not get lifesaving healthcare, or *my* siblings' lives were threatened by unjust violence, we would certainly engage the government, even though it might be perceived as political. Within the church we indeed have family members—in Christ—in each of these situations, and many of our neighbors are in these situations too. Keila Garcia of the Association for a More Just Society (ASJ, for its initials in Spanish) in Honduras, says that truly biblical justice includes our insistence that other people's children should have the same rights as our own children.[10]

Our individualistic focus also makes it difficult for evangelicals to recognize that, as Kaitlyn Schiess observes, "evil worms its way into our structures and institutions just as much as it does our own hearts."[11] Repenting of and rectifying the effects of our own individual sins toward others is vital, to be sure, but genuinely loving our neighbors also compels us to engage dysfunctional structures. These systems of injustice are often sustained by a government's authority and thus can only be rectified by addressing government. There are clear cases in US history where (at least some) Christians have challenged systemic injustices heroically, such as clergy who opposed the Chinese Exclusion Act near the end of the nineteenth century,[12] the Black church–led civil rights movement in the United States,[13] or, more recently, the work of many US evangelicals to address the HIV/AIDS pandemic in Africa.[14] But there are certainly many other instances where (at least most) Christians were notably silent or even complicit in perpetuating systems of injustice.

If Christians are to seek justice, it is not enough to minister to the individual needs of those harmed by sin-marred systems. We must also advocate for more just systems, which necessitates getting political in some cases. As Dietrich Bonhoeffer argued, the church's response to evil and injustice "is not just to bandage the victims under the wheel, but to put a spoke in the wheel itself."[15] Thankfully, the Bible can help guide us to engage systemic issues without falling into idolatrous forms of partisanship.

THE BIBLE AND GOVERNMENT

For most Christians, Romans 13 is the Bible's most comprehensive description of how our relationship to the state should look. The apostle Paul begins by making clear that God has established human government:

Let everyone be subject to the governing authorities, for there is no authority except that which God has established. The authorities that exist have been established by God. Consequently, whoever rebels against the authority is rebelling against what God has instituted, and those who do so will bring judgment on themselves. (Rom 13:1-2)

Romans 13 has been misused at various points in history to essentially imply that the state is always right and that dissent is thus unbiblical. In 2018, for example, after many Christians, including prominent conservative evangelicals,[16] decried the separation of children from their parents at the US-Mexico border, Attorney General Jeff Sessions critiqued his "church friends," saying they should take their cues from Paul's instructions in Romans 13 and simply respect the law as he'd interpreted it.[17] Of course, such invocations of Romans 13 tend to be used only selectively; by the same logic, Christians who believe that abortion is morally wrong would have no other option but to accept the practice without objection, since for decades it has been allowed under US law.

While Christians are generally called to obey their rulers as part of their submission to God, that does not mean the government is always right and should never be critiqued. Paul's instructions in Romans 13 could not possibly have meant that a Christian should *only* submit to and never resist a government or policy. In the same letter, Paul extols Moses for having been used by God not to merely submit to Pharaoh, but to judge him (Rom 9:17).[18] As Origen of Alexandria wrote in his commentary on Romans 13, God himself will judge the authorities "if they have used the powers they have been given according to their own ungodliness and not according to the laws of God."[19]

Moreover, Paul also defines the appropriate role of government as holding "no terror for those who do right" and functioning as "God's servant for your good" (Rom 13:3-4). He goes on to specify that the ultimate law to which all other laws are subject is "to love one another" (Rom 13:8). And, as Martin Luther King Jr. observed, loving one's neighbor requires that we challenge unjust structures that are harming them.[20]

As McCaulley notes, Romans 13 "does not place limits on our ability as Christians to call evil by its name. . . . The state has duties, and we can hold them accountable even if it means that we suffer for doing so peacefully."[21] Romans 13 can indeed be hard to follow faithfully in a nation where we do not always prefer the leadership that is in place, but it asks far less of us than it does of Christians who live or have lived under tyranny in places like North Korea, Iran, China, Burma, or Iraq—or ancient Rome for that matter. Unlike the Roman imperial context in which Paul wrote, being subject to the governing authorities in the United States allows for peaceful advocacy for changes to laws we believe are unjust.

The Scriptures include various models of heroic figures who confronted unjust governments even at considerable personal cost. Moses, for example, repeatedly confronted Pharaoh, insisting that he liberate the enslaved people of Israel. To be sure, he could have made a different choice. Unlike most of his fellow Israelites, Moses, who had been raised by Pharaoh's daughter, could have lived a life of wealth and privilege. Instead, "he chose to be mistreated along with the people of God rather than to enjoy the fleeting pleasures of sin" (Heb 11:25). Those of us who either were born or made our way into positions of influence and privilege may also face the temptation to be willfully blind to injustice when we are aware that speaking up may cost us—but we are called to sacrifice like Moses, who "was looking ahead to his reward" (Heb 11:26).

Esther, like Moses, found herself as part of the household of a powerful, pagan king. As Malawian theologian Lapani Nkhonjera notes, Esther similarly responded to God's call to liberate the people of Israel.[22] Esther faced a great risk in confronting the king about a plot to exterminate the Jewish people. Ultimately, though, she recognized that God had given her a position of influence precisely for that moment, and, after fasting, she approached the king uninvited and strategically persuaded him to intervene, saving her people (Esther 4:14; 7:3-4). Contemporary Christians who find themselves in positions of influence with governmental leaders would do well to learn from Esther's example. God has entrusted them with such relationships not to enjoy the trappings of wealth or proximity to power, but to speak up on behalf of the vulnerable, even if that means jeopardizing their position.

Nehemiah similarly chose to leverage his proximity to governing authorities—in his case, as the cupbearer to Persian king Artaxerxes—to assist the Jewish remnant who had survived the exile and remained in Jerusalem. Notably, before approaching the king, Nehemiah repeatedly prayed, asking God to give him favor before the king (Neh 1:4-11; 2:4). His prayer included a confession, both for his own sins and for those of his people and his "father's family" (Neh 1:6), for which he acknowledged that God had justly sent them into exile (Neh 1:8). As the authors of *Forgive Us* write, "He opened his heart to godly grief on behalf of the sins of his people, confessed them, then busied himself with doing what he could to make things right,"[23] which included risking his livelihood and his unique access to political power.

While contemporary Christians are unlikely to find themselves married to a monarch or serving wine to a king, president, or prime minister, we are not without influence. In our democratic form of government, each citizen has a role in setting the direction of government and the freedom to use our voice to advocate for change. Some will find themselves uniquely situated to influence elected officials, whether because of a personal relationship, the clout that comes with financial resources, or the spiritual authority of a pastor, and—like Moses, Esther, and Nehemiah—we are called to speak on behalf of the vulnerable, even if doing so comes with risk.

Indeed, we see this involvement with governmental leaders modeled by the Hebrew prophets throughout the Hebrew Scriptures. Nathan challenged David's adultery and murder (2 Sam 12:1-14). Elijah confronted King Ahab for abandoning God's commands and leading the people to idolatry (1 Kings 18:18). Amos rebuked Jeroboam II, the king of Israel, for having sold "the innocent for silver" and denying "justice to the oppressed" (Amos 2:6-7). Obadiah called to account the leaders of Edom, who further harmed, rather than rendering help to, refugees who were fleeing destruction in Judah (Obad 1:10-14).

These biblical prophets, Eugene Peterson wrote,

sniff out injustice, especially injustice that is dressed up in religious garb. They sniff it out a mile away. Prophets see through hypocrisy, especially hypocrisy that assumes a religious pose. Prophets are not impressed by position or power or authority. They aren't taken in by numbers, size, or appearance of success. They pay little attention to what men and women say about God or do for God. They listen to God and rigorously test all human language and action against what they hear. . . . A spiritual life that doesn't give a large place to prophet-articulated justice will end up making us worse instead of better, separating us from God's ways instead of drawing us into them.[24]

Many of these prophets, like John the Baptist in the New Testament, paid a steep cost for confronting the injustice of a governing authority. In the US context, confronting the unjust policies of a governing authority is unlikely to lead to death or imprisonment, but there are real costs to count: pastors can lose church members and ministries may lose donors. But we can take courage from examples of Christians in other contexts who continue to face much greater threats for their advocacy.

In Honduras, ASJ has drawn on biblical principles to hold governmental institutions accountable with great effect, but also at significant cost.[25] In 2016, for example, Pastor Jorge Machado, executive director of Honduras's Evangelical Fellowship of Churches, was the victim of an attempted assassination that killed his bodyguard after serving on a commission focused on police accountability. That commission, instigated by ASJ with pressure from brave Honduran Christians, led to the dismissal of more than twenty-seven hundred members of the national police force who were found to be corrupt.[26]

The model of both the biblical prophets and many sisters and brothers around the globe should encourage us to be brave

Christians who are willing to confront injustice, regardless of what party or politician is perpetuating it. Even the most faithful among the biblical prophets, however, were still flawed human beings. The only perfect biblical model of advocacy is found in God himself.

CHRISTLIKE ADVOCACY IN BOTH ENDS AND MEANS

Just as Scripture has been our primary guide in our journey to this point, the Bible also gives us a clear picture of how advocacy should be done. In the first-century world of the New Testament, the Greek word for "advocate" (*paraklētos*) was part of common speech. An advocate was one who stood alongside another person in order to plead their case, defend their worth, provide for their needs, or do all three at once. The word was often used for a lawyer appointed to defend a client in court. There were also many other common examples, including someone who helped a blind person find his or her way, comforted a grieving widow or parent, tended to the needs of an elderly person, bound up the wounds of an injured person, welcomed and provided for the immigrant and exile, stood up for victims of injustice, or was simply a loyal and devoted friend.[27]

In the New Testament itself, however, the word is only used to describe Jesus (1 Jn 2:1-2) and the Holy Spirit (Jn 14:16; 14:26; 15:26; 16:7). Therefore, we may rightly say that advocating for others and giving of ourselves for them are among the most Christlike and Spirit-filled things we can do.

There are, without question, some key issues we care deeply about precisely because we are Christians. As a practical help, the National Association of Evangelicals' *For the Health of the Nation* outlines a series of policy priorities,[28] not all of which fit neatly into a single political platform. Whereas those on the right would likely be more favorable toward the emphases on protecting religious freedom, safeguarding the sanctity of human life (both unborn and born), and strengthening marriage and families, other issues such as seeking justice for the poor, confronting systemic racism, and caring for God's creation might resonate more with those on the political left.

Of course, we suspect most people are neither surprised nor offended that our faith influences our politics. On many occasions, however, that which has repulsed many outside the church the most has not been, as Ben Lowe notes, "*what* is being fought over but *how* it's being fought . . . in an overwhelmingly combative and divisive way, focused on building walls instead of bridges . . . demonizing the other side in order to further galvanize the base rather than respectfully trying to negotiate areas of agreement."[29]

Though *meek* is not the usual adjective that comes to mind when we think of someone doing politics well, meekness is a characteristic that Christ praised (Mt 5:5) and modeled (2 Cor 10:1). Political goals are not a justification for forsaking Christlikeness. Simply put, since we are called to be "Christ's ambassadors" (2 Cor 5:20), we better not earn a reputation for being "jerks for Jesus."[30]

The political tendency to view those with a different view from us as enemies is often the first step to abandoning kindness and grace as we engage with others. Yet, even in the case that our political opponent proves in fact to be an enemy, Christ has commanded us to love our enemy (Mt 5:44-48).

Similarly, whereas political advocacy from a worldly perspective tends to focus on those in power with the authority to change a policy as "targets," Alexia Salvatierra and Peter Heltzel argue that Christians cannot replicate this language.[31] Instead, we are to see those elected leaders—just as we do the marginalized communities for whom we may be advocating—as human beings, made in God's image (Gen 1:27), whom we want to help honor God in their consequential decisions. For example, when pastors organized by the Evangelical Immigration Table visit a member of Congress and invite her or him to accept a forty-day Bible-reading challenge focused on God's heart for immigrants, they're not only hoping to change the lawmaker's vote on an immigration bill. They also seek to guide that elected official pastorally to subject their views on this sensitive political issue to the Word of God, for their own good.

Some may find it difficult to believe that there are politicians in both parties who genuinely love Jesus and occasionally vote in a way that defies political expediency *because* they believe it is right and what God is calling them to do. Salvatierra and Heltzel argue that Christians make a unique contribution to the political process because of our belief in the power of prayer, of truth told in love, and of moral authority.[32] There are certainly times when evangelical advocacy is effective not because a politician is convicted by the Scriptures or the Holy Spirit but because they are keenly aware of the share of their electorate who are evangelical Christians and who, if alienated, may not vote for their reelection—but we err if we act as if that is all there is.

Indeed, in a polarized partisan climate such as ours, a sense of political expediency often pollutes the political ends we pursue and the means by which we pursue them. We must remember, however, that Christlike advocacy has eternal significance. As Schiess argues, our political identities and locations, much like the "earthly city" in Augustine's *City of God*,[33] are temporary and should always be in full alignment with the love of God and neighbor Christ commands. As a result, she writes, "political work can be right and good without being successful or permanent, so Christians are freed from attachment to any particular political structure and flexible enough to remain faithful in whatever context or circumstances they find themselves."[34] This kind of freedom in Christ releases us from the pressure of gaining temporal victories at the expense of our character and witness, which has often been the justification for pursuing ostensibly Christian policies by distinctly un-Christlike means.

DISCIPLESHIP FREED FROM PARTISANSHIP

Dallas Willard defined discipleship as when a person decides "to be with another person, under appropriate conditions, in order to become capable of doing what that person does or becoming what that person is."[35] If we were to conduct an audit of our own lives, we might ask ourselves: who or what is discipling me? Is it the Bible itself? A pastor, teacher, or leader who presents the Bible faithfully? A local church community? A Sunday school class or small group?

Someone in my family? A school or some form of higher education? Politicians? Platforms? Cable news? Talk radio? Podcasts? Social media algorithms?

For some of us, the likely answer is "all of the above" in one form or another. The truth is that we are all being discipled by many relationships and in many directions. For those seeking to "make disciples" as modeled by Christ himself, it is hard to compete when we only have someone for an hour a week while so many of those other sources have them the rest of the time.

As a pastor, I (Eric) understand this tension all too well. As many other pastors can also attest, there is something of a vicious cycle when it comes to shepherding a community of faith to respond strategically in Christlike ways to the complex cultural and political issues of our day. We lament the fact that our congregants fail to think biblically about issues in many cases because they are largely informed by a myriad of sources other than the Bible itself or someone actively living out its teachings. At the same time, we may be reluctant to address those same issues for fear of upsetting our congregants, who may then leave and find a church down the street that does not challenge them on those issues, taking their pocketbook with them. Yet by avoiding the hard topics, we also leave our congregations misinformed, and the cycle repeats.

In my own church, immigration could easily have been one of those issues. A few years ago, just as the topic was heating up before a major election, we noticed that several parts of our neighborhood were shifting toward immigrant and refugee populations. Around the same time, LifeWay Research released a poll that found that just 12 percent of evangelical Christians said the Bible was the primary influence on their views toward immigrants—which is at least partially explained by the finding that only around 20 percent could ever remember actually hearing a message on the topic in their churches.[36] We began a months-long process of praying, reading Scripture, and educating our congregation about the many opportunities that were before us to serve our neighbors. This did not come without conflict, of course, but God was at work. As we opened our doors to our immigrant and refugee neighbors, God brought them to us in droves. At the same time, the generous and kind hearts of many in our congregation were further opened, and God has continued to move in this ministry in ways unique to anything else we do.[37]

Whether we're pastors or laypeople, we also need to take responsibility for our own discipleship, submitting ourselves to habits and practices throughout our week that more fully form us to be like Christ. As Tish Harrison Warren notes, "We don't wake up daily and form a way of being-in-the-world from scratch, and we don't think our way through every action of our day. We move in patterns that we have over time, day by day. These habits and practices shape our loves, our desires, and ultimately who we are and what we worship."[38]

For many American Christians, one of the most commonly affirmed yet least practiced of these disciplines is prayer. Jesus taught his disciples to pray as if emulating a persistent widow who doggedly pleads for justice, assuring us that God will "bring about justice for his chosen ones, who cry out to him day and night" (Lk 18:7).

Several of the global Christians we interviewed believe the American church can learn much from those in their churches who pray and fast regularly, often day and night, and sometimes *all* night. For example, Joseph Bataille says, "The Haitian church really believes in prayer . . . like *really* believes in prayer . . . and really depends on God," noting that many local churches will have multiple corporate prayer services each week, and that they're the most well-attended services.[39]

Like Bataille, others also point to the importance of discipleship and disciplines in the context of community. Schiess makes this point as well, helping us see that proximity and fellowship with those who think and live differently than us is a part of both our spiritual formation and our commitment to advocacy:

> The community of God has always been shaped—morally, spiritually, and politically—by gathering together. If we want

the truths of Scripture to push back against the strong politically formative forces in our lives, that change will not come
about in isolated study that disconnects us from the community of faith. . . . The idea that our identity is based in a
messy group of people who are not like us is a politically
radical idea. When we read Scripture with the needs and
burden of other people in mind, it changes our perspective.
This makes it much more difficult to remain neutral on the
issues the vulnerable and oppressed face in your own community when you read scriptural commands about caring for
them while sitting just a pew away from people in need.[40]

For me (Matthew) and my family, seeking this kind of community
was one reason we joined a Spanish-speaking church. In addition
to being formed by the diverse experiences of the people with whom
we read the Bible, I've also been formed by reading the Bible in a
different language. For example, while in some English-speaking
congregations the word *justice* is seen as suspect, in my Spanish
language Bible, Jesus commands me to seek first the kingdom of
God and his *justicia* ("justice" rather than "righteousness" for the
Greek *dikaiosynē* in Mt 6:33). If justice, which is related to right-
eousness but implies a social dimension that goes beyond just personal holiness, has become a more central focus of my political
engagement in recent years, it is likely because I am reading the
Bible in a different language and with people who in some cases
have been victims of injustice.[41]

If the church in the United States is to recover our gospel witness,
we will need to be more deeply discipled toward Christlikeness and
freed from the idol of partisanship that has malformed us in recent
years. We need to see advocating as an inalienable part of our
mandate—a way to love our neighbors by addressing the structures
of injustice that hinder them from flourishing. And we need to be
focused not on gaining or maintaining political power, but on the
multifaceted mission that God has given us.

QUESTIONS FOR REFLECTION AND DISCUSSION

▸ In light of faithful Christian citizenship, how do we avoid the two extremes of blind partisanship or apoliticality?

▸ What are some current issues or humanitarian emergencies that require us to "get political" using a biblical framework?

▸ How do evil and sin affect systems and structures as well as human hearts?

▸ How do we apply Paul's teaching about government in Romans 13 faithfully and honestly to American civil life no matter which person or party holds power?

▸ What are some practical ways you have applied biblical advocacy on behalf of others?

▸ How does true Christian discipleship reveal itself in ways that are different from partisanship to a tribe, party, or group?

ACTION STEPS

▸ Listen to and reflect on Jon Guerra's song "Citizens," available at http://hyperurl.co/citizenssong.

▸ Choose a contentious political issue about which you have strong feelings and find at least three passages or stories from Scripture that challenge or at least better inform your views. Don't cherry-pick a verse, but rather do a deeper study of the texts in their original context.

▸ Identify a public policy issue that your faith speaks to, determine who is in a position of influence regarding that area (e.g., a US senator, a governor, a city councilperson, etc.), and write a letter or email respectfully expressing your perspective.

9

AMERICAN RELIGION OR THE GREAT COMMISSIONS?

God blessed them and said to them,
"Be fruitful and increase in number;
fill the earth and subdue it. Rule over the fish
in the sea and the birds in the sky and over every
living creature that moves on the ground."

GENESIS 1:28

Therefore go and make disciples of all ethnē [nations],
baptizing them in the name of the Father and of the Son
and of the Holy Spirit, and teaching them to obey
everything I have commanded you. And surely
I am with you always, to the very end of the age.

MATTHEW 28:19-20

IN 2013, I (DANIEL) moved my family from Southlake, Texas, where I'd been serving on the staff of a large, predominantly White church, to start a new church in downtown Toronto, Ontario, Canada.

Although I'd grown up in inner-city Detroit, my recent ministry context was in an affluent suburb in what was not just the South, but the Texas South! My newly acquired southern culture came right along with me to Toronto, even though it was very different from both the one in which I grew up and the one I was entering. The American couple my wife, Linda, and I partnered with, Mike and Missy Seaman, had relocated from North Carolina just before we arrived. Together as Americans, we began learning more about Canada and Toronto, and more specifically about a neighborhood called Regent Park, one of the city's lower-income neighborhoods with a long history of re-development and nonprofit services.

About three months in, we hosted our first public gathering and shared the vision for our new church with around thirty people. That evening I met an Afro Caribbean man who was a longtime resident of Regent Park. He enjoyed some of the snacks we provided and listened politely as I enthusiastically shared with him our plans for the soon-to-be church.

When I finished my spiel, he calmly responded: "Don't bring any of that American religion up here."

He wasn't rude, just honest. I wasn't offended, just humbled. It's hard to pinpoint exactly what it was, but something led him to see what we felt called by God to do as advancing "American religion." I don't think we were wrong in what we were doing, as that wasn't our aim or sense of calling, but I don't think he was wrong either. He taught us something very important about what it means to really understand Jesus' mission for his followers.

THE GREAT COMMISSION DOES NOT MEAN EXPORTING AMERICAN RELIGION

What led our team to Toronto and what has led untold numbers of Christians across borders—both literal and metaphorical—is what we call the Great Commission.

The best-known version of the Great Commission is what's recorded in Matthew 28:19-20, which is focused on going into the world, making disciples, and baptizing and teaching them.

Variations of this charge from Jesus are also found in the other three Gospels and in the book of Acts. While Matthew's version uses the phrase "all nations" (Mt 28:19), Mark's Gospel reads, "Go into all the world and preach the gospel to all creation" (Mk 16:15). In Luke, Jesus, explaining and quoting Scripture, says, "Repentance for the forgiveness of sins will be preached in his [Jesus'] name to all nations, beginning at Jerusalem" (Lk 24:47), while John records Jesus saying simply, "As the Father has sent me, I am sending you" (Jn 20:21). Jesus' commission in Acts has a Spirit-led, geographic outflow: "You will receive power when the Holy Spirit comes on you; and you will be my witnesses in Jerusalem, and in all Judea and Samaria, and to the ends of the earth" (Acts 1:8).

In each case, Jesus sent his disciples out with a clear mission—to make disciples—and that mission clearly transcends national boundaries. While a few take Jesus' words as directives given only to his first-century disciples, most Christians have historically believed that Jesus' commission is for all his followers, in all places, for all time. And though we don't know for certain how the original disciples understood Jesus' words in the moment, their actions over time tell us how they came to process what he meant. As Justin Martyr, who lived in the generation after the first disciples, attested, "A band of twelve men went forth from Jerusalem, and they were common men, not trained in speaking, but by the power of God they testified to every race of humankind."[1]

As of late, however, at least in the US context, many Christians seem to roughly understand Jesus' commission to mean growing local churches and bringing new members "into the fold." At times, we have focused almost exclusively on the goal of conversion—the profession of faith in Christ, followed, ideally, by baptism as a marker of initiation into a new faith—with far less emphasis on an ongoing process of discipleship guided by the fullness of Christ's teaching. And too often, we've called people to be converted not to biblical faith, but to White American evangelical culture, which often means a certain way of doing church or a certain level of influence in society.

A deficit of discipleship within the American church is partly to blame for such misapplications. Had we valued, above all else, obedience to *all* that Christ commanded in the whole of the Great Commission—things that cannot be easily measured by congregation size, church programming, or public acclaim—our commitments would not be misplaced. But unhealthy ambition and the misappropriation of American church-growth ideas have sometimes led some to serve two masters (Mt 6:24)—God and a triumphant notion of American Christianity. This makes all the more troubling the results of a 2020 survey, analyzed by scholar Joshua Wu, which found that just 13 percent of White evangelicals (and a minority of evangelicals of all ethnic backgrounds) affirm that their faith is more important to their identity than "being an American."[2]

We personally know many American crosscultural missionaries who place their identity in Christ over their American identity. But what happens when American Christians who place more importance on their identity as Americans go to make converts? To what exactly are people being converted?

ALLOWING JESUS TO CONFRONT OUR CONVERSION EFFORTS

Before we go further into Jesus' commission, we as Christians and as Americans must heed Jesus' warnings to Jewish leaders regarding the hypocrisy in *their* conversion efforts:

> Woe to you, teachers of the law and Pharisees, you hypocrites! You shut the door of the kingdom of heaven in people's faces. You yourselves do not enter, nor will you let those enter who are trying to. [They devour widows' houses and for a show make lengthy prayers. These men will be punished most severely.][3]
>
> Woe to you, teachers of the law and Pharisees, you hypocrites! You travel over land and sea to win a single convert, and when you have succeeded, you make them twice as much a child of hell as you are. (Mt 23:13-15)

These sharp words by Jesus were also indictments on the Jewish system in which he, and several of his disciples, were raised and educated. Zambian pastor Joe M. Kapolyo observes that the teachers of the law and the Pharisees were directing people's attention to non-essentials, effectively facilitating a structure that led people away from the kingdom of God. Instead of the kind of freedom that Jesus came to give, Kapolyo explains, "the Pharisees had developed a burdensome religious legalism that weighed people down."[4] Their ethnocentric system displayed the showiness of their leaders at the expense, rather than for the benefit, of the most vulnerable among them, especially widowed women. Moreover, their converts were taught to be ambitious and were encouraged to build the system stronger, so as to create higher pedestals than their predecessors.

But God was doing something different. Pharisaism was a pathway toward self-destruction, and Jesus called for their expansion activity to come to a full stop.

"Woe to you" was not just an expression of disapproval or an angry emotional outburst. This phrase, which Matthew records Jesus using seven times in this discourse, was a prophetic utterance that signaled the end of their brand-building religious structure that distracted people away from true humanity and the kingdom of God. The Pharisees had created a system to build more of themselves, and Jesus wanted that manmade idol factory shut down.[5] He spoke with power and authority against the powers and authorities that had maintained an unjust system for far too long. In ways far more divine than anything spoken by any great orator or revolutionary leader, Jesus' words had a binding and loosing effect. Something broke loose in the system and something broke through from the kingdom of God. Pronouncing "woe to you" was an exact measure he took to stop the hypocrisy.

Pharisaism was a small worldview that was maintained to support its Jewish followers and benefit its Jewish leaders. But this structure isn't unique to just nationalistic and ethno-religious groups. All humans belong to systems that support them and benefit their leaders. How Americans talk about ourselves says something of how we view the American system we belong to—for example: "I'm a citizen/immigrant," "I'm a Christian/atheist," "I'm a theological conservative/progressive," "I'm a northerner/southerner," or "I'm a Democrat/Republican."

The late sociologist Peter Berger calls the labels we ascribe to ourselves and others our *plausibility structures*—the mindset of a person or a group of people that determines how they interact with others inside and outside of their social group.[6] A simplistic metaphor for plausibility structure would be a tribe of people surrounded by many other tribes, perhaps even living in proximity to each other in a particular region. Each tribe has their own way of thinking and doing things. "Winning a single convert" for one group would mean socializing another person into their own plausibility structure, or getting someone from one tribe to experience and understand the world through the view of another tribe.

Our initial entry into a new tribe can seem odd at first, but over time, odd can become comfortable. Our leaders—who may be winsome, intelligent, and organizational geniuses—live with us inside the tribe, and they've constructed good arguments for staying inside, bringing others in, and growing our numbers. Those outside the tribe are either pitied or demonized and can only be saved by initiation. New recruits are usually vulnerable and needy, or eager and ready to do whatever is required of them to grow the group and perhaps even expand the territory of the tribe. Eventually, some hope to rise in the ranks. Everything that seems real in the world is mentally and culturally contained inside this tribe.

As an example, I (Daniel) have watched Hmong Christian friends get caught up in theological pet issues such as Reformed theology, charismatic gifts, women in ministry, denominationalism, and even Christian homeschooling. With so many unique issues and tensions already in our Hmong churches, I often wondered why some of us opt to fight and debate the battles of White American churches. Many in my generation entered American seminaries with the best intentions of getting equipped to better serve our home churches.

However, in that experience, some of us were won over into the plausibility structures of specific streams of (White) American Christianity, buying into sophisticated and elaborate theological systems. We not only graduated from American seminaries but, almost with condescension, felt like we graduated from our immigrant churches now prepared to serve in White spaces. Admittedly, this also reflects my own experience and the personal tensions I navigate daily.

These metaphorical tribes are not limited to religion, nor are religious people the only ones who seek to make converts. In fact, even American-style democracy functions as a plausibility structure. Its growth and expansion has done tremendous good in much of the world; in many laudable instances, America has traveled over land and sea to make successful converts to democracy and capitalism, uplifting some impoverished nations. But it has also, at other times and in other places, had a suppressive and even oppressive impact on many groups of people.[7] In those cases, we have made those nations twice as much a child of hell as we are.[8]

American democracy and culture should never be equated with the kingdom of God, and neither should evangelicalism or any other particular theological expression. If necessary, we must allow Jesus to bring our own systems to a full stop or at least give them a major course correction, especially if they keep us from genuine kingdom activity and inhibit our obedience to what is actually Christ's Great Commission.

COUNTING THE COST AT HOME FOR TAKING AMERICAN RELIGION ABROAD

Chrissy Stroop writes frequently about her upbringing as an evangelical and her path away from the church and Christianity altogether. In the exvangelical anthology *Empty the Pews: Stories of Leaving the Church*, Stroop wrote a chapter titled, "Now Defunct: Confessions of a Former Short-Term Youth Missionary to Russia," in which she credits the intersection of American nationalism and

Christian missionary work as a major reason for her exit from the church:

> In the evangelical subculture I grew up in, sending college, high-school, and even middle-school students all over the world on short-term mission trips is regarded not just as normal, but as praiseworthy. My story can't provide a comprehensive answer as to why, but it can provide a window into the weird world of white American evangelicalism as it manifests on the global stage—and how the anti-intellectualism, colonialist attitudes, and general confusion I encountered among missionaries became a key factor in my protracted process of losing faith.[9]

Stroop goes on to share about her mission trips to Russia and how she came to believe modern evangelicals still have colonialist tendencies with condescending attitudes toward Christians of other traditions, specifically Orthodox Christians in Russia.

Many lifelong American Christians can tell stories of attending retreats and conferences meant to inspire teenagers or college students to "reach the nations." To be clear, we certainly believe it is a central mandate of the church to proclaim the good news of Christ's kingdom to those who have never had the opportunity to hear it (Rom 10:14-15). But we also recognize that the American missionary lens through which we've taught many of our young (and older) people to understand the world has kept American Christianity at the center. Which is to say that, in addition to imposing Pharisee-like structures on others, we've projected a sense of superiority to sisters and brothers in Christ of other cultures and nationalities. Indeed, rather than teaching our young people to uphold the dignity of those with whom we engage cross-culturally, we've further exoticized other cultures, over-romanticized our ability to help, unnecessarily demonized those who reject our efforts, and sometimes disenfranchised the sisters and brothers we've claimed to help.

Joseph Bataille reflects on this dynamic in the context where he has pastored in Haiti:

> I've heard it many times—and it sounds so innocent—when a missionary at the end of a trip is speaking to the church or whoever they're visiting and they say, "Wow, I came here expecting to be a blessing, but I didn't imagine how much you would bless me." I think the real tragedy in that statement is that *they didn't imagine it.*[10]

As a result, a generation or more of American Christian young people were taught to see the peoples of the nations mainly as the *object* and recipient of their Christian service, as opposed to assuming that people from among the nations have valuable contributions to offer on their own. In many cases, we've set out to "bring Jesus to the lost people" of countries in which a higher share of the population are evangelical Christians than in the United States.[11] Luis Luna conveys one such example:

> One time, I was translating for this missionary—a really lovely person, a very quality person—who did not understand that there are a lot of people in Honduras who are *already* Christians. We're a country with 17,000 churches, and we were in a village in which there were *a lot* of Christians, and the missionary goes, "Are you ready to give your life to Christ?"
> And they said, "Yeah, we're part of this church."
> "But just to be sure?" he asked. And I saw him taking notes of how many people he could get to raise their hands.
> I totally get it that it makes sense to go back to the churches that paid for the mission trip and report 500 people gave their lives to Christ, but the fact that I understand doesn't make it right.[12]

Such sentiments by American Christians demonstrate a lack of imagination and a failure to see and appreciate the maturity of the global church. Perhaps in our American eagerness to mobilize the next generation into global missions, we have forgotten that by learning and appreciating the robust faith traditions of global Christians, we can find rest and healing for some of our older and tired ways of thinking.

It is important to note here that we are not referring to what Lamin Sanneh calls the "Western guilt complex" of missionaries, prevalent in more liberal streams of Christianity, which saw Western missions primarily as a shameful imposition of Western culture. Sanneh, a Gambian theologian and scholar whose voice is well respected in global Christianity, argues that it is condescending and dismissive to demean the autonomy of African conversions to Christianity simply because of colonialism. Many Africans chose Christian conversion after having received the gospel of Jesus Christ from honorable missionaries who themselves had first "converted" by becoming like the Indigenous people, learning their language and culture. Sanneh also notes that in some cases, missionaries even helped to preserve the local language and customs from other destructive forces.[13]

These missionaries were tools and reference guides in the hands of the Africans who were learning to preserve and advance their culture as they were confronted by a biblical understanding of the kingdom of God. When we fail to understand the process by which Africans and other global Christians heard about and believed upon Jesus, we perpetuate a guilt complex that still sees the world through American-centric Christianity, which is not much different from colonial Christianity.

As American Christians, and especially as evangelicals, the solution is certainly not to stop engaging in mission. While there is much that has been done in the name of the Great Commission that can be critiqued, challenged, and—when it has been done inadequately or from wrong motives—repented of, making disciples of all nations can never be abandoned because it is an inalienable responsibility.

Though the biblical mandate of mission does not change, the details of our social narrative have. As a result, we must talk about the global church and global missions accurately, reflecting in a matter-of-fact way that America and the West are not the centers. We must also update our theological and mobilization rhetoric accordingly. As C. René Padilla argued, Western Christians must break loose from the assumption that they, "because of their (supposedly) superior education, must always be not on the receiving end as learners but on the giving end as teachers."[14]

The failure to take seriously and to learn from the growing intellectual and spiritual traditions from around the world—whether Christian or not—will only prolong the cycle of creating and sending out well-meaning but naive Americans who have trained for a nineteenth-century world that no longer exists. While it is worthwhile to affirm the contributions of Western missionaries, both past and present, to human flourishing, we must also learn from their blind spots, especially when it comes to operating from a premise of cultural superiority. If we do not begin seeing with a better lens, then the naivete of our youth could turn into even more cynical apostasy. Part of seeing the world situation more clearly is recognizing paradigm shifts that must occur in the American church, which will more closely align us with the kingdom, and will help us better understand the Great Commission for our time.

REMEMBERING THE FIRST GREAT COMMISSION

The reality is that the message of American religion has not always been "good news to the whole creation" (Mk 16:15 NRSV). But the whole story of the gospel is—and that starts in Genesis 1.

Millennia before Jesus left the disciples with *the* Great Commission before ascending into heaven, God had another great commission for humanity—what some have called the Creation Mandate:[15] the agreement made within God himself to imbue and dignify humanity with his own likeness and creative work (Gen 1:24-31; 2:15; 9:1-2).

The value of life and work, which are attributes initially unique to God, were conferred and embedded into the first humans as the world was becoming. No longer would it be only God who had life and work, but now also something and someone outside of himself.

Although God would still rule the vast number of galaxies and beyond, the planetary domain of earth was meant to be enjoyed peaceably and ruled through a partnership between humanity and God himself. He would not take care of this world without the help of humans because it was created as the place where he would have personal communication and fellowship with creation. Every human was and is meant to participate meaningfully in this fellowship, and intended to live in conditions where that can happen.

This is a foundational narrative from which civilizations have emerged, and the Hebrew Bible is its most ancient source. At the same time, the Scriptures were not written primarily as an origin story but rather as a global invitation for all of humanity to return to this divine-human social contract, which God calls a *covenant*.

Covenant implies a personal relationship between God and humankind, bound at the deepest level, much like a husband and wife or a parent and child. The covenant relationship of being "God's people" is not meant to create ethnically, religiously, or geopolitically fenced-in groups. Instead, our covenant identity communicates and facilitates the strongest basis for relationships among disparate groups of peoples, who otherwise are too culturally separated to belong to one another, especially given distance and time.

True conversion, then, is a process of being turned toward one another by having God in common. It is both communal and missional. In seeking conversion, we desire to bring out the likeness of God in others so that the community of believers can more fully express the body of Christ in the world. And it is missional in that people are invited into the mission of God to learn how to steward with others the world which we share with him and with one another.

Identity-based living in the context of community and mission is not unique to Christians, however, because all human beings bear these aspects of God's image. If Christians fail to recognize this, we miss one of the greatest connection points we have with people of other faiths and traditions. Whether someone is a Christian, Buddhist, or secular humanist, there is an innate longing to partner with something or someone "bigger than us" to care for the world and for one another. No one should be denied that longing. The first great commission, in essence, is the plausibility structure that validates and incites this basic longing. It underscores purpose and meaning for human life and acknowledges the image of God in others to find common ground, validating their longing to participate as caretakers of the world.

Though the first great commission was meant to build bridges, somewhere early in the plot, humanity instead built fences. The religious leaders of Jesus' day also built fences instead of bridges. And somewhere along our way, American Christianity (and perhaps particularly American evangelicalism) has built as many fences as we have bridges. Whenever we don't recognize the image of God in others, we are tempted to demonize them by what makes them different. If in our time we lose the essence of Genesis 1 and 2, we will join the teachers of the law and the Pharisees in committing the same errors Jesus condemned in Matthew 23. In Christ's Great Commission, in light of his suffering, death, and resurrection, he steered his followers away from this error to reimagine what the first great commission meant for them in their time.

REHEARING THE GREAT COMMISSION

Each generation's commitment to the Great Commission requires a restart process in which we acknowledge our need for renewal, repentance, and reimagination. As part of this process, we must examine our own obedience and adherence to Jesus' teachings before we transmit them to others. Like the crowd who was present when Jesus gave the Great Commission (Mt 28:17), we must be honest about whether we are among those who worship him or those who doubt him. To make disciples without seriously undergoing this soul-searching process is to risk propagating nothing more than American religion.

In some ways, American Christianity may need to be "reevangelized," as Kwame Bediako suggests,[16] through the message of God's kingdom. If our message is anything other than the gospel of his kingdom, we will brand the mission and begin exporting it as if it is our own. The Great Commission came as a revelation to Jesus' first disciples that the proper context for the gospel of the kingdom was *the world*—not just the *Jewish* world. They would need to receive and contextualize his words for their own generation if they were going to be able to proclaim the kingdom winsomely to the nations and also teach them to do the same.

In all his commissions, Jesus was not looking to the distant future of Christendom or to a time when Western Christianity was staving off church membership decline. He also was not thinking about the beginnings of what we call "modern missions" or strategies such as people groups, the 10/40 window, short-term trips, or business as mission. These may be conventions for how we conceive of Jesus' commissions today, but they cannot be the lens through which we reread and reimagine his words to us in our own cultural moment.

We must resist boiling down the Great Commission to what Samuel Escobar and C. René Padilla called *managerial missions,* or evangelicalism's penchant to turn "the strategy for the evangelization of the world into a problem of technology," where the gospel is a commodity and a "product . . . to distribute among the greatest number of consumers."[17] In fact, it is not uncommon for American missionaries to undergo a deprogramming process and their own "conversion," as Sanneh talks about, where they move from seeing mission as primarily a problem to be solved by well-framed American strategies to seeing themselves as ambassadors of God's kingdom, unmotivated by selfish ambition or conceit, emptying and humbling themselves in the interest of others just as Jesus modeled (Phil 2:3-8). We are called to a great, multiethnic collaboration, as the gospel message of Christ's kingdom goes "from everywhere to everywhere."[18]

BEING CHANGED BY THE GREAT COMMISSION

I (Daniel) took to heart those words spoken to me at the end of our vision night in Toronto: "Don't bring any of that American religion up here."

Although it didn't keep me from making mistakes, it gave me a constant awareness of how much my Americanness was embedded into every word that I said and every decision that I made. Each time I was able to distance myself a little more from the metrics of success that I had learned from my professional training (the number of people who show up to a service, the financial sustainability of our organization, and the facilities we were seeking to acquire), I was able to embrace the humaneness of the Great Commission. I experienced my own deeper conversion into the values and ethics of the kingdom, and it changed the way that I thought about disciple-making among non-Americans.

Conversion from power to weakness. I realized that although all authority in heaven and earth had been given to Jesus, my training, fundraising, and credentials gave me little influence or power among those I was called to serve in Toronto. Learning to embrace limitation and weakness was not subsequent to strategy; it *was* the strategy. Those who would eventually join the new church were not attracted to our qualifications, speaking ability, or the organizations that supported us. They were mainly attracted to how vulnerable we were and how much they could contribute from their own passions and experiences. A young woman with strong leadership gifts named Michelle eventually became the president of our church board of directors. She was born and raised in Toronto and worked at a mission empowering inner-city youth. Michelle once joked with us that the reasons she was compelled to join the new church were because of (1) our faith to move to a city like Toronto and (2) how lost we seemed as Americans in Canada.

Conversion from confidence to empathy. Similarly, just as we embraced weakness, we also learned how much more important empathy was over our need to feel confident. Missionaries often deal with feelings of insecurity or discouragement. Their temptation is to look for some semblance of confidence, sometimes as a way to project strength or even as a way to "fake it until you make it." At the same time, the search for confidence can sometimes blind a missionary to the more important skills of learning to genuinely listen and to be meaningfully present. As time went on, we learned that you can only bring true change to people and places you truly care about. Superficial care brings superficial change. Leading with empathy as both a means and an end ensures that the focus is on people rather than just on accomplishing a plan. While confidence ebbs and flows with changing situations, empathy developed within us a moral compass for what the best thing to do was for the people we were called to serve.

Conversion from segregation and assimilation to incarnation. Admittedly, learning how to do incarnational ministry started first with acknowledging our privilege. We had the ability to enter but also to leave this new place. We could retreat away across the border and be home again with our American families. And then a few days later, we could reenter and pick up where we left off. But in time, this process of entering, then leaving, and then reentering (sometimes physically leaving the country but usually mentally and metaphorically leaving our work) challenged what we truly understood to be the core of our identity. As long as we segregated ourselves as Americans in our own minds, we risked having an underlying expectation that others would adjust to who we were. But as we became aware of that privilege to enter and leave, we were more mindful to look out for any segregationist and assimilationist tendencies. Deepening our identity in Christ and his kingdom transformed our privilege into freedom, which allowed us to go deeper into incarnational ministry, which meant preferring the culture and expectation of others over our own.

Conversion from projects to partnership. Over time, we did fewer and fewer events and projects on our own. We went from the mentality of being a church that "served the city" to being a church that "served *with* the city." As a growing but young church, we learned how to sit at tables with others and contribute when called upon. For example, even before having many people or any formal gatherings, a few of our team members volunteered at the Kiwanis Boys and Girls Club to support and underscore the good work that was already happening in the neighborhood. In time, we were able to rent their space for special community events as well as our own weekend gatherings. Because of our commitment and partnership, one of our members was eventually asked to join their board with a focus on helping raise funds for the club. We developed a posture of learning and asked other groups how we could help them accomplish more of what they were already better positioned to do. In turn, they did not measure our value so much by what we could give but more so by how present we were when it mattered to them.

SEEING THE GREAT COMMISSION AS A GREAT COLLABORATION

Just as the Great Commission in our time calls us away from a mono-ethnic, one-directional approach to missional community, it also requires a conversion of American Christians away from a material-wealth mindset. Affluence-based strategies can only imagine the rich reaching the poor but cannot imagine the poor reaching the rich.[19] Our models of mission will always be deemed oppressive to the marginalized if they are not authentically designed along with the marginalized. The twenty-first-century church in America will likely be marked by whether or not we figure this out.

Our teachers are speaking loudly to us from the margins about our attitudes of cultural superiority and self-reliance. Whereas American Christians often think of seeking justice and affecting change from the "top down," hoping that policies and structures might accomplish spiritual ends, many global Christians have no ability to influence anything at the systemic level. Instead, they take an active role in engaging physical and social needs from the "bottom up," empowered by Scripture in the face of the worst conditions.[20] Again, may they be our teachers.

We cannot wrestle Christian missions away from an enterprise mindset if it is heavily dependent on a corporate strategy with no ethnic diversity and in which the poor and marginalized among us are not able to meaningfully participate. If we fail to take practical and meaningful steps to see Christian mission not only happening to the marginalized but also from the marginalized, we will perpetuate the misconception that mission is a ploy of the powerful. This is far from the true commissions given to Jesus' first disciples and far from the pattern of partnership established in the book of Acts and Paul's epistles to the early churches.

Stepping back to allow others to step forward is often seen as an opportunity to neglect one's role in a relationship. But this is not the time for neglect. Today, the American church has been given an opportunity to forge equitable partnerships both locally and globally. The interest, respect, and tenacity we bring to those partnerships will prove the unity we have in Jesus Christ, which he says is necessary for the world to know that God has truly sent him (Jn 17:23).

QUESTIONS FOR REFLECTION AND DISCUSSION

- ▶ What is the most important message in your life that you want the world to know about? How can you relate that to the task of the Great Commission?
- ▶ What do you think are the systems in our time that Jesus would want to come to a full stop? Do you see the American church cooperating more with Jesus or more with those systems?
- ▶ How might the next generation of church leaders reimagine the Great Commission in a way that is both consistent with the Creation Mandate and relevant to the fast-changing world of the twenty-first century?
- ▶ Why is it important to acknowledge God's present work among people of other ethnicities, faiths, and traditions?
- ▶ Daniel mentioned the four conversions he experienced while planting a church in Toronto. Which one resonates with you most and why?

ACTION STEPS

- ▶ Take time to evaluate the church systems and programs that you are a part of. Deeply reflect on (1) whether they are effective in accomplishing the Great Commission, and (2) whether they might be further alienating or even marginalizing certain groups. Determine what the next breakthrough conversation you may need to have is and with whom in order to align more of what you are doing with how God is working around you.

▶ Reach out to two or three other Christians who have a different ethnic or racial background from you. If you don't already have a close relationship, find ways to deepen your relationship in a way that is mutual. Perhaps even commit to a series of regular social gatherings or intentional times of being present in each other's lives. When it is the right time, begin thinking about ways you can be on mission together in your city. The important thing here is to intersect your lives in a meaningful way and see how that intersection leads you to make a collective impact together.

▶ Find one way that you and your church's leadership can meaningfully be present in your community to listen and to learn from leaders of other faith communities and traditions. Some evangelicals are fearful of being branded "liberal" for working with people of other faiths. However, some of our greatest opportunities for evangelism come from honoring the image of God in others and affirming how God is at work in their community.

CONCLUSION

A Declaration of Dependence

Far from being hostile toward Jesus' message,
my experience has been that our society is hungry for precisely
the kind of integrity, gentleness, kindness, and love
Jesus reveals. . . . We who claim to be Jesus' followers
and seek a life shaped by His kingdom hold
the antidote to the division and anger
that is poisoning our culture.

SKYE JETHANI

VANESSA IS A THIRTY-YEAR-OLD who is rethinking whether or not she will remain a Christian.[1] People who know her would describe her as quiet, calm-natured, and intellectual. She lives with her boyfriend and their young children in the suburbs of Detroit and has built a good career as an architect, fulfilling part of her immigrant parents' hopes for coming to the United States in pursuit of the American dream. After arriving in the United States, her parents became Christians and raised her and her siblings in the kind of evangelical church upbringing we three authors know all too well.

As a teenager and young adult, Vanessa read and studied the Bible from cover to cover. For a time, Christian apologetics and spiritual formation were her hobbies. Her father is a staunch Republican who posts many of his political views on social media. He often chides undocumented immigrants because, in his words, his family immigrated here "the right way." Vanessa's parents attend church faithfully every week, and she even has a sister doing campus ministry. But Vanessa stopped going to church after university and has admitted publicly to others, "I'm not sure if I would consider myself a Christian anymore." Like many at her stage of life, she is unsure if what she grew up with is *real* or just some cultural way of life.

This book isn't an attempt to explain all the conditions or complex reasons why someone like Vanessa, who was raised in the American church, might choose to leave it. Nor is it our goal to provide simple answers for how to prevent disaffected people like Vanessa from leaving. At the same time, we want to begin our conclusion with the reminder that she matters. Vanessa's story, and the stories of a wave of young adults like her, need to be heard. We believe Vanessa's generation can still depend on the American church and that the future of the American church depends on her generation. What we've written in these pages describes hope for the American church, and so we finish our journey with hopeful signs of a new direction.

HOW LOCAL CHURCH PASTORS ARE BEING CHANGED

Long before the iPhone, internet, or television, Søren Kierkegaard wrote: "Suppose someone invented an instrument, a convenient little talking tube which could be heard over the whole land—I wonder if the police would not forbid it, fearing that the whole country would become mentally deranged if it were used."[2]

Every pastor knows all too well the challenges of shepherding people in a world with countless "talking tubes." An hour or two each week is not long enough to help a church navigate the misinformation, conspiracy theories, and inflammatory messaging with which its congregants are bombarded hours upon hours each day. There is also the fear that taking a stand on any controversial issue might not only cause people to get upset, but also result in being "canceled" by or at least distanced from other pastors and colleagues who do not want to be labeled something that might cause them their own conflicts. The sad reality is that a growing number of pastors have recently considered leaving or have already left the pastorate altogether.[3]

This last season has also brought a sharpened focus to many of us. We've had far too many reminders that we truly are not in control, which has driven us to a deeper level of dependence on Christ in our ministries than perhaps we had before. We see that the only way forward that truly matters is the advancement of God's kingdom, and our priorities are shifting in that direction. We are not nearly as interested in politics or partisan loyalties as we are in influencing policies and people through Christlike means for Christ-honoring ends.

A kingdom-oriented mindset also affects our character, which means we are just as concerned with how those we shepherd are living out righteousness and seeking justice as we are with their doctrinal soundness and church attendance. We are willing to direct more energy into a wider pro-life view, stressing the value of every human life—from the womb to refugees and their families, migrants at the border, those in prison, the sick, the disabled, and the elderly.

These things take courage, but we are often heartened by the faithfulness of our sisters and brothers in Christ from all over the world and the reminder that we are part of a global community of faith and do not struggle alone. At the same time, the more we remember the stories of the early church and other Christians from the past, the more we realize we are just one of many generations who have been commissioned to speak and act as if "Jesus is Lord" of every aspect of our lives, come what may. It is the kingdom of God that drives how we shepherd our families and churches, and nothing is more important.

HOW GLOBAL LEADERS ARE BRINGING CHANGE

The pulpit at Parklands Baptist Church rests above an image of the continent of Africa marked with the words "Arise and Shine." Pastor

Simon Mwangi preaches from John 6:1-15, the story of Jesus miraculously multiplying a young boy's five barley loaves and two fish to feed a crowd of more than five thousand. Like that boy who gave up what he had for God's purposes, like a single seed that, when sacrificed to death, multiplies (Jn 12:24), Pastor Mwangi believes that God has miraculous purposes for the African continent.

"What God has put in your hands is what is needed," he tells his congregation, gathered in a large arena-style building in Nairobi, and many others listening online throughout Africa, which is now home to more Christians than any other continent in the world.[4] "Africa is blessed. . . . This is a place that is carrying the gift needed by the rest of the world. . . . Revival will flow from Africa. And what the rest of the world needs is actually here."[5] Like that young boy who offered all he had for lunch, he concludes, they also must be willing to release their gifts and offer themselves sacrificially for God's kingdom purposes.

Listening to Pastor Mwangi preach this message in early 2020, I (Matthew) couldn't help but cringe when he also called Africa "a despised continent," on account of the many disparaging things he'd heard said about his native land.[6] I was heartbroken thinking of the vulgarities that the then–US president had recently used to describe African nations,[7] and of the US policy announced just the previous month restricting all immigrant visas from Africa's most populous country and adding new restrictions on visas from three other African nations.[8]

That policy change barely registered as a news story for most Americans, but for pastors like my friend Gregory Ijiwola, who leads a mostly Nigerian congregation in Chicago with many families who were directly affected, it was "devastating."[9] God has gifted Africa, and Africans are offering themselves up to help lead the global church—and yet it seems like our country, at least on a formal legal level, does not want them. We must have the humility to receive their gifts, and those of Christians from other parts of the Global South.

The three of us, in the different contexts where we live and work, have been blessed by brothers and sisters from Africa (and from many other places in the Global South) who have invested in us. One reason we're still hopeful about the future of the church in America, and think that it can be saved, is precisely because we've seen much more of the church than just the American versions. Christians from other parts of the world, including many who lack the same level of financial resources available in the United States, are offering up their perspectives, gifts, and leadership to the struggling American church.

Indeed, God created the church to be a single, interdependent body, and "those parts of the body that seem to be weaker are indispensable" (1 Cor 12:22). The Global South may never have actually been the weaker or "less honorable" (1 Cor 12:23) part of the church, but it certainly has been regarded as marginal by many North American Christians. For far too long we've associated Africa and other materially poorer regions of the world solely with poverty, and not with potential. We believe it is indeed time for the church in the Global South to arise and shine, and for the American church to learn to look to their leadership, because we need them as much as they need us.

HOW NEXT GENERATION LEADERS ARE THE CHANGE

We must also recognize that God is at work in the next generation. As much as we cannot forget the Vanessas of America, we also can't forget the Hannahs. Hannah Gronowski Barnett is a millennial who was raised in the suburbs of Chicago. She describes herself as being born "with a neon soul and freedom in my lungs."[10] Hannah has attended church all of her life and is neither ignorant of nor immune to the issues we describe in this book. She sees the hypocrisy in our churches, especially given the relatively recent moral failures of high-profile pastors in her hometown. She's also well aware of the spiritual trauma that many in her generation (and the ones before) have experienced, whether from abusive church leadership or the conflation of faith and partisan politics. Where many have been jaded by these stories, Hannah has somehow managed to find a deep motivation to advocate for her generation of the American church.

Hannah and her friends are part of a budding movement called Generation Distinct, which, among other things, includes cohort-based mentorship for young adults wrestling with cultural injustices of our time. Participants are led through a process of exploring their unique passions and discovering where their personal interests might converge with addressing these issues.[11]

Seeing environments created for young adults to process pain and uncertainty along with hope and purpose gives us more encouragement than meeting the church-growth success metrics that were defined by previous generations. Indeed, this generation of American Christianity cannot healthily evolve without safe spaces created for and by young Christ followers who are wisely choosing empathy, lament, and hope over notoriety, spin, and shallow results. Although American Christianity has long weathered cultural upheaval and theological controversy, the uniqueness of the cultural convulsions in this generation will undoubtedly create spiritual trauma for many. This is not a dissimilar consequence from that experienced by trauma survivors from around the world.

Diane Langberg's book *Suffering and the Heart of God: How Trauma Destroys and Christ Restores* solidly argues that trauma is the mission field of the twenty-first century.[12] Her work with missionaries and trauma survivors offers tremendous insight into what kind of church leaders are needed for now and in the future. In the most difficult circumstances in the world, those who are effective in helping people are those who lead with empathy. How much more, then, should we learn these lessons and heed the voices from around the world prophetically speaking to American Christians about the wounded and the tired among us? Many like Hannah are answering this challenge by creating environments that will carry her generation forward—and perhaps with them, the future of American Christianity.

Where we've focused on the shortcomings of American Christianity in this book, we've done so with younger Christians in mind who are already being led and shaped by voices from the margins. Both Vanessa and Hannah *are* the future of American Christianity, and we are hopeful that those like Hannah will remain compassionately aware of the Vanessas and do their best to keep space open for them.

ENCOURAGEMENT FOR THE JADED

For those struggling within evangelical churches, we've not intended this book to be a rationale to stay. Instead, we're acknowledging some of the ways we've strayed from God and are calling on all of us within the American church to repent, even if it means putting on sackcloth and lying in the dust. For those not holding their breath for this to happen—we understand. Many before us have called out the glaring idols of American Christianity, and many people we love have been damaged by so-called Christian leaders who have proliferated idolatry in the name of Jesus. There are still many days when we say to ourselves, *this is such a mess.* But there are also days when the beauty of Jesus and his kingdom shine through, giving us a fresh glimpse of God's incredible love and mercy.

Those people Jesus described as being close to the kingdom during his ministry often looked like those most wounded by the religious leaders. Nevertheless, they were also among the ones actively seeking him in the crowds. Belonging to Jesus means that anything we leave behind will eventually be given back to us in manifold ways. Jesus is not a toxic Savior, even if some who claim to follow him are themselves toxic. Though the Spirit of God may wound us at times, it is only with the intention to heal us and to use us, and not in the ways religious people often wound and use others.

If you have been jaded by American Christianity, we mourn the ways in which the church has failed you, and we admire your courage to speak up and stir our consciences and those of many others.

ENCOURAGEMENT FOR THE REMNANT

What if maybe, just maybe, the many political, social, and cultural tensions within American churches of late are signs that there is soon to be a changing of the guard? Perhaps, through God's sovereignty, self-serving and destructive leaders will fade away and new, humble, Spirit-led leaders will emerge. Whether in local churches, Christian institutions, or models for ministry, we are prayerful that this changing of the guard will be about far more than just personnel. We have hope that new leaders will examine our root systems and foundations to find that solid framework upon which it is still worth building.

If anything other than the kingdom of God is the framework for Christianity in America, let's be okay with God removing it and let's pray with Jesus for his kingdom to come. God is doing a similar thing in our time to that which the writer of Hebrews describes:

> At that time his voice shook the earth, but now he has promised, "Once more I will shake not only the earth but also the heavens." The words "once more" indicate the removing of what can be shaken—that is, created things—so that what cannot be shaken may remain.
>
> Therefore, since we are receiving a kingdom that cannot be shaken, let us be thankful, and so worship God acceptably with reverence and awe, for our "God is a consuming fire." (Heb 12:26-29)

In his mercy, God is shaking things up in our house and the furniture is moving. Though our instinct is to bolt down the couch and fridge and straighten up the photos hanging on the wall, it's time to get underneath the basement, find where the foundation has cracked, and get to repairing it.

ENCOURAGEMENT—AND A CHALLENGE— FOR PASTORS AND CHURCH LEADERS

To say this last season has been challenging for pastors who shepherd people is much like saying the ocean has lots of water.

Pastors are used to feeling pressure to grow attendance and keep people giving in order to keep the church doors open. In the Covid-affected world, however, many previously unheard-of challenges have emerged that make ministry and communication more essential and yet more complex than ever. In our current cultural climate it may feel perilous to challenge a congregation with a message, no matter how biblical, that they may not like. Taking such risks requires not only wisdom and courage but also a realistic assessment of the costs and energy that potential conflicts will require.

Even so, the pastor's primary calling is not to make people come back next Sunday, to balance a ministry budget, or to make people feel comfortable and secure. The pastoral call is the Great Commission call—to make disciples. As Bob Roberts asserts, we need to "push against the American mentality 'This isn't going to grow my church,'" because the church belongs to Christ, not us. If we compromise God's inalienable, biblical truths to placate "happy" church consumers, what we're growing will ultimately be a perversion of authentic Christian faith.[13]

We're convinced that our sisters and brothers around the world, particularly in contexts where poverty is prevalent, have modeled this for us. They've demonstrated that the church can grow with or without significant resources so long as we stay faithful to God's kingdom character and values. When any church fails to do so, it ceases to be Christ's church. That the church has endured for millennia by the promise of our Savior himself (Mt 16:18) secures our hope that even as individual congregations come and go, Christ's church will endure until he returns. No matter the cost, may we as ministers of the gospel keep our eyes fixed on Jesus (Heb 12:2), take care of his sheep (Jn 21:16), and trust that he will build his church (Mt 16:18).

WHERE WE GO FROM HERE

So, can American Christianity be saved? Is the evangelical version of it worth saving? We're still writing as insiders, hopeful that the influence of global Christianity and the more noble elements of our history will help spur a renewal within the American church. We are praying for a true revival, centered not on seizing political power or refurbishing a tarnished brand, but on recommitting ourselves to the inalienable truths of the Christian faith—namely, the *kingdom of God*, the *image of God*, the *Word of God*, and the *mission of God*.

Ultimately, though, we're less concerned with whether the American brand of Christianity survives than we are with the mission we believe God has entrusted to his church, with Jesus at the center. Some will need to distance themselves from the evangelical label; some will need to find a new church or denomination. Whatever the case, we pray *you* will not walk away from Jesus, nor pursue Jesus in isolation, but rather find a safe and healthy Christian community.

The world and all that is within it are awaiting the salvation we proclaim, whether they articulate it that way or not. As Paul wrote, "For the creation waits in eager expectation for the children of God to be revealed" (Rom 8:19). People from every perspective—especially those traumatized by the church—are waiting for American Christians to return to our greatest identity as children of God, following the example of love and sacrifice modeled for us by the Son of God.

When we prefer our social or political identities over the divine one, we are bound to make enemies of all who differ from us, whether physically or ideologically. We cannot demonize a group and then later romanticize to our tribe how difficult it is to reach them. Our failure to hear the critiques about who we are in this cultural moment, especially from the ones we want to reach, may be us muting the voice that matters the most: God's voice.

If left to itself, the American church is totally and utterly lost. Thankfully, by God's mercy, we are not left alone. Through our constant dependence on Jesus and in the power of the Holy Spirit, we are part of an interconnected global body, where each part needs every other part. We believe God may yet use the testimony and collective wisdom of the ancient church, our partnership in the gospel with the global church, and the experiences and strength from the margins to save the American church.

ACKNOWLEDGMENTS

ERIC

First and foremost I want to thank my wife, Rebecca, and my children, Adin, Noah, Abigail, and Kynzleigh, for your enduring patience and encouragement on this project (and in life and ministry). God has given each of you such faithful and loving hearts, and I pray this book and its impact will lead your hearts to follow Christ more passionately.

I also want to thank my parents—both Bill and Terri, and Glenn and Carol—and my grandparents Harold and Teresia for the investments you've made in me and the great interest you've shown in my endeavors.

Thank you also to my church family for the many ways in which you model the Christlike character and commitment we've written about in this book. This is especially true of my fellow ministers and our other staff members. This last season has been the hardest, yet sweetest, time I've had in ministry. I thank you all for that.

As always I am incredibly blessed by our growing immigrant population in Tulsa. To all who are part of our Rising Village family and South Tulsa Baptist Church international and refugee ministry—I can think of no other individuals and families who've inspired my contributions to this book more than you. I especially want to thank Hau Suan Khai, who I interviewed for this book, and the entire Zomi community of Oklahoma who enrich our communities in so many ways.

Thank you also to Marissa Carter, Kelsey Carter, and Cindy Seay who gave of your personal time to help me think through and articulate my thoughts in better ways. Your insights are truly invaluable, and I look forward to working together more in the future.

Thank you, InterVarsity Press—you were our first choice as a publisher and you've believed in this project from the beginning. Al Hsu, you and your team are first-class.

Lastly and certainly not least, thank you, Daniel Yang and Matthew Soerens. This project could never have happened without you. I am proud to call you both colleagues and friends.

DANIEL

I'd like to first acknowledge my dad, Ed (Yaj Neej Thoob), and my mom, Chue (Paj Tswb), who passed away in 2016.

My mom's only formal education was ESL classes and my dad had an education equivalent to middle school before taking a welding course at a local community college. And yet they raised children whose careers include a physician, a food distributor, an attorney, an engineer, and a missiologist.

My parents never uttered these phrases, whether in English or in Hmong: "I am an evangelical" or "I am an American Christian." In fact, to attempt to say those simple phrases in Hmong is cumbersome and awkward. When asked about their faith, their response would be: "Kuv ntseeg Yexus" or "I trust Jesus."

Together they had a simple life with simple faith. Yet they modeled for me the best of what it means to be American and what it means to be Christian.

I also want to thank my wife, Linda. She led the prayer team that's been praying for us and this book. She's also processed with me my concerns about the state of American Christianity and evangelicalism! I love you.

Thank you, Justin, Conor, Joel, John-Abraham, and Sara—my kids! I thought about you often as I wrote. Have faith, and have courage.

I want to thank the good folks at InterVarsity Press, the Church Multiplication Institute, the Wheaton College Billy Graham Center, the North American Mission Board, Trinity Evangelical Divinity

School, and The Prodigal Network for being my community for the past few years!

Eric and Matt, it's been a joy and honor to serve alongside you in this project. I've learned so much from you and about myself in this process. Thank you, and let's do it again!

And finally, to my few friends who don't fit the religious labels used to describe Christians in America: thank you for sharing with me your sacred stories of hurt from the church. Your faces came to mind and your voices rang in my ear every time I sat down to write. Even though you can no longer say, "I am an evangelical," I hope you will say, "I trust Jesus."

MATTHEW

Christianity Today executive editor Ted Olsen recently reflected on the devastating experience of reporting on one moral failure after another among prominent Christian leaders. The experience never shook his own faith in God, he says, but he began to question the church, wondering if there were any *real* Christians who actually believed what they professed to believe.

I can identify with those questions. I'm so grateful for the Christian sisters and brothers of integrity who have, with their lives and their words, actually helped me to love the church more, even in a season when many prominent Christian leaders have left me disenchanted.

Many of those folks have been colleagues at World Relief, both in the United States and in Africa, Asia, Latin America, and the Caribbean. Special thanks to Jenny Yang, who has been an incredibly supportive boss. Our partners with the Evangelical Immigration Table and the National Immigration Forum have similarly been a regular source of encouragement.

My community in Aurora, including at Iglesia San Pablo, have likewise been a hopeful reminder of the value of Christian community. Thanks, too, to my *compadres,* Janvier Decise and Marie Josee Furaha, Jacob and Tessa Rodriguez, Eric and Kelly Stade, and Rigo and Elizabeth Ortiz.

Special thanks to those who lent me their time and wisdom to be interviewed in the process of writing this book, including Nina Balmaceda, Joseph Bataille, Morna Gallagher, Keila Garcia, Luis Luna, Dennis Mwangwela, Moses Ndahiro, Cesalie Nicimpaye, Jean Nyandwi, and Ruth Padilla DeBorst. And to the many authors whose books shaped this one.

InterVarsity Press has been a joy to work with, both on my first book project, *Welcoming the Stranger*, and on this one.

I counted both Eric and Daniel as friends before we started working on this project together, in the early months of a global pandemic, but hours and hours of Zoom calls (and a few actual in-person interactions) have made me value their friendship all the more.

Lastly, my family—my mom and dad; parents-in-law; siblings and siblings-in-law; my remarkable children Zipporah, Zephaniah, Zoë, and Zacchaeus; and especially, Diana. I love you all!

NOTES

1. WHY THE AMERICAN CHURCH NEEDS SAVING

[1]Beth Moore, "Beth Moore Sounds the Alarm," interview by Esau McCaulley, *The Disrupters* (podcast), October 10, 2020, www.christianitytoday.com/partners/intervarsity-press/disrupters-change-what-is/beth-moore-sounds-alarm.html; see also Emma Green, "The Tiny Blond Bible Teacher Taking On the Evangelical Political Machine," the *Atlantic*, October 2018, www.theatlantic.com/magazine/archive/2018/10/beth-moore-bible-study/568288/.

[2]"U.S. Adults See Evangelicals Through a Political Lens," Barna, November 21, 2019, www.barna.com/research/evangelicals-political-lens/.

[3]Jacob Chansley, quoted in Jack Jenkins, "The Insurrectionists' Senate Floor Prayer Highlights a Curious Trumpian Ecumenism," Religion News Service, February 25, 2021, https://religionnews.com/2021/02/25/the-insurrectionists-senate-floor-prayer-highlights-a-curious-trumpian-ecumenism/; Emma Green, "A Christian Insurrection: Many of Those Who Mobbed the Capitol on Wednesday Claimed to Be Enacting God's Will," the *Atlantic*, January 8, 2021, www.theatlantic.com/politics/archive/2021/01/evangelicals-catholics-jericho-march-capitol/617591/.

[4]Jemar Tisby, *The Color of Compromise: The Truth About the American Church's Complicity in Racism* (Grand Rapids, MI: Zondervan, 2019); Kristin Kobes Du Mez, *Jesus and John Wayne: How White Evangelicals Corrupted a Faith and Fractured a Nation* (New York: Liveright Publishing Co., 2020).

[5]Russell Moore, "Enraged by Ravi (Part 1): The Wreckage of Ravi Zacharias," February 15, 2021, www.russellmoore.com/2021/02/15/enraged-by-ravi-part-1-the-wreckage-of-ravi-zacharias/.

[6]"U.S. Adults See Evangelicals."

[7]Glenn Packiam, *Blessed Broken Given: How Your Story Becomes Sacred in the Hands of Jesus* (Colorado Springs, CO: Multnomah, 2019), 175.

[8]"State of the Church 2020," Barna, March 4, 2020, www.barna.com/research/changing-state-of-the-church/.

[9]Daniel Cox and Amelia Thomson-DeVeaux, "Millennials Are Leaving Religion and Not Coming Back," FiveThirtyEight, December 12, 2019, https://fivethirtyeight.com/features/millennials-are-leaving-religion-and-not-coming-back/.

[10]Jeffrey M. Jones, "U.S. Church Membership Falls Below Majority for First Time," Gallup, March 29, 2021, https://news.gallup.com/poll/341963/church-membership-falls-below-majority-first-time.aspx.

[11]The Public Religion Research Institute finds that just 14.5 percent of Americans identified as White evangelical or born-again Christians in 2020, down from more than 20 percent just a decade earlier ("The American Religious Landscape in 2020," Public Religion Research Institute, July 8, 2021, www.prri.org/research/2020-census-of-american-religion/). We should note that the data on evangelical affiliation and the

extent of its decline is disputed, with different and seemingly contradictory results from different polls emerging, depending in part on how one categorizes *evangelical* (i.e., whether that term should include those who self-identify as evangelical or only those who self-identify both as evangelical and Protestant, whether it should apply based on affiliation with an evangelical denomination or by affirmation of particular beliefs, etc.). Even those who believe self-identified evangelicals are actually remaining a roughly stable portion of the American population, however, observe a troubling trend: the share of self-identified evangelicals who say they seldom or never attend church more than doubled from 2008 to 2019 (see Ryan P. Burge, "So, Why Is Evangelicalism Not Declining? Because Non-Attenders Are Taking On the Label," *Religion in Public*, December 10, 2020, https://religioninpublic.blog/2020/12/10/so-why -is-evangelicalism-not-declining-because-non-attenders-are-taking-on-the-label/).

[12]Rabbi Shimon bar Yochai, *Vayikra Rabbah* 4, trans. Sefaria community, available from www.sefaria.org/Vayikra_Rabbah.4.6?ven=Sefaria_Community_Translation&lang=bi& with=all&lang2=en.

[13]In the drafts of the Declaration of Independence written by Thomas Jefferson and housed in Philadelphia, New York, and Boston, the word *inalienable* is used rather than the synonymous *unalienable,* which appears in the official copy displayed at the National Archives in Washington, DC. *Inalienable* is more widely used in contemporary English; see more from the Independence Hall Organization at www.ushistory.org /declaration/document/unalienable.html.

[14]Martin Luther King Jr., "I Have a Dream," August 28, 1963, Washington, DC, https:// avalon.law.yale.edu/20th_century/mlk01.asp.

[15]Joseph Bataille, former country director of World Relief Haiti, interview with Matthew Soerens, December 10, 2020.

[16]Luis Luna, interview with Matthew Soerens, December 11, 2020.

[17]"Religious Landscape Study: Religious Tradition," Pew Research Center, accessed August 6, 2021, www.pewforum.org/religious-landscape-study/religious-tradition /#gender-composition-trend.

[18]Data Visualization Tool, "Enrollment by Category," The Association of Theological Schools, accessed December 31, 2020, www.ats.edu/data-Visualization; "Women in Leadership," The Association of Theological Schools, accessed December 31, 2020, www.ats.edu/resources/current-initiatives/women-in-leadership.

[19]Jo Saxton, *Ready to Rise: Own Your Voice, Gather Your Community, Step into Your Influence* (Colorado Springs, CO: WaterBrook, 2020), 37. Saxton notes that Jesus affirms the faith of a woman who was treated as an outcast because of persistent bleeding (Lk 8:48); he engages in a theological discussion with a Samaritan woman, who ultimately becomes one of the first to recognize Jesus as the Messiah (Jn 4:1-29); he affirms Mary's decision to sit at his feet, a position that was usually reserved for men as part of theological education from a rabbi (Lk 10:38-42); and he included various women among his disciples (Lk 8:2-3) and entrusted them to be the first witnesses of the resurrection (Lk 24:1-10).

[20]G. K. Chesterton, *Orthodoxy* (New York: John Lane Co., 1909), 85.

[21]Roberta Green Ahmanson, "Covering Our Tracks," *Comment,* December 1, 2015, www .cardus.ca/comment/article/covering-our-tracks/.

[22]James K. A. Smith, "The Future Is Catholic: The Next Scandal for the Evangelical Mind," in *The State of the Evangelical Mind: Reflections on the Past, Prospects for the Future,* ed. Todd C. Ream, Jerry Pattengale, and Christopher J. Devers (Downers Grove, IL: IVP Academic, 2018), 153.

[23]Elements of Matthew's introduction are drawn from Matthew Soerens, "We Didn't Memorize the Bible Verses About Immigrants," *Christian Post,* March 5, 2021,

www.christianpost.com/voices/we-didnt-memorize-the-bible-verses-about
-immigrants.html.

²⁴As a sheltered evangelical kid, of course, I had no idea what a virgin was, as I'd not yet
found and furtively read James Dobson's *Preparing for Adolescence* on our bookshelf.

²⁵Matthew Soerens and Jenny Yang, *Welcoming the Stranger: Justice, Compassion and
Truth in the Immigration Debate* (Downers Grove, IL: InterVarsity Press, 2018), 86.

²⁶Sam George, *Asian Diaspora Christianity*, vol. 3 (Minneapolis, MN: Fortress Press, 2022), 97.

²⁷We credit Blake Chastain for giving the exvangelical movement a name and a platform.
Chastain is host of the *Exvangelical* and *Powers & Principalities* podcasts and writer of
the *Post-Evangelical Post* newsletter. He started the #exvangelical hashtag and helped
popularize the term. See www.exvangelicalpodcast.com/about/.

2. KINGDOM CENTERED

¹Jason Feifer, "The Most Important Political Platitude of our Lifetime," *Slate*, November
2, 2020, https://slate.com/news-and-politics/2020/11/most-important-election-of-our
-lifetimes-history.html.

²Alexander Schmemann, *For the Life of the World* (Crestwood, NY: St. Vladimir's Seminary Press, 1973), 29.

³For some historic examples among American Christian theologians, see Carl F. H. Henry,
The Uneasy Conscience of Modern Fundamentalism (Grand Rapids, MI: Eerdmans, 1947);
George Eldon Ladd, *The Gospel of the Kingdom* (Grand Rapids, MI: Eerdmans, 1959), 20;
E. Stanley Jones, *The Unshakable Kingdom and the Unchanging Person* (Potomac, MD:
The E. Stanley Jones Foundation, 2017); Dallas Willard, *The Divine Conspiracy:
Rediscovering Our Hidden Life in God* (San Francisco: HarperOne, 1998), 25.

⁴Hau Suan Khai, interview with Eric Costanzo, July 9, 2021.

⁵Kathleen Schuster, "6 Facts About Catholic and Protestant Influence in Germany,"
Deutsche Welle, January 24, 2021, www.dw.com/en/6-facts-about-catholic-and
-protestant-influence-in-germany/a-43081215; Elisabeth Braw, "In Martin Luther's
Church the Pastor Asks: Where Have All the Protestants Gone?," *Newsweek*, February
24, 2014, www.newsweek.com/2014/02/28/martin-luthers-church-pastor-asks-where
-have-all-protestants-gone-245572.html?amp=1; Jonathan Evans, "Once a Majority,
Protestants Now Account for Fewer than a Third of Germans," Pew Research Center,
February 12, 2019, www.pewresearch.org/fact-tank/2019/02/12/once-a-majority
-protestants-now-account-for-fewer-than-a-third-of-germans/.

⁶Jonathan Evans and Chris Baronavski, "How Do European Countries Differ in Religious
Commitment?," Pew Research Center, December 5, 2018, www.pewresearch.org/fact
-tank/2018/12/05/how-do-european-countries-differ-in-religious-commitment/.

⁷Martin Knispel, interview with Eric Costanzo, July 22, 2019.

⁸Harriet Sherwood, "'Christianity as Default Is Gone': The Rise of a Non-Christian
Europe," *Guardian* (US edition), March 20, 2018, www.theguardian.com/world/2018
/mar/21/christianity-non-christian-europe-young-people-survey-religion.

⁹Lesslie Newbigin, *Signs Amid the Rubble: The Purposes of God in Human History* (Grand
Rapids, MI: Eerdmans, 2003), 100-101. See also Allan Aubrey Boesak and Curtiss Paul
DeYoung, *Radical Reconciliation: Beyond Political Pietism and Christian Quietism*
(Maryknoll, NY: Orbis Books, 2012), 157-58.

¹⁰Christian Smith, *American Evangelicalism: Embattled and Thriving* (Chicago: University
of Chicago Press, 1998), 89.

¹¹Mark Shaw and Wanjiru M. Gitau, *The Kingdom of God in Africa: A History of African
Christianity*, rev. ed. (Carlisle, UK: Langham Global Library, 2020), 16.

¹²Anthony Taylor, "The Kingdom of God: A Biblical Paradigm for Mission," in *Understanding Insider Movements: Disciples of Jesus Within Diverse Religious Communities*, ed.
Harley Talman and John Jay Travis (Pasadena, CA: William Carey Library, 2015), 177.

13"Backing Trump, White Evangelicals Flip Flop on Importance of Candidate Character," Public Religion Research Institute, October 19, 2016, www.prri.org/research/prri-brookings-oct-19-poll-politics-election-clinton-double-digit-lead-trump/; see also David Campbell and Geoffrey Layman, "How Trump Has Changed White Evangelicals' Views About Morality," *Washington Post,* April 25, 2019, www.washingtonpost.com/politics/2019/04/25/how-trump-has-changed-white-evangelicals-views-about-morality/.

14D. L. Mayfield, "Politics and Piety: Trump's Relationship with White Evangelicals," interview by Marty Moss-Coane, *Radio Times,* September 8, 2020, https://whyy.org/episodes/trumps-relationship-with-white-evangelicals/.

15Ruth Padilla DeBorst, "'Unlikely' Contributions Toward a Global Social Ethic: Can Anything Good Come from There?," in *First the Kingdom of God: Global Voices on Global Missions,* ed. Daniel K. Darko and Beth Snodderly (Pasadena, CA: William Carey International University Press, 2013), 107.

16C. René Padilla, "Contextual Scripture Engagement and Transcultural Mission," in *First the Kingdom of God: Global Voices on Global Missions,* ed. Daniel K. Darko and Beth Snodderly (Pasadena, CA: William Carey International University Press, 2013), 217.

17Jonathan Edwards, *History of Redemption* 2.1 (London: S. Gosnell, 1791), 52. Edwards for all of his theological insights, enslaved human beings for much of his life, demonstrating that, tragically, doctrinal acumen does not always translate to just living and holiness.

18J. N. Kanyua Mugambi, *From Liberation to Reconstruction: African Christian Theology After the Cold War* (Nairobi, Kenya: East African Educational Publishers Ltd., 1995), 176. See also Agbonkhianmeghe E. Orobator, "The Idea of the Kingdom of God in African Theology," *Studia Missionalia* 46 (January 1997): 327-57, https://epublications.marquette.edu/cgi/viewcontent.cgi?article=1510&context=theo_fac.

19Ellen Vaughn, *Time Peace: Living Here and Now with a Timeless God* (Grand Rapids, MI: Zondervan, 2007), 195.

20N. T. Wright, *Surprised by Hope: Rethinking Heaven, the Resurrection, and the Mission of the Church* (New York: HarperCollins, 2008), 208.

21Vilma "Nina" Balmaceda, interview with Matthew Soerens, December 4, 2020.

22Martin Luther King Jr., *Strength to Love* (Boston: Beacon Press, 1963), 51.

3. DECENTERING THE (WHITE) AMERICAN CHURCH

1"The 2020 Census of American Religion," Public Religion Research Institute, https://s3.documentcloud.org/documents/20985213/prri-census-of-american-religion.pdf, 8.

2Todd Johnson, "Christianity in Its Global Context, 1970–2020: Society, Religion, and Mission," *International Bulletin of Mission Research* 37, no. 3 (2013): 164, 14.

3Gina Zurlo, "The World as 100 Christians," Gordon-Conwell Theological Seminary, January 29, 2020, www.gordonconwell.edu/blog/100christians/.

4This idea comes from Stephen Bevans in an article where he says, "The 'average Christian' today is female, black, and lives in a Brazilian favela or an African village" (Stephen B. Bevans and Roger P. Schroeder, "Missiology After Bosch: Reverencing a Classic by Moving Beyond," *International Bulletin of Missionary Research* 29, no. 2 [April 2005]: 70, https://doi.org/10.1177/239693930502900202).

5Jehu J. Hanciles, *Beyond Christendom: Globalization, African Migration, and the Transformation of the West* (Maryknoll, NY: Orbis Books, 2013), 109.

6Hanciles, *Beyond Christendom,* 110. It's also important to note that Christianity has deep roots in Africa as well as Asia and, of course, the Middle East. See also Vince Bantu, *A Multitude of All Peoples: Engaging Ancient Christianity's Global Identity* (Downers Grove, IL: IVP Academic, 2020).

[7]For an in-depth discussion regarding the growth of Christianity around the world and its impact, see Philip Jenkins, *The Next Christendom: The Coming of Global Christianity,* 3rd ed. (Oxford, England: Oxford University Press, 2011).

[8]Tish Harrison Warren, "Why I Claim the 'Global Evangelical' Label," *Christianity Today,* November 23, 2020, www.christianitytoday.com/ct/2020/december/global-church -american-politics-evangelicalism.html.

[9]Abby Budiman, "Key Findings About U.S. Immigrants," Pew Research Center, August 20, 2020, www.pewresearch.org/fact-tank/2020/08/20/key-findings-about-u-s -immigrants/.

[10]Steven R. Warner, "Coming to America: Immigrants and the Faith They Bring," *The Christian Century* 121, no. 3 (February 2004): 20-23.

[11]Phillip Connor, *Immigrant Faith: Patterns of Immigrant Religion in the United States, Canada, and Western Europe* (New York: NYU Press, 2014), 19.

[12]Hau Suan Khai, interview with Eric Costanzo, July 2021.

[13]Saba Imtiaz, "A New Generation Redefines What It Means to Be a Missionary," the *Atlantic,* March 8, 2018, www.theatlantic.com/international/archive/2018/03/young -missionaries/551585/; "Missionaries from the Global South Try to Save the Godless West," *The Economist,* January 12, 2019, www.economist.com/international/2019/01/12 /missionaries-from-the-global-south-try-to-save-the-godless west.

[14]Ed Stetzer, "If It Doesn't Stem Its Decline, Mainline Protestantism Has Just 23 Easters Left," *Washington Post,* April 28, 2017, www.washingtonpost.com/news/acts-of-faith /wp/2017/04/28/if-it doesnt-stem-its-decline-mainline-protestantism-has-just -23-easters-left/.

[15]Michael Lipka, "The Most and Least Racially Diverse U.S. Religious Groups," Pew Research Center (July 27, 2015), www.pewresearch.org/fact-tank/2015/07/27/the-most -and-least-racially-diverse-u-s-religious-groups/.

[16]"Church Giving Drops $1.2 Billion Reports 2012 Yearbook of Churches," National Council of the Churches of Christ, March 20, 2012, www.ncccusa.org/news/120209 yearbook2012.html.

[17]"Southern Baptists Grow in Number of Churches, Plant 588 New Congregations Amid COVID-19 Pandemic," Baptist Press, May 20, 2021, www.baptistpress.com/resource -library/news/southern-baptists-grow-in-number-of churches-plant-588-new -congregations-amidst covid-19-pandemic.

[18]Allison Young, "Annual of the Southern Baptist Convention 2020" (Nashville, TN: SBC Executive Committee, 2020), 55.

[19]"Race and Ethnicity of AG U.S. Churches, 2020," Assemblies of God, August 18, 2021, www.ag.org/-/media/AGORG/Downloads/Statistics/Churches/2020-Race-and -Ethnicity-of-Churches.pdf.

[20]"Statistics on the Assemblies of God (USA)," Assemblies of God, accessed February 27, 2021, https://ag.org/about/statistics.

[21]"AG USA Adherents by Race 2001 to 2020," Assemblies of God, July 19, 2021, www .ag.org/-/media/AGORG/Downloads/Statistics/Attendance-and-Adherents/Adherents -by-Race-2001-through-2020.pdf.

[22]Dennis R. Edwards, *Might from the Margins: The Gospel's Power to Turn the Tables on Injustice* (Harrisonburg, VA: Herald Press, 2020), 26.

[23]Paul Mumo Kisau, "Acts," in *Africa Bible Commentary: A One-Volume Commentary Written by 70 African Scholars,* ed. Tokunboh Adeyemo, rev. ed. (Grand Rapids, MI: Zondervan Academic, 2010), 4466.

[24]This history, which ought to inform how Christians today relate to questions of race, is summarized well in historian Jemar Tisby's book *The Color of Compromise: The Truth About the American Church's Complicity in Racism* (Grand Rapids, MI: Zondervan, 2019).

[25]Esau McCaulley, *Reading While Black: African American Biblical Interpretation as an Exercise in Hope* (Downers Grove, IL: InterVarsity Press, 2020), 171, 174.

[26]Damares Alves is the Minister of Human Rights, Family, and Women in Brazil. She is also an attorney and a Pentecostal pastor. She is well-known for her conservative evangelical views and activism. Although few Americans would know Alves, she has over 1.2 million followers on Twitter, which speaks to the significance of her work.

[27]Joshua Wong is a student and political activist in Hong Kong who has repeatedly been imprisoned for his advocacy to keep Hong Kong separate from China. In 2014, he was named one of *TIME Magazine*'s most influential teens and was nominated as Person of the Year. Wong's family is Christian and credits his oratory and leadership skills to his involvement in church.

[28]John Stott, "The Lausanne Covenant: An Exposition and Commentary" (Lausanne Occasional Paper 3, Lausanne Committee for World Evangelization, 1975), www.lausanne.org/content/lop/lop-3.

[29]The Lausanne Covenant (Lausanne International Congress on World Evangelization, Lausanne, Switz., August 1, 1974), www.lausanne.org/content/covenant/lausanne-covenant.

[30]Ruth Padilla DeBorst, "'Unlikely' Contributions Toward a Global Social Ethic: Can Anything Good Come from There?," in *First the Kingdom of God: Global Voices on Global Missions*, ed. Daniel K. Darko and Beth Snodderly (Pasadena, CA: William Carey International University Press, 2013), 110.

[31]Robert Chao Romero, *Brown Church: Five Centuries of Latina/o Social Justice, Theology, and Identity* (Downers Grove, IL: IVP Academic, 2020), 10.

[32]Romero, *Brown Church*, 11-12.

[33]"The Cape Town Commitment," Lausanne Movement (Cape Town, S.Afr., 2010), sec. I7A, https://lausanne.org/content/ctcommitment#p1-7.

[34]"ACTS Group of Institutions," accessed February 27, 2021, https://actsgroup.org.

[35]Ken Gnanakan, "Creation and the Environment," in *South Asia Bible Commentary: A One-Volume Commentary on the Whole Bible,* ed. Brian Wintle et al. (Grand Rapids, MI: Zondervan Academic, 2015), 2115.

[36]*Glocalization* is a concept developed first by the sociologist Roland Robertson. To read further how he nuances the term, read his article "Globalisation or Glocalisation?," *The Journal of International Communication* 18, no. 2 (August 2012): 191-208, https://doi.org/10.1080/13216597.2012.709925.

[37]To learn more about Glocal Ventures, Inc., visit www.glocalventures.org.

[38]I (Daniel) worked with Bob Roberts Jr. at his church, Northwood Community Church, from 2010 to 2012 as a staff pastor. I've traveled with him on many occasions and have seen firsthand how his church in Keller, Texas, has been shaped by their work in Vietnam.

[39]Bob Roberts Jr., *Glocalization: How Followers of Jesus Engage a Flat World* (Grand Rapids, MI: Zondervan, 2016), 34.

[40]The following sections are adapted from an article Daniel wrote for the Send Institute titled "Our Modern Ephesian Moment: Four Markers of Meaningful Ethnic Belonging in Multiethnic Congregations," August 15, 2019.

[41]Andrew Walls, *The Cross-Cultural Process in Christian History: Studies in the Transmission and Appropriation of Faith* (Maryknoll, NY: Orbis Books, 2002), 77.

[42]Walls, *Cross-Cultural Process in Christian History,* 78.

[43]Andrew Walls, *The Missionary Movement in Christian History: Studies in the Transmission of Faith* (Maryknoll, NY: Orbis Books, 1996), 7.

[44]Walls, *Missionary Movement in Christian History,* 9.

[45]Denise Kimber Buell, *Why This New Race: Ethnic Reasoning in Early Christianity* (New York: Columbia University Press, 2005), 138.

[46]Lola Romanucci-Ross, George A. De Vos, and Takeyuki Tsuda, eds., *Ethnic Identity: Problems and Prospects for the Twenty-First Century*, 4th ed. (Lanham, MD: AltaMira Press, 2006), 212.

4. AMERICAN CHRISTIAN IDOLS

Joshua Rhodes Balme, *American States, Churches, and Slavery* (London: Hamilton, Adams, and Co., 1864), 525-26. Balme mentions specifically the idols of the eagle symbol, the state itself, liberty, and the Union to the detriment of human flourishing.
[1]Ben Kirby, *PreachersNSneakers: Authenticity in an Age of For-Profit Faith and (Wannabe) Celebrities* (Nashville, TN: Thomas Nelson, 2021), 4-5.
[2]Vinoth Ramachandra, *Gods That Fail: Modern Idolatry and Christian Mission*, rev. ed. (Eugene, OR: Wipf and Stock, 2016), 109.
[3]See also Psalm 135:15-18. This psalm repeats many of the same words as Psalm 115:4-8, with the additional phrase "nor is there breath in their mouths" (Ps 135:17). The sections in both psalms end with the words "Those who make them will be like them, / and so will all who trust in them."
[4]Ramachandra, *Gods That Fail*, 104.
[5]Tertullian of Carthage, *On Idolatry* 1.
[6]See also Ezekiel 16:1-63 and the story of Hosea and Gomer (Hos 1–4). Tertullian also completed his discourse on idolatry by equating the worship of idols among Christians with adultery against Christ, since the church is his bride. See Tertullian, *On Idolatry* 1.
[7]Examples: Gen 31:19, 34; Ex 20:4; 34:13; Lev 18:21; 19:4; 20:1-5; 26:30; Num 25:2; 33:52; Deut 5:8; 7:5; 12:3; 16:21; 29:17; 32:21; Judg 2:13; 6:25-32; 10:6; 11:24; 1 Sam 7:3-4, 12:10; 31:9; 1 Kings 11:2-13; 14:15-23; 15:13; 16:31-33; 18:26; 2 Kings 3:2, 10:21-28; 11:18; 13:6; 17:9-16; 18:4; 21:3-21; 23:4-24; 1 Chron 10:9; 16:26; 2 Chron 11:15; 14:3-5; 15:16; 17:3; 23:17; 24:18; 28:2; 33:3-22; 34:7-33; Ps 31:6; 78:58; 96:5; 97:7; 106:36-38; 115:4-8; 135:15-18; Is 1:29; 10:11; 17:8; 27:9; 30:22; 37:19; 41:28; 48:5-13; 57:5-9; Jer 3:6; 7:9; 9:14; 11:13; 14:22; 16:19; 19:5; 32:35; Ezek 6:4-13; 8:10; 16:16; 18:12; 23:39; 36:18-25; 37:23; 44:12; Dan 3:1-30; 5:4-23; 11:8; Hos 2:8; 4:17; 8:4; 11:2; 13:2; 14:8; Mic 1:7; 5:14; Hab 2:18; Zeph 1:4-5; Zech 13:2.
[8]Timothy Keller, *Counterfeit Gods: The Empty Promises of Money, Sex, and Power, and the Only Hope That Matters* (New York: Penguin Books, 2009), xxi-xxv, 203-4; Ed Stetzer, *Subversive Kingdom: Living as Agents of Gospel Transformation* (Nashville, TN: Broadman and Holman, 2012), 144.
[9]Catherine McNiel, *Fearing Bravely: Risking Love for Our Neighbors, Strangers, and Enemies* (Colorado Springs, CO: NavPress, 2022). See also Randolph E. Richards and Brandon J. O'Brien, *Misreading Scripture with Western Eyes: Removing Cultural Blinders to Better Understand the Bible* (Downers Grove, IL: InterVarsity Press, 2012), 95-112.
[10]Joseph Bataille, interview with Matthew Soerens, December 10, 2020.
[11]Soong-Chan Rah, *The Next Evangelicalism: Freeing the Church from Western Cultural Captivity* (Downers Grove, IL: InterVarsity Press, 2009), 29-30.
[12]David J. Bosch, *Transforming Mission: Paradigm Shifts in Theology of Mission* (Maryknoll, NY: Orbis Books, 1991), 529.
[13]A prominent example is the sexual abuse scandal in the Southern Baptist Convention, which became public in 2019. See Robert Downen, Lise Olsen, and John Tedesco, "Abuse of Faith: 20 Years, 700 Victims: Southern Baptist Sexual Abuse Spreads as Leaders Resist Reforms," *Houston Chronicle*, February 10, 2019, www.houstonchronicle.com /news/investigations/article/Southern-Baptist-sexual-abuse-spreads-as-leaders -13588038.php.
[14]J. Daryl Charles, *The Unformed Conscience of Evangelicalism: Recovering the Church's Moral Vision* (Downers Grove, IL: InterVarsity Press, 2002), 27.

[15]Gregory of Nazianzus in Richard Newhauser, *The Early History of Greed: The Sin of Avarice in Early Medieval Thought and Literature* (New York: Cambridge University Press, 2000), 31.
[16]The Greek word *pleonexia*, often translated as "greed or covetousness," is perhaps best translated in its New Testament usage as "an insatiable desire for more." Clement of Alexandria, writing in the second and third centuries CE, defined *pleonexia* as that which "is opposed to contentment with what one possesses, and as idolatry is an abandonment of the one God to embrace many gods." See Clement of Alexandria, *Stromata* III 12.89.
[17]Ramachandra, *Gods That Fail*, 105.
[18]William Wilberforce, *A Practical View of the Prevailing Religious System of Professed Christians with the Higher and Middle Classes Contrasted with Real Christianity* (New York: Leavitt, Lord, & Co., 1835), 32, 195.
[19]Miroslav Volf, "On Being a Christian Public Intellectual," in *Public Intellectuals and the Common Good: Christian Thinking for Human Flourishing,* ed. Todd C. Ream, Jerry A. Pattengale, and Christopher J. Devers (Downers Grove, IL: IVP Academic, 2021), 6; Volf credits German sociologist Hartmut Rosa for the final sentence in this quote.
[20]Ruth Padilla DeBorst, interview with Matthew Soerens, December 16, 2020.
[21]Sharon Marcus, *The Drama of Celebrity* (Princeton, NJ: Princeton University Press, 2019), 9.
[22]Vilma "Nina" Balmaceda, interview with Matthew Soerens, December 4, 2020.
[23]Moses Ndahiro, interview with Matthew Soerens, December 16, 2020.
[24]Alexis de Tocqueville, *Democracy in America,* trans. Henry Reeve (London: Saunders and Otley, 1835; Project Gutenberg, 1997), 1.17.3, www.gutenberg.org/ebooks/815.
[25]Stewart Davenport, *Friends of the Unrighteous Mammon: Northern Christians and Market Capitalism 1815–1860* (Chicago: University of Chicago Press, 2008), v.
[26]Kristin Kobes Du Mez, *Jesus and John Wayne: How White Evangelicals Corrupted a Faith and Fractured a Nation* (New York: Liveright Publishing Co., 2020), 11-12.
[27]The church still had its Easter Sunday services, of course, but just did not host its traditional concert on the resurrection theme. Also, while this is true to the best of my recollection, I have not been able to independently verify my decades-old memory, which certainly is prone to error; should I be mis-remembering this situation, please take it as an unfortunately all-too-plausible hypothetical example.
[28]C. S. Lewis, "Meditation on the Third Commandment," in *God in the Dock: Essays on Theology and Ethics,* ed. Walter Hooper (Grand Rapids, MI: Eerdmans, 1970), 214-15. We want to note that Lewis's use of the word *Christendom* was likely not meant as a pejorative, as it's often used today, but rather simply as the church's advancement.
[29]Lewis, "Meditation on the Third Commandment," 215.
[30]Mark Charles and Soong-Chan Rah, *Unsettling Truths: The Ongoing, Dehumanizing Legacy of the Doctrine of Discovery* (Downers Grove, IL: InterVarsity Press, 2019), 72. For example, despite its affirmation of the inalienable truth that "all men are created equal," the Declaration of Independence also references Native Americans as "merciless Indian savages," an apparent contradiction that has borne itself out in the mistreatment of Native Americans, African Americans, and others throughout US history; see *Unsettling Truths,* 83.
[31]Richard Twiss, *Rescuing the Gospel from the Cowboys: A Native American Expression of the Jesus Way* (Downers Grove, IL: InterVarsity Press, 2015), 37.
[32]Kevin Singer, "Why I Ditched the Evangelical Persecution Complex," *Sojourners,* May 15, 2019, https://sojo.net/articles/why-i-ditched-evangelical-persecution-complex; Emma Green, "White Evangelicals Believe They Face More Discrimination than Muslims," the *Atlantic,* March 10, 2017, www.theatlantic.com/politics/archive/2017/03/perceptions-discrimination-muslims-christians/519135/.
[33]Padilla DeBorst, interview with Matthew Soerens, December 16, 2020.

[34]Randall Balmer, "The Real Origins of the Religious Right," *Politico*, May 27, 2014, www .politico.com/magazine/story/2014/05/religious-right-real-origins-107133.

[35]"White Christians Have Become Even Less Motivated to Address Racial Injustice," Barna, September 15, 2020, www.barna.com/research/american-christians-race-problem/.

[36]Lucas Kwong, "Christian Opponents of CRT Peddle a Hollow Salvation," *Sojourners*, June 24, 2021, https://sojo.net/articles/christian-opponents-crt-critical-race-theory -peddle-hollow-salvation; Tara Isabella Burton, "Study: When It comes to Detecting Racial Inequality, White Christians Have a Blind Spot," Vox, June 23, 2017, www.vox .com/identities/2017/6/23/15855272/prri-study-white-christians-discrimination -blind-spot.

[37]This question was asked by Australian journalist Kylie Beach, as cited in Morgan Lee, "How American Evangelicals Lost Credibility with the Global Church," *Quick to Listen* (podcast), *Christianity Today*, January 27, 2021, www.christianitytoday.com/ct/podcasts /quick-to-listen/global-church-american-evangelicals-trump-trust-podcast.html.

[38]The Homogeneous Unit Principle (HUP) was first introduced by Donald McGavran. He defined a homogeneous unit as "a section of society in which all the members have some characteristic in common." See Donald A. McGavran, *Understanding Church Growth* (Grand Rapids, MI: Eerdmans, 1970), 85. Some have touted HUP as helpful in understanding human social behavior while others have decried it, claiming in particular that it leads to pragmatism and discrimination. In 1978, the Lausanne Movement investigated its usefulness and critiques and released a paper stating its position on HUP. The paper is available here: https://lausanne.org/content/lop/lop-1.

[39]Alejandro Mandes, *Embracing the New Samuria: Opening Our Eyes to Our Multiethnic Future* (Colorado Springs, CO: NavPress, 2021), 161.

[40]Glenn Bracey et al., *Beyond Diversity: What the Future of Racial Justice Will Require of U.S. Churches* (Ventura, CA: Barna Group, 2021), 75-80; InterVarsity Christian Fellowship, *InterVarsity Report: Christian Student Attitudes Amid the COVID-19 Pandemic*, July 2021, https://pinkston.co/docs/2021-Student-Survey.pdf.

[41]Ramachandra, *Gods That Fail*, 206.

[42]Hau Suan Khai, interview with Eric Costanzo, July 2021.

[43]Volf, "On Being a Christian Public Intellectual," 5, 7-9.

[44]Vinoth Ramachandra, "Global Society: Challenges for Christian Mission," *Anvil* 21, no. 1 (2004): 20.

[45]Morris Bishop, *The Horizon Book of the Middle Ages*, ed. Norman Kotker (Boston: Houghton Mifflin Company, 1968), 137.

[46]Vinoth Ramachandra, "Politics and the Occult," *Vinoth Ramachandra* blog, July 24, 2009, https://vinothramachandra.wordpress.com/2009/07/24/politics-and-the-occult/.

[47]Ramachandra, "Politics and the Occult."

[48]D. L. Mayfield, *The Myth of the American Dream: Reflections on Affluence, Autonomy, Safety, and Power* (Downers Grove, IL: InterVarsity Press, 2020), 4-6, 13.

[49]This phrasing came from Padilla DeBorst, interview with Matthew Soerens, December 16, 2020. She specifically mentions the cultural norms of autonomy, individualism, racism, competition, activism, consumerism, and aimlessness.

5. IMAGO DEI AND NEIGHBOR

Sami DiPasquale is the founder of Abara | Borderland Connections in El Paso, Texas. This statement was recorded at the Evangelical Immigration Table that convened in Washington, DC, in November 2019.

[1]Michael Lipka, "The Continuing Decline of Europe's Jewish Population," Pew Research Center, February 9, 2015, www.pewresearch.org/fact-tank/2015/02/09/europes -jewish-population/.

[2]Soong-Chan Rah, *Prophetic Lament: A Call for Justice in Troubled Times* (Downers Grove, IL: InterVarsity Press, 2015), 137-38.

[3]Dietrich Bonhoeffer, *Ethics*, Touchstone ed. (New York: Simon and Schuster, 1995), 108.

[4]"The International Covenant on Civil and Political Rights," United Nations Human Rights, December 16, 1966, www.ohchr.org/en/professionalinterest/pages/ccpr .aspx.

[5]Richard J. Middleton, *The Liberating Image: The Imago Dei in Genesis 1* (Grand Rapids, MI: Brazos Press, 2005), 18.

[6]Thomas Aquinas commenting on Genesis 1:26-28 in *Summa Theologia*, Ia. Q93 A2.

[7]Unknown, *Opus Imperfectum in Matthaeum*, in *Patrologia Graeca* 56:867-68.

[8]Martin Luther, *Luther's Works, Vol. 1: Lectures on Genesis: Chapters 1–5*, ed. Jaroslav Pelikan et al. (St. Louis, MO: Concordia, 1999), 337.

[9]The first division among peoples was between man and woman generally (Gen 3:16), and later between ethnic groups, languages, and cultures at Babel (Gen 11:1-9). Soon after the Fall in Genesis 3 came the first murder in Genesis 4, when Cain killed his brother Abel.

[10]John of Damascus, "Annunciation of the Most Holy Theotokos," in *The Festal Menaion*, trans. Mother Mary and Archimandrite Kallistos Ware (London: Faber and Faber: 1969), 440, 443.

[11]Jaroslav Pelikan, *Jesus Through the Centuries: His Place in the History of Culture*, rev. ed. (New Haven, CT: Yale University Press, 1999), 32.

[12]In one (long) sentence in the original Greek, Hebrews 1:3 provides a succinct yet detailed Christology using the word *character* to describe the way God himself is seen in Jesus, the Son: "The Son is the radiance of God's glory and the exact representation [Gk: *character*] of his being, sustaining all things by his powerful word. After he had provided purification for sins, he sat down at the right hand of the Majesty in heaven."

[13]Simon Chan, *Grassroots Asian Theology: Thinking the Faith from the Ground Up* (Downers Grove, IL: IVP Academic, 2014), 82.

[14]Howard Thurman, *Jesus and the Disinherited*, rev. ed. (Boston: Beacon Press, 1996), 7.

[15]Leo Tolstoy, *Anna Karenina* (New York: Thomas Y. Crowell, 1899), 3:244-45.

[16]See Marlo Safi, "The Porn Industry and Human Trafficking Reinforce Each Other," *National Review*, August 1, 2018, www.nationalreview.com/2018/08/porn-human -trafficking-reinforce-each-other/; John-Henry Western, "Want to Stop Sex Trafficking? Look to America's Porn Addiction," *Huffington Post*, March 30, 2015, www .huffpost.com/entry/want-to-stop-sex-traffick_b_6563338.

[17]William Barbieri Jr., "The Migrant *Imago*: Migration and the Ethics of Human Dignity," in *Christian Theology in the Age of Migration: Implications for World Christianity*, ed. Peter C. Phan (Lanham, MD: Lexington Press, 2020), 172.

[18]A Cato Institute analysis of terrorist attacks perpetrated by immigrants of various statuses concludes that "the chance of an American being murdered in a terrorist attack by a refugee is about 1 in 3.86 billion per year, while the annual chance of being murdered in an attack committed by an illegal immigrant is zero" (Alex Nowrasteh, "Terrorists by Immigration Status and Nationality: A Risk Analysis, 1975-2017," May 7, 2019, www.cato.org/publications/policy-analysis/terrorists-immigration-status-nationality -risk-analysis-1975-2017). Similarly, various studies have found that immigrants, whether lawfully present in the United States or not, commit crime at significantly lower rates than native-born US citizens (see Michael T. Light, Jingying He, and Jason P. Robey, "Comparing Crime Rates between Undocumented Immigrants, Legal Immigrants, and Native-Born US Citizens in Texas," *Proceedings of the National Academy of Sciences*, December 2020, www.pnas.org/content/117/51/32340/tab-figures -data).

[19]See Todd C. Ream, Jerry Pattengale, and Christopher J. Devers, eds., *Public Intellectuals and the Common Good: Christian Thinking and Human Flourishing* (Downers Grove, IL: IVP Academic, 2021), xviii.

[20]Miroslav Volf, "'Honor Everyone!': Christian Faith and the Culture of Universal Respect," in *First the Kingdom of God: Global Voices on Global Missions*, ed. Daniel Dark and Beth Snodderly (Pasadena, CA: William Carey International University Press, 2013), 65, 72.

[21]Andrea Zaki Stephanous, "Culture and Identity," in *Arabic Christian Theology: A Contemporary Global Evangelical Perspective*, ed. Andrea Zaki Stephanous (Grand Rapids, MI: Zondervan, 2019), 456.

[22]John S. Mbiti, *African Religions and Philosophy*, 2nd ed. (London: Heinemann, 1989), 106.

[23]Kofi Asare Opoku as cited in Cephas N. Omenyo, "Essential Aspects of African Ecclesiology: The Case of the African Independent Churches," *Pneuma* 22, no. 2 (2000): 236.

[24]Mojalefa L. J. Koenane, "*Ubuntu* and Philoxenia: *Ubuntu* and Christian Worldviews as Responses to Xenophobia," *HTS Teologiese Studies/Theological Studies* 74, no. 1 (2018): 4668, https://doi.org/10.4102/hts.v74i1.4668.

[25]Paul John Isaak, "Luke," in *Africa Bible Commentary*, ed. Tokunboh Adeyemo (Grand Rapids, MI: Zondervan, 2006), 1251. See also MelindaJoy Mingo, *The Colors of Culture: The Beauty of Diverse Friendships* (Downers Grove, IL: InterVarsity Press, 2020), 3-5.

[26]Vinoth Ramachandra, *Gods That Fail: Modern Idolatry and Christian Mission*, rev. ed. (Eugene, OR: Wipf and Stock, 2016), 113.

[27]Dennis Mwangwela, interview with Matthew Soerens, December 2020; see also Soong-Chan Rah, *The Next Evangelicalism: Freeing the Church from Western Cultural Captivity* (Downers Grove, IL: InterVarsity Press, 2009), 75. Rah contends that though White evangelicals are incredibly vocal about overturning *Roe v. Wade*, in issues related to the mistreatment of immigrants and the need for immigration reform, many American Christians have again demonstrated a selective silence.

[28]Christena Cleveland, *Disunity in Christ: Uncovering the Hidden Forces That Keep Us Apart* (Downers Grove, IL: InterVarsity Press, 2013), 153-54.

[29]Aristides the Philosopher, *Apology* (Syriac) 2.

[30]Allan Aubrey Boesak and Curtiss Paul DeYoung, *Radical Reconciliation: Beyond Political Pietism and Christian Quietism* (Maryknoll, NY: Orbis Books, 2012), 66-74.

[31]Andrew B. McGowan, *Ancient Christian Worship: Early Church Practices in Social, Historical, and Theological Perspective* (Grand Rapids, MI: Baker Academic, 2014), 135-67; see also Michael W. Holmes, ed. and trans., *The Didache* 7:1-4, in *The Apostolic Fathers: Greek Texts and English Translations*, 3rd ed. (Grand Rapids, MI: Baker Academic, 2007), 355.

[32]Catherine McDowell, "In the Image of God He Created Them: How Genesis 1:26-27 Defines the Divine-Human Relationship and Why It Matters," in *The Image of God in an Image Driven Age: Explorations in Theological Anthropology*, ed. Beth Felker Jones and Jeffrey W. Barbeau (Downers Grove, IL: InterVarsity Press, 2016), 46.

6. THE BIBLE WITH EYES TO SEE AND EARS TO HEAR

[1]Southern Baptist Convention, *The Baptist Faith and Message 2000*, https://bfm.sbc.net/bfm2000.

[2]Jesus is quoting Isaiah 6:9-10. See also John 9:40-41.

[3]See also Luke 10:23-24, where Jesus said to his disciples: "Blessed are the eyes that see what you see. For I tell you that many prophets and kings wanted to see what you see but did not see it, and to hear what you hear but did not hear it."

[4]Augustine, *Tractates on the Gospel of John* 111.2.

[5]Hans Denck, as quoted in Clarence Bauman, *The Spiritual Legacy of Hans Denck: Interpretation and Translation of Key Texts* (New York: E. J. Brill, 1991), 97, 157; see also Thomas N. Finger, *A Contemporary Anabaptist Theology: Biblical, Historical, Constructive* (Downers Grove, IL: IVP Academic, 2004), 337.

[6]Malcolm B. Yarnell III, *The Formation of Christian Doctrine* (Nashville, TN: B&H Academic, 2007), 12.

[7]Soong-Chan Rah, *The Next Evangelicalism: Freeing the Church from Western Cultural Captivity* (Downers Grove, IL: InterVarsity Press, 2009), 161-62.

[8]Daniel Hill, *White Awake: An Honest Look at What It Means to Be White* (Downers Grove, IL: InterVarsity Press, 2017), 173.

[9]Korie Little Edwards, "The Multiethnic Church Movement Hasn't Lived up to Its Promise," *Christianity Today,* February 16, 2021, www.christianitytoday.com/ct/2021/march/race -diversity-multiethnic-church-movement-promise.html.

[10]Charlie Dates, "Forever Word in a Fading World," plenary talk at The Gospel & Our Cities: Chicago 2018, October 18, 2018, The Moody Church, Chicago, IL, www.youtube .com/watch?v=KJLU0Xkf4qg&t=1420s.

[11]Veli-Matti Kärkkäinen, *An Introduction to Ecclesiology* (Downers Grove, IL: IVP Academic, 2002), 213.

[12]Graham Hill, *GlobalChurch: Reshaping Our Conversations, Renewing our Mission, Revitalizing our Churches* (Downers Grove, IL: InterVarsity Press, 2016), 276.

[13]K. K. Yeo, "Asian and Asian American Biblical Interpretation," in *Scripture and Its Interpretation: A Global, Ecumenical Introduction to the Bible,* ed. Michael J. Gorman (Grand Rapids, MI: Baker Academic, 2017), 333-34.

[14]Peter T. Cha, "Doing Theology in a Multicultural Theological Community," *Torch Trinity Journal* 10, no. 1 (2007): 98.

[15]Francisco Goldman, "Matthew," in *Revelations: Personal Responses to the Books of the Bible,* ed. Richard Holloway (London: Canongate, 2005), 210.

[16]M. Daniel Carroll R., "Latino/Latina Biblical Interpretation," in *Scripture and Its Interpretation: A Global, Ecumenical Introduction to the Bible,* ed. Michael J. Gorman (Grand Rapids, MI: Baker Academic, 2017), 312-13.

[17]Darren Carlson, "When Muslims Dream of Jesus," The Gospel Coalition, May 31, 2018, www.thegospelcoalition.org/article/muslims-dream-jesus; see also Tom Doyle, *Dreams and Visions: Is God Awakening the Muslim World?* (Nashville, TN: Thomas Nelson, 2012); Nabeel Qureshi, *Seeking Allah, Finding Jesus: A Devout Muslim Encounters Christianity* (Grand Rapids, MI: Zondervan, 2014).

[18]Yeo, "Asian and Asian American Biblical Interpretation," 326-29, 333; Vinoth Ramachandra, *Gods That Fail: Modern Idolatry and Christian Mission,* rev. ed. (Eugene, OR: Wipf and Stock, 2016), 206.

[19]Monty Mowery, interview with Eric Costanzo, January 2021. Mowery has worked with the Wa people for nearly two decades; see also Kosuke Koyama, *Water Buffalo Theology* (Maryknoll, NY: Orbis Books, 1974). Koyama was a Japanese missionary and scholar who developed the term *water buffalo theology* working among Thai Buddhists to describe the ways in which the Bible is applied in the context of Asian worldviews related to farming and husbandry as opposed to more educated classes.

[20]Bungishabaku Katho, "African Biblical Interpretation," in *Scripture and Its Interpretation: A Global, Ecumenical Introduction to the Bible,* ed. Michael J. Gorman (Grand Rapids, MI: Baker Academic, 2017), 291.

[21]Andrea Zaki Stephanous, "Culture and Identity," in *Arabic Christian Theology: A Contemporary Global Evangelical Perspective,* ed. Andrea Zaki Stephanous (Grand Rapids, MI: Zondervan, 2019), 11-12, 212.

[22]Visit https://theglobalchurchproject.com.

[23]Terry M. Wildman, ed., *First Nations Version: An Indigenous Translation of the New Testament* (Downers Grove, IL: InterVarsity Press, 2021), available from www.ivpress.com /first-nations-version.

[24]Hau Suan Khai, interview with Eric Costanzo, July 2021.

[25]The traditional English version of the Nicene Creed noting the inclusion of the *Filioque* may be viewed here: www.ccel.org/creeds/nicene.creed.html. The more contemporary version used among many Reformed and Anglican traditions may be found here: www .crcna.org/welcome/beliefs/creeds/nicene-creed. See also Lewis Ayres, *Nicaea and Its Legacy: An Approach to Fourth-Century Trinitarian Theology* (Oxford, England: Oxford University Press, 2004), 30-36.

[26]For a great summary of this term and insights from Ayres's book, see Andrew Arndt, "What Does It Mean to Be a 'Nicene Christian'?," *Jesus Creed* (blog), Patheos, November 15, 2019, www.patheos.com/blogs/jesuscreed/2019/11/15/what-does-it-mean-to-be-a -nicene-christian.

[27]The Masai (Maasai) Creed, in *Creeds & Confessions of Faith in the Christian Tradition,* ed. Jaroslav Pelikan and Valeri Hotchkiss (New Haven, CT: Yale University Press, 2003), 568-69.

[28]Vinoth Ramachandra, "Global Society: Challenges for Christian Mission," *Anvil* 21, no. 1 (2004): 20.

[29]G. Campbell Morgan, *The Birth of the Church: An Exposition of the Second Chapter of Acts,* ed. Jill Morgan (Old Tappan, NJ: Fleming H. Revell, 1968), 157.

[30]Hear the Maasai Creed read online by Jaroslav Pelikan at https://onbeing.org/blog /creeds-that-span-continents/.

7. GOD'S INCLINATION TOWARD THE POOR, OPPRESSED, AND VULNERABLE

[1]Elements of this chapter are drawn from that sermon, given on September 16, 2018, at Flood Church in San Diego, California, https://diveintoflood.com/media/misquoted -persistent-poverty/misquoted-persistent-poverty-2/.

[2]Elaine Storkey and Rowan Williams, "At the Margins," December 23, 2017, in *Nomad* (podcast), www.nomadpodcast.co.uk/elaine-storkey-rowan-williams-advent -04-margins/.

[3]"COVID-19 to Add as Many as 150 Million Extreme Poor by 2021" The World Bank, October 7, 2020, www.worldbank.org/en/news/press-release/2020/10/07/covid-19 -to-add-as-many-as-150-million-extreme-poor-by-2021.

[4]"Under-Five Mortality," World Health Organization, accessed November 4, 2021, www.who .int/data/gho/data/indicators/indicator-details/GHO/under-five-mortality-rate -(probability-of-dying-by-age-5-per-1000-live-births).

[5]Kate Hodal, "One in 200 People Is a Slave. Why?," *Guardian* (UK edition), February 25, 2019, www.theguardian.com/news/2019/feb/25/modern-slavery-trafficking-persons -one-in-200.

[6]David Platt, *Something Needs to Change: A Call to Make Your Life Count in a World of Urgent Need* (Danvers, MA: Multnomah, 2019), 178.

[7]"2019 Data Report," Polaris Project, 1, https://polarisproject.org/wp-content /uploads/2019/09/Polaris-2019-US-National-Human-Trafficking-Hotline-Data-Report.pdf.

[8]"Uniquely Vulnerable: The Nexus Between Human Trafficking and Immigration," Faith Alliance Against Slavery and Trafficking, accessed November 4, 2021, https:// s3.amazonaws.com/media.cloversites.com/33/336bad01-3ae4-41f0-aaab-dde25ca8746f /documents/Uniquely_Vulernable_the_nexus_between_human_trafficking_and _immigration.pdf.

[9]Pulcherie Kindoho, "I Escaped. Now I'm Using My Voice for Victims Trafficked to the U.S.," *The Better Samaritan* (blog), *Christianity Today,* January 29, 2021, www.christianity

today.com/better-samaritan/2021/january/i-escaped-now-im-using-my-voice-for
-victims-trafficked-to-u.html.

[10]According to the U.S. Department of Labor, at least 156 different goods from 77 different countries have been tied directly to forced and child labor as of June 23, 2021. Some of the most common products include things one might expect like diamonds and clothing; others include chocolate, coffee, alcohol, beef, parts for mobile devices, rubber, and countless other things. Details are updated regularly at "List of Goods Produced by Child Labor or Forced Labor," Bureau of International Labor Affairs, U.S. Department of Labor, www.dol.gov/agencies/ilab/reports/child-labor/list-of-goods.

[11]Ruth Padilla DeBorst, "'Unlikely' Contributions Toward a Global Social Ethic: Can Anything Good Come from There?," in *First the Kingdom of God: Global Voices on Global Missions*, ed. Daniel K. Darko and Beth Snodderly (Pasadena, CA: William Carey International University Press, 2013), 108, 110.

[12]Daniel G. Groody and Gustavo A. Gutierrez, eds., *The Preferential Option for the Poor Beyond Theology* (South Bend, IN: University of Notre Dame Press, 2013).

[13]For example, Ex 23:3; Lev 19:15; Acts 10:34; Rom 2:11; Gal 2:6; Eph 6:9; Col 3:25; 1 Tim 5:21; Jas 2:1-9.

[14]Nicholas Wolterstorff, *Justice: Rights and Wrongs* (Princeton, NJ: Princeton University Press, 2008), 75-76. Examples include Deut 10:18; 24:17; 27:19; 1 Sam 2:8; Ps 82:3-4; 113:7-8; 140:12; 146:9; Is 1:17; 10:1-2; Jer 7:5-7; 22:3; Ezek 18:12-13; 22:29; Zech 7:9-10; Jas 1:27.

[15]Margo Schlanger, "Illegal Immigration and the Book of Ruth," *Tablet*, May 25, 2017, www.tabletmag.com/sections/belief/articles/illegal-immigration-book-of-ruth.

[16]The "year of the Lord's favor" refers to the Year of Jubilee (Lev 25:8-55), which God commanded the Israelites to observe every fiftieth year in order to free fellow Israelites from debts, restore property, and establish generous relationships among all.

[17]Howard Thurman, *Jesus and the Disinherited*, rev. ed. (Boston: Beacon Press, 1996), 7, 23.

[18]Bekele Deboch Anshiso, *Jesus's Identification with the Marginalized and the Liminal: The Messianic Identity in Mark* (London: Langham Publishing, 2018), chap. 1, Kindle.

[19]Liz Theoharis, *Always with Us?: What Jesus Really Said About the Poor* (Grand Rapids, MI: Eerdmans, 2017), 99.

[20]C. René Padilla, "Jesus' Galilean Option and the Mission of the Church," Micah Network, May 25, 2016, 2, https://fliphtml5.com/capw/qdso/basic.

[21]Derwin L. Gray, *Building a Multiethnic Church: A Gospel Vision of Love, Grace, and Reconciliation in a Divided World* (Nashville, TN: Thomas Nelson, 2021), 5.

[22]"Figures at a Glance," The UN Refugee Agency (UNHCR), June 18, 2021, accessed November 4, 2021, www.unhcr.org/en-us/figures-at-a-glance.html. According to the UNHCR, more than eighty-two million were displaced globally as of the end of 2020, including more than thirty-four million children.

[23]Hannah Hartig, "Republicans Turn More Negative Toward Refugees as Number Admitted to U.S. Plummets," Pew Research Center, May 24, 2018, www.pewresearch.org/fact-tank /2018/05/24/republicans-turn-more-negative-toward-refugees-as-number-admitted -to-u-s-plummets/.

[24]With the arrivals of Afghans fleeing the persecution of the Taliban, many because of their service to the U.S. military, new polling suggested a dramatic reversal, with evangelicals suddenly even *more* supportive of refugee resettlement processes than Americans as a whole (see National Immigration Forum, *Bullfinch Group National Survey*, September 2021, https://immigrationforum.org/wp-content/uploads/2021/09/Forum -Bullfinch-Sept21-Polling-Q-Adults.pdf). But even this encouraging shift speaks to the ongoing challenge that evangelicals' views toward refugees tend to be fickle, swayed by changing headlines and political circumstances, rather than steadily rooted in the unchanging commands of Scripture.

[25]Jenny Yang, "Supporting Hong Kong's Pro-Democracy Movement Through U.S. Refugee Policy" (testimony to the U.S. Senate Subcommittee on Border Security and Immigration, Washington, DC, December 16, 2020), www.judiciary.senate.gov/imo/media /doc/Yang%20Testimony1.pdf.

[26]We've used a pseudonym to protect Lah's privacy.

[27]For example, sociologist Rodney Stark's *The Triumph of Christianity: How the Jesus Movement Became the World's Largest Religion* (San Francisco: HarperOne, 2011) documents how Christianity's ethic of concern for the sick and poor as well as its relatively dignifying treatment of women, children, and others who were vulnerable fueled the movement's remarkable early growth. More recently, as political scientist Robert Woodberry demonstrates, Protestant missionary efforts contributed to literacy and education that, in turn, contributed to more stable, democratic forms of government; see Robert Woodberry, "The Missionary Roots of Liberal Democracy," *American Political Science Review* 106, no. 2 (May 2012): www.researchgate.net/publication/235503 063_The_Missionary_Roots_of_Liberal_Democracy.

[28]Esa Autero, *Reading the Bible Across Contexts: Luke's Gospel, Socio-Economic Marginality, and Latin American Biblical Hermeneutics*, Biblical Interpretation Series 145 (Boston: Brill, 2016), 251.

[29]John Chrysostom, *Seven Sermons on Lazarus* 1.10.

[30]Diane Langberg, *Suffering and the Heart of God: How Trauma Destroys and Christ Restores* (Greensboro, NC: New Growth Press, 2015), 84.

8. ADVOCACY AND DISCIPLESHIP
FREED FROM PARTISANSHIP

[1]Leith Anderson and Galen Carey, *Faith in the Voting Booth: Practical Wisdom for Voting Well* (Grand Rapids, MI: Zondervan, 2016), 32.

[2]Anderson and Carey, *Faith in the Voting Booth*, 32.

[3]Michele F. Margolis, *From Politics to the Pews: How Partisanship and the Political Environment Shape Religious Identity* (Chicago: University of Chicago Press, 2018), 4.

[4]Jenny Yang, "Politics Isn't the Answer. But It's an Answer," *Christianity Today*, March 2, 2020, www.christianitytoday.com/ct/2020/march-web-only/politics answer-jenny -yang.html.

[5]Eugene Cho, *Thou Shalt Not Be a Jerk: A Christian's Guide to Engaging Politics* (Colorado Springs, CO: David C. Cook, 2020), 23.

[6]Esau McCaulley, *Reading While Black: African American Biblical Interpretation as an Exercise in Hope* (Downers Grove, IL: InterVarsity Press, 2020), 49.

[7]Dennis Mwangwela, interview with Matthew Soerens, December 16, 2020.

[8]Mark R. Glanville and Luke Glanville, *Refuge Reimagined: Biblical Kinship in Global Politics* (Downers Grove, IL: InterVarsity Press, 2021), 9.

[9]Dave Ferguson and Matthew Soerens, "'Family Win' and How Our Churches Care for Each Other and the World," *The Exchange with Ed Stetzer* (blog), *Christianity Today*, January 29, 2018.

[10]Keila Garcia, interview with Matthew Soerens, December 18, 2020.

[11]Kaitlyn Schiess, *The Liturgy of Politics: Spiritual Formation for the Sake of Our Neighbor* (Downers Grove, IL: InterVarsity Press, 2020), 141.

[12]See Robert Seager II, "Some Denominational Reactions to Chinese Immigration to California, 1856-1892," *Pacific Historical Review* 28, no. 1 (February 1959).

[13]See Charles Marsh, *God's Long Summer: Stories of Faith and Civil Rights* (Princeton, NJ: Princeton University Press, 2008).

[14]See Jennifer E. Dyer, "The Politics of Evangelicals: How the Issues of HIV and AIDS in Africa Shaped a 'Centrist' Constituency in the United States," *Journal of the American*

Academy of Religion, 82, no. 4 (December 2014): 1010-32, https://doi.org/10.1093/jaarel /lfu041.

[15]Quoted in Renate Wind, *Dietrich Bonhoeffer: A Spoke in the Wheel*, trans. John Bowden (Grand Rapids, MI: Eerdmans, 1992), 69.

[16]For example, Franklin Graham called the separation of children from parents "disgraceful," prominent Iowa evangelical Bob Vander Plaats called it "cruelty," and Faith and Freedom Coalition leader Ralph Reed called it "heartbreaking and tragic." They echoed condemnations of the policy from evangelical leaders who criticized Trump administration immigration policies more regularly, such as the Ethics & Religious Liberty Commission of the Southern Baptist Convention, the National Association of Evangelicals, World Relief, and World Vision. See Niall Stanage, "The Memo: Religious Right Hits Trump on Border Crisis," *The Hill*, June 20, 2018, https://thehill.com/homenews/the-memo/393120-the -memo-religious-right-hits-trump-on-border-crisis, as well as "Evangelical Leaders Urge President Trump to Keep Families Together," Evangelical Immigration Table, June 1, 2018, https://evangelicalimmigrationtable.com/evangelical-leaders-urge-president-trump -to-keep-families-together/.

[17]Quoted in Emily McFarlan Miller, "The 'Splainer: Why Is Jeff Sessions Quoting Romans 13 and Why Is It So Often Invoked?," Religion News Service, June 15, 2018, https://religionnews.com/2018/06/15/the-splainer-why-is-jeff-sessions-quoting -romans-13-and-why-is-it-so-often-invoked/.

[18]McCaulley, *Reading While Black*, 32.

[19]Origen of Alexandria, *Commentarii in Epistulam ad Romanos*, ed. T. Heither, vol. 5 (New York: Herder, 1995), 94.

[20]Martin Luther King Jr., "Beyond Vietnam," April 4, 1967, Riverside Church, New York City, audio from the Martin Luther King, Jr. Center for Nonviolent Social Change, www .youtube.com/watch?v=AJhgXKGldUk.

[21]McCaulley, *Reading While Black*, 32.

[22]Lapani Langford Sankhani Nkhonjera, "Esther as the New Moses: Deliverance Motifs in the Book of Esther" (master's thesis, Stellenbosch University, 2015), 105, https:// scholar.sun.ac.za/bitstream/handle/10019.1/98067/nkhonjera_esther_2015.pdf ?sequence=2&isAllowed=y.

[23]Mae Elise Cannon, Lisa Sharon Harper, Troy Jackson, and Soong-Chan Rah, *Forgive Us: Confessions of a Compromised Faith* (Grand Rapids, MI: Zondervan, 2014), 24.

[24]Eugene Peterson, "Introduction to Amos," *The Message* (Colorado Springs, CO: NavPress, 2002), 1641.

[25]ASJ cofounder Kurt Ver Beek dialogues with Christian philosopher Nicholas Wolterstorff on how biblical justice is at the root of ASJ's work in Honduras in their coauthored *Call for Justice: From Practice to Theory and Back* (Eugene, OR: Cascade Books, 2019).

[26]"AJS Condemns Assassination Attempt Against AJS-Honduras Board Member Jorge Machado That Resulted in Death of Bodyguard," Association for a More Just Society, December 16, 2016, www.ajs-us.org/stories/news/ajs-condemns-assassination-attempt -against-ajs-honduras-board-member-jorge-machado-that-resulted-in-death-of -bodyguard.

[27]Gustav Stählin, "Comfort and Comforters in Non-Biblical Antiquity," in *Theological Dictionary of the New Testament*, ed. Gerhard Friedrich (Grand Rapids, MI: Eerdmans, 1970), 5:780-81.

[28]National Association of Evangelicals, *For the Health of the Nation: An Evangelical Call to Civic Responsibility*, March 8, 2018, www.nae.net/wp-content/uploads/2018/09/For-the -Health-of-the-Nation_spreads.pdf.

[29]Ben Lowe, *Doing Good Without Giving Up: Sustaining Social Action in a World That's Hard to Change* (Downers Grove, IL: InterVarsity Press, 2014), 73.

[30]Cho, *Thou Shalt Not Be a Jerk*, 63.

[31]Alexia Salvatierra and Peter Heltzel, *Faith-Rooted Organizing: Mobilizing the Church in Service to the World* (Downers Grove, IL: InterVarsity Press, 2014), 107.

[32]Salvatierra and Heltzel, *Faith-Rooted Organizing*, 74.

[33]Augustine, *The City of God*, trans. Marcus Dods (Peabody, MA: Hendrickson Publishers, 2009), 4.

[34]Schiess, *The Liturgy of Politics*, 160-61.

[35]Dallas Willard, *The Divine Conspiracy: Rediscovering Our Hidden Life in God* (San Francisco: HarperOne, 1998), 282.

[36]LifeWay Research, "Evangelical Views on Immigration," February 2015, http://lifeway research.com/wp-content/uploads/2015/03/Evangelical-Views-on-Immigration -Report.pdf.

[37]See some of Eric's articles on his church's ministry: Eric Costanzo, "Pastor: For Me, Immigration Is Biblical—Foreign-Born Congregants Are Human Beings, Not Political Problems," Fox News, February 10, 2019, www.foxnews.com/opinion/pastor-for-me -immigration-is-biblical-foreign-born-congregants-are-human-beings-not-political -problems; Costanzo and Cesar Quintero, "God Blessed My Church with Migrants," *Christianity Today*, July 23, 2019, www.christianitytoday.com/ct/2019/july-web-only /god-blessed-church-migrants-refugee-leaders-south-tulsa-bap.html.

[38]Tish Harrison Warren, *Liturgy of the Ordinary: Sacred Practices in Everyday Life* (Downers Grove, IL: InterVarsity Press, 2016), 30.

[39]Joseph Bataille, interview with Matthew Soerens, December 10, 2020.

[40]Schiess, *The Liturgy of Politics*, 79-80.

[41]Sidney Rooy, who served as a missionary in Argentina and Costa Rica for more than thirty-five years, came to the same etymological realization several decades before I did, and makes a compelling argument for why the Spanish language translation is actually closer to the meaning of the original Greek term; see Sidney Rooy, "Right-eousness and Justice," *Evangelical Review of Theology* 6, no. 2 (October 1982): 65-77, https://theology.worldea.org/wp-content/uploads/2020/12/ERT-06-2.pdf.

9. AMERICAN RELIGION OR THE GREAT COMMISSIONS?

[1]Justin Martyr, *First Apology* 39.

[2]Joshua Wu (@joshswu), "This #July4th weekend, I'm thankful for the liberties/privi-leges of being an American, but unquestionably value my faith more than my nation-ality," Twitter with graphic of results from a Nationscape 2020 survey, July 2, 2021, https://twitter.com/joshswu/status/1411110436498509829/photo/1.

[3]The early manuscripts of Matthew did not include verse 14. This particular rendering was taken from the equivalent passage in Mark 12:40.

[4]Joe M. Kapolyo, "Matthew," in *Africa Bible Commentary: A One-Volume Commentary Written by 70 African Scholars*, ed. Tokunboh Adeyemo, rev. ed. (Grand Rapids, MI: Zondervan Academic, 2010), 1186, 1159.

[5]This phrase is borrowed from John Calvin, who described human nature as "a perpetual factory of idols." See John Calvin, *Institutes of the Christian Religion*, vol. 1, trans. Ford Lewis Battles (Louisville, KY: Westminster John Knox Press, 2006), 108.

[6]Peter L. Berger, *The Many Altars of Modernity: Toward a Paradigm for Religion in a Plu-ralist Age* (Boston: De Gruyter, 2014), 31.

[7]To this day, the United States is still the only nation to detonate a nuclear bomb against a warring enemy state. Moreover, it also made Laos the most bombed country by dropping more than two million tons of ordnance during 580,000 bombing missions from 1964 to 1973, equal to a planeload of bombs every eight minutes, twenty-four hours a day, for nine years. To learn more, see http://legaciesofwar.org/about-laos /secret-war-laos.

[8]Some reputable critics argue this was the case with ISIS, which emerged as a response to American military involvement in Iraq. Hassan Hassan, coauthor of *ISIS: Inside the Army of Terror,* explains the idea of how ISIS was formed as a response to the US invasion into Iraq in 2003 in "The True Origins of ISIS," the *Atlantic,* November 30, 2018, www.theatlantic.com/ideas/archive/2018/11/isis-origins-anbari-zarqawi/577030.

[9]Chrissy Stroop and Lauren O'Neal, eds., *Empty the Pews: Stories of Leaving the Church* (Indianapolis, IN: Epiphany Publishing, 2019), 159.

[10]Joseph Bataille, interview with Matthew Soerens, December 10, 2020.

[11]For example, per the Pew Research Center, between 36 percent and 41 percent of people in Honduras, El Salvador, Guatemala, and Nicaragua are Protestants (*evangélico/as*), compared to about 25 percent who are evangelical Protestants in the United States. See Benjamin Wormald, "Religion in Latin America: Widespread Change in a Historically Catholic Region," Pew Research Center, November 13, 2014, www.pewforum.org/2014/11/13/religion-in-latin-america/, and "America's Changing Religious Landscape," Pew Research Center, May 12, 2015, www.pewforum.org/2015/05/12/americas-changing-religious-landscape/.

[12]Luis Luna Jr., interview with Matthew Soerens, December 11, 2020.

[13]Lamin Sanneh, "Christian Missions and the Western Guilt Complex," *The Christian Century* 104, no. 11 (1987): 331–34.

[14]C. René Padilla, "Contextual Scripture Engagement and Transcultural Mission," in *First the Kingdom of God: Global Voices on Global Missions,* ed. Daniel K. Darko and Beth Snodderly (Pasadena, CA: William Carey International University Press, 2013), 220-21.

[15]Ranald Macaulay, "The Great Commissions," *Cambridge Papers* 7, no. 2 (1998): 1-4.

[16]Kwame Bediako, *Jesus and the Gospel in Africa: History and Experience* (Maryknoll, NY: Orbis Books, 2004), 116.

[17]Quoted in David P. King, *God's Internationalists: World Vision and the Age of Evangelical Humanitarianism* (Philadelphia: University of Pennsylvania Press, 2019), 149.

[18]Michael Cassidy, quoted in Dion Forster, "Missionaries from Everywhere to Everywhere," Lausanne Movement, October 25, 2010, https://lausanne.org/about/blog/missionaries-from-everywhere-to-everywhere.

[19]Jon Bonk, *Missions and Money: Affluence as a Missionary Problem—Revisited* (Maryknoll, NY: Orbis Books, 2006), 82.

[20]C. René Padilla, "Contextual Scripture Engagement and Transcultural Mission," 217.

CONCLUSION: A DECLARATION OF DEPENDENCE

[1]We've changed Vanessa's name and a few identifying details to respect her privacy.

[2]Søren Kierkegaard, *Søren Kierkegaard's Journals and Papers,* vol. 2, ed. and trans. Howard V. Hong and Edna H. Hong (Bloomington, IN: Indiana University Press, 1970), 482-83.

[3]Bob Smietana, "For Some Pastors, the Past Year Was a Sign from God It Was Time to Quit," Religion News Service, May 7, 2021, https://religionnews.com/2021/05/07/for-some-pastors-the-past-year-was-a-sign-that-it-was-time-to-quit/.

[4]Gina Zurlo, "The World as 100 Christians," Gordon-Conwell Theological Seminary, January 29, 2020, www.gordonconwell.edu/blog/100christians/.

[5]Simon Mwangi, "Seeding Your Miracle," February 23, 2020, Parklands Baptist Church, Nairobi, Kenya, https://parklandsbaptist.org/sermons/seeding-your-miracle/.

[6]Mwangi, "Seeding Your Miracle."

[7]Alan Fram and Jonathan Lemire, "Trump: Why Allow Immigrants from 'Shithole Countries'?," Associated Press, January 11, 2018, https://apnews.com/article/immigration-north-america-donald-trump-ap-top-news-international-news-fdda2ff0b877416c8ae1c1a77a3cc425.

[8]Michelle Hackman, "Trump Administration Imposes New Travel Restrictions on Six Countries," *Wall Street Journal*, January 31, 2020, www.wsj.com/articles/trump -administration-imposes-new-travel-restrictions-on-six-countries-11580500874.

[9]Quoted in World Relief, "World Relief Laments Expanded Restrictions on Lawful Immigration," February 17, 2020, https://worldrelief.org/world-relief-laments-expanded -restrictions-on-lawful-immigration/.

[10]Hannah Gronowski and Danielle Strickland, *Generation Distinct: Discover the Wrong You Were Born to Make Right* (Colorado Springs, CO: NavPress, 2020), 14.

[11]"You Want to Live a Life That Matters. We Want to Show You *How*," 6-Month Program, Generation Distinct, 2021, www.generationdistinct.com/6month-program.

[12]Diane Langberg, *Suffering and the Heart of God: How Trauma Destroys and Christ Restores* (Greensboro, NC: New Growth Press, 2015).

[13]Bob Roberts Jr., "Discipleship in Politically Polarized Times," interview by Beth Cossin, Evangelical Immigration Table Convening, January 7, 2021, https://evangelicalimmi grationtable.com/2021convening/.

NAME INDEX

SCRIPTURE INDEX